Walking Wounded

Written by OLIVIER MOREL   Art by MAËL

Translated by EDWARD GAUVIN

NANTIER • BEALL • MINOUSTCHINE
Publishing inc.
new york

Mama, Mama, Can't You See?

Summer, 2008. Jason had just gotten out of the hospital, but he didn't tell me that until near the end of our phone call. Almost six years ago to the day, this young man, now in his thirties, had tried to take his life. Ironically, it wasn't the invasion of Iraq, but rather the return to his homeland that nearly proved fatal to this National Guard volunteer.

Jason Moon's decision to embrace life after his brush with death coincided with my desire to make a film on this subject. I wanted to get to know him. I wanted to make sure the voices of men and women like him were more widely heard—men and women no one was talking about back then. Individuals who, having participated in the post-9/11 wars, could no longer live with "it."

What was "it"? How and why did "it" lead many of them to kill themselves? And in such great numbers? I couldn't believe it at first. After all, no one ever heard anything about it back then. Today, however, it has almost become a cliché. A common occurrence, tragically, every day. And in a society where we are exposed to nonstop violence, we are becoming accustomed to everything. We're used to it. Nothing surprises us anymore.

When it became clear that we were in the war for the long haul, young soldiers—men and women alike—rallied to have their say in the face of shocking public indifference. Then came a number of towering films, like Delphine Dhilly's *Far From Iraq* (2008), Sara Nesson's *Poster Girl* (2010), Kirby Dick's *The Invisible War* (2012), and even Laurent Bécue-Renard's more recent *Of Men and War* (2014), among many others, each with its own take, its own vision and different things to say. Documentary films; veterans who bravely broke the silence and spoke up; in-depth reporting from journalists like Amy Goodman, Aaron Glantz, and Bob Koehler; scandals like the one that recently broke out concerning the VA—all these have played their part in the (far too) gradual rise in public awareness of the intensity of veterans' suffering. In this book, *Walking Wounded,* the characters who figure prominently in my documentary film *On the Bridge* (2010) are transfigured. For those familiar with the experiences of veterans who have returned from these recent wars, the stories depicted here are anything but revelations.

In many ways, this is a book that sublimates and transcends. It provides an account of how human beings can survive trauma so great that the medical establishment deems it insurmountable. But that's not all. It also addresses the subconscious elements of society, the unspoken values that make war possible, not only in the United States, but everywhere. What readers will find in this book are not simple "memories of war," but a profound representation of the ways in which violence has made an indelible mark on the lives of its protagonists—as well as my own. Along the way, what proved to be the urgent impetus driving this book was the indefinable feeling of friendship. A friendship for the ages—like all lasting friendships, as great a mystery as existence itself. These and other contradictions can be found in my relationship with my "characters." One thing is certain: I love them, and I seek to pay them heartfelt tribute in these pages.

Among the most powerful attributes of the genre known as the graphic novel is its ability to make visible and to render legible all that is vague and uncanny—feelings and sensations, the incorporeal and uncertain, even visions and phantasmagoria—while remaining firmly in the realm of the factual, the documentary. The work of the great documentary filmmakers of our time, such as Ari Folman, Joshua Op-

word

penheimer and Rithy Panh, can do the same. But through their work on the printed page, graphic novels are able to accomplish something unique. Aided by the artistic ingenuity of my collaborator Maël, I was able to recount and to report what I witnessed photographically and cinematically, while also giving shape to the indispensable aspects of the narrative that do not fall into the category of what could be considered as strictly "documentary." If these non-factual, indecisive elements of a real experience are at the heart of war, they are also the building blocks of peace. For although peace, like forgiveness and reconciliation, needs signals, words, and actions, it remains an act of *sublimation*, a performance that is *impalpable and improbable:* an art.

This book is located within a fragile artistic borderland: part imagination, part fact, part symbol, and part fiction. Joe Sacco, the undisputed master of the nonfiction graphic novel, once said that "Drawing is interpretative, and I am a filter." This book's "truth" is "filtered" through that of trauma. If trauma can do this—can be at once prophetic and threatening, capable of transforming not so much the documentary "truth" of what our protagonists have survived, as our *relationship* to that truth—then *Walking Wounded* also heralds a metamorphosis of characters who challenge the reigning post-9/11 narrative that sent them to war. By working through their trauma, these protagonists report what they did, or lived through, in Iraq, and the way shock has strained or splintered, fractured or shattered their grasp of history—our history. Iraq, suddenly and literally, bursts through: on a bridge in Milwaukee; through a ghostly apparition in the Mojave Desert; by the Chicago suburbs; in a photo of a dead Iraqi that a soldier brought back. These distortions are not "distortions of the truth," but *truths about the trauma of war* that refract historical "reality." In this upended world that effaces solid shapes and straight lines, truth is the very embodiment of distortion, one that war works upon the wounded heart, upon the torn and beaten body, upon the blood-stained human soul.

Hence the shock I felt right from the moment I met Jason, like all the others. Confronted with societal institutions quick to prescribe drugs and assign a label to their suffering (PTSD), these veterans were way ahead of me. They had grasped the significance of all of "it."

What is "it"?

"It" is this: Cyclist, banjo player, poet, and singer, Jacob George served three tours in Afghanistan. There, he witnessed the horror in person. He repeatedly came face-to-face with devastating fear: in himself, but also in the eyes of the Afghans around him. Inspired to help the country after his deployments, he opted to return to that war-torn land with a peace delegation. But it wasn't enough. In Chicago, during a protest against the NATO summit held in May 2012, he publicly discarded his military decorations and vehemently denounced the wars, chanting over and over, "Mama, Mama, can't you see / What Uncle Sam has done to me?" He was an active member of Iraq Veterans Against the War, like Jason Moon and other protagonists featured in this book.

Just three weeks ago, Jacob George committed suicide. He was thirty-two years old.
We are supposed to become accustomed to things, to learn to get used to all of it.
But we have to start over again, each time.
We never get used to *anything*.

Olivier Morel October 2014

"I carry with me a cargo of memories, some painful and some pleasant, which have remained locked in the hold of my mind."
Will Eisner, A Contract With God

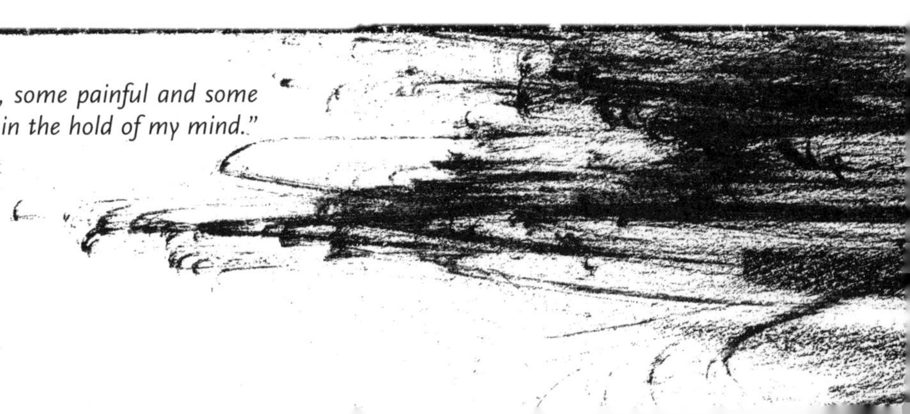

"They'll say we're disturbing the peace,
but there is no peace. What really bothers them
is that we are disturbing the war."

Speech against the Vietnam War on Boston Common, Massachusetts,
May 5, 1971. Howard Zinn, Collected Speeches 1963-2009, Haymarket
Books, Chicago, 2012, p. 18.

In memoriam, Jean-Florian Tello, who was in my thoughts
while I was working on this book.
M.

This work is a tribute to Wendy, Lisa, Joyce, Debbie, Kevin L.,
Vinny, Ryan, Jason, & Kevin S., and through their voices, to
the veterans who were silenced by the moral injuries of war.
It is dedicated to Paul Rozenberg.
O.M.

Other comics journalism available from NBM:
To Afghanistan & Back, Ted Rall
Contrarian view on the Afghan War, hc $15.95, sc $12.99
War Fix, David Axe, Steve Olexa
A journalist gets hooked on the adrenaline of war, hc, $15.95

See our complete list and Morel's blog at:
NBMPUB.COM
We have over 200 titles available
NBM Graphic Novels
160 Broadway, Suite 700, East Wing
New York, NY 10038
Catalog available by request
If ordering by mail add $4 P&H 1st item, $1 each addt'l

This book was published with the financial support of the Institute for
the Scholarship in the Liberal Arts of the University of Notre Dame.

ISBN 9781561639823
© 2013 Futuropolis, Olivier Morel, Mael
Library of Congress Control Number: 2015943276
Translation by Edward Gauvin, assisted by Mercedes Claire Gilliom,
Olivier Morel, Alison Rice, Claire-Elizabeth Gonnard
Lettering by Mercedes Claire Gilliom

Printed in China
First printed October 2015
Also available wherever e-books are sold

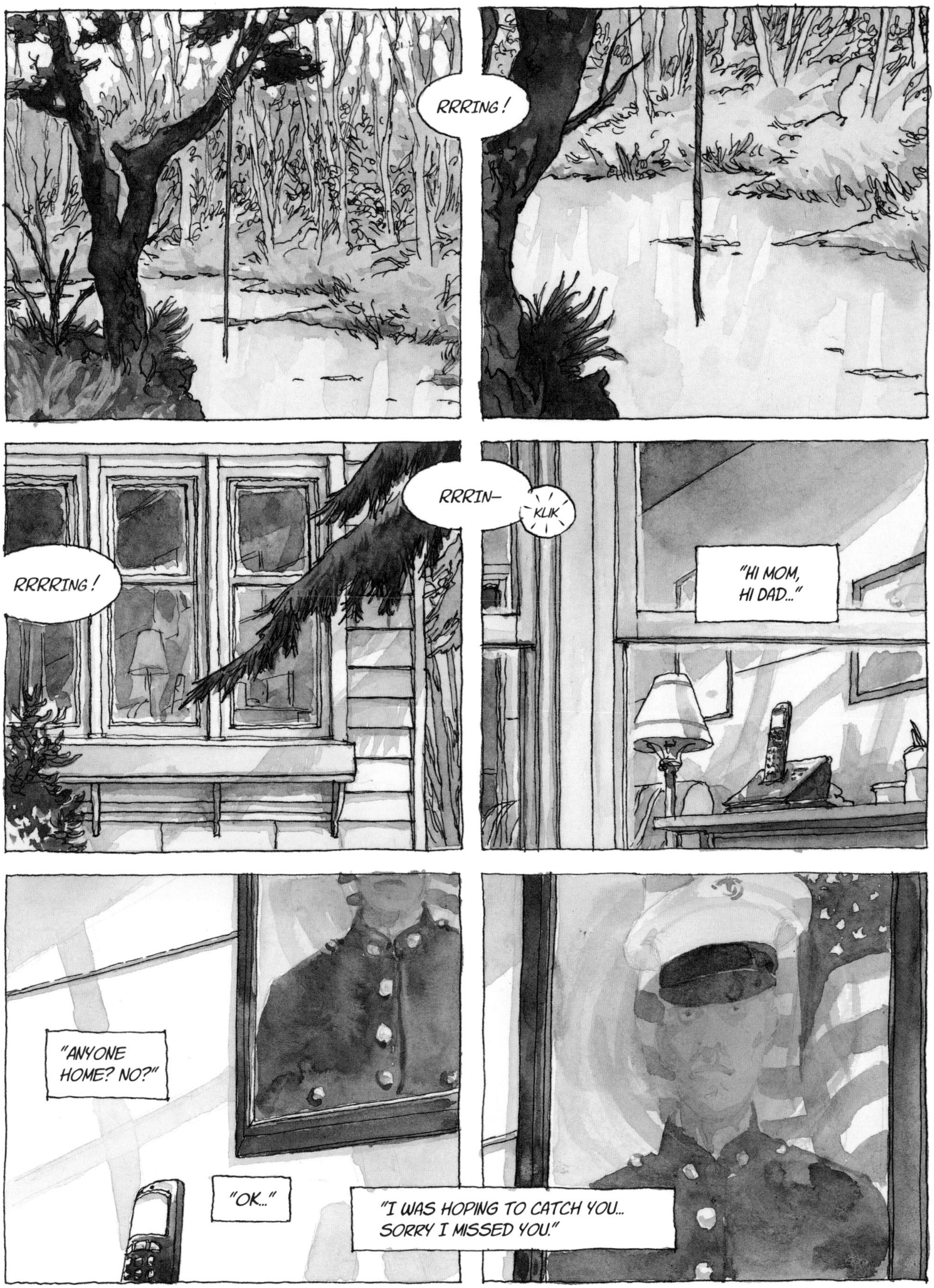
RRRING!
RRRRING!
RRRIN—
KLIK
"HI MOM,
HI DAD..."
"ANYONE
HOME? NO?"
"OK..."
"I WAS HOPING TO CATCH YOU...
SORRY I MISSED YOU."

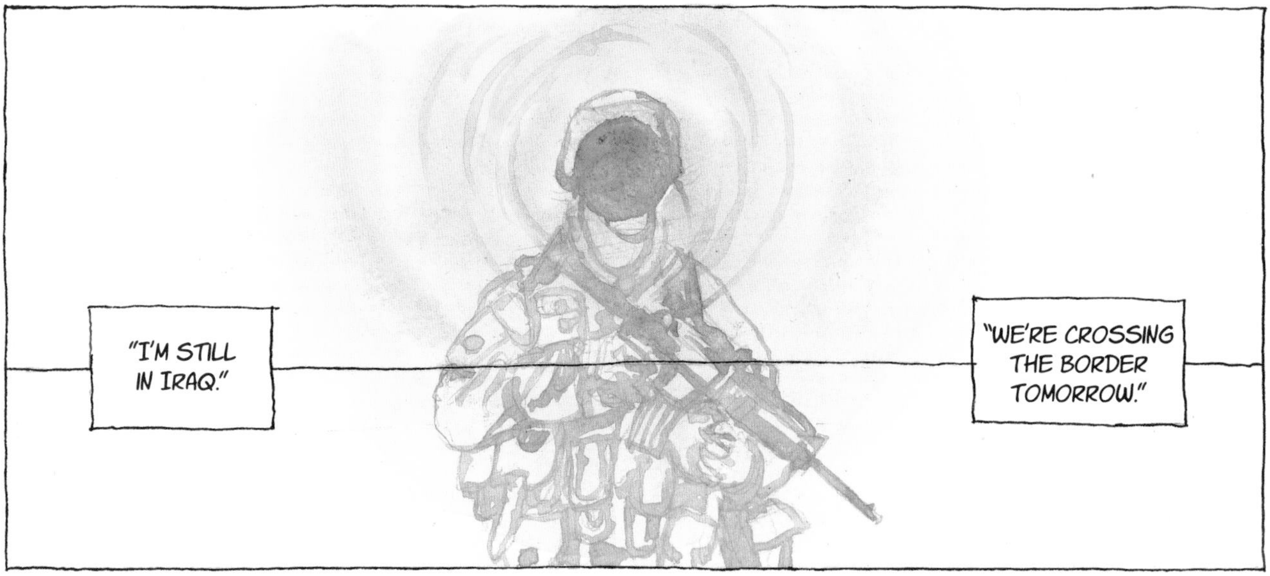
"I'M STILL IN IRAQ."
"WE'RE CROSSING THE BORDER TOMORROW."

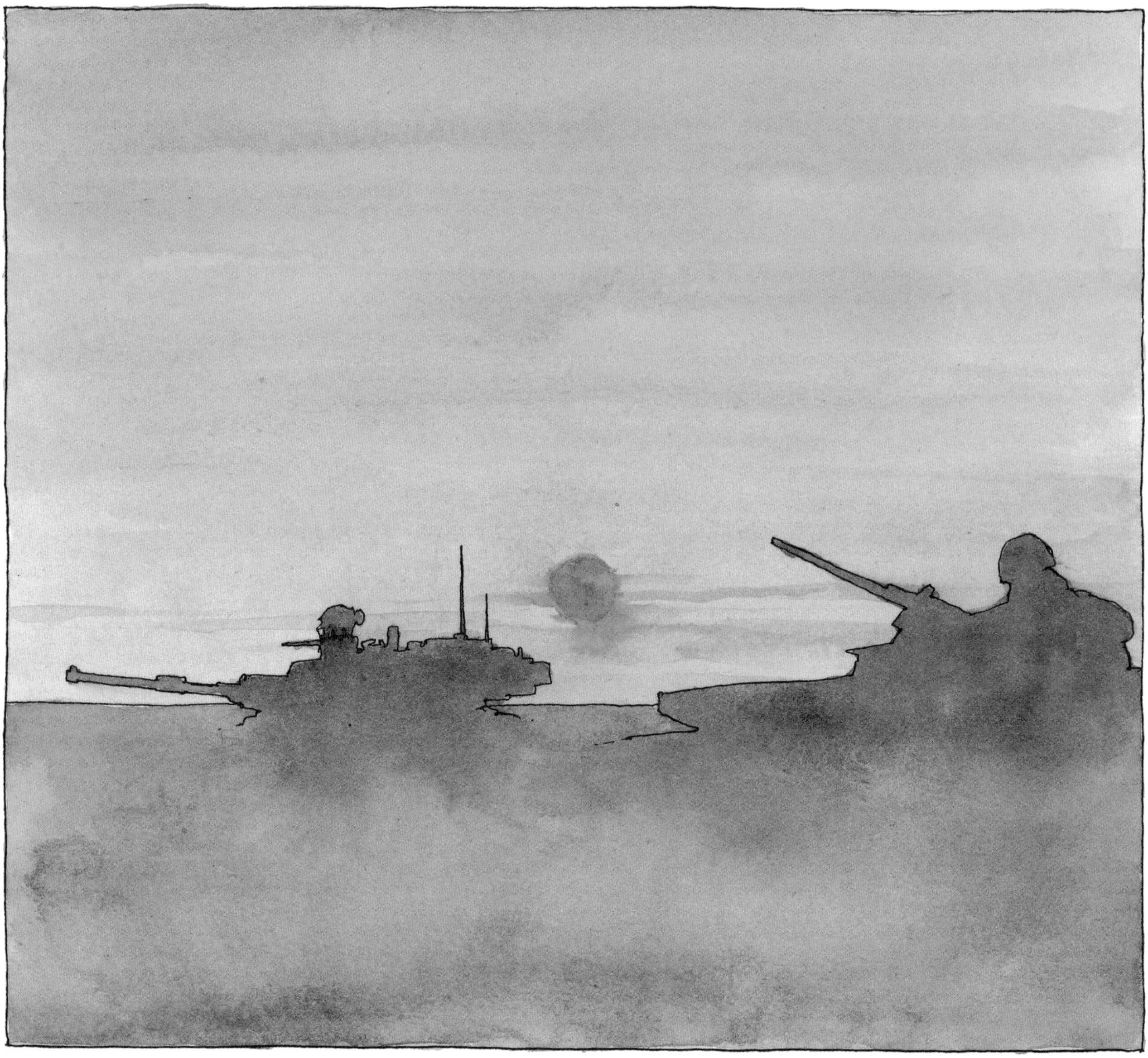

chapter 1

Haunted

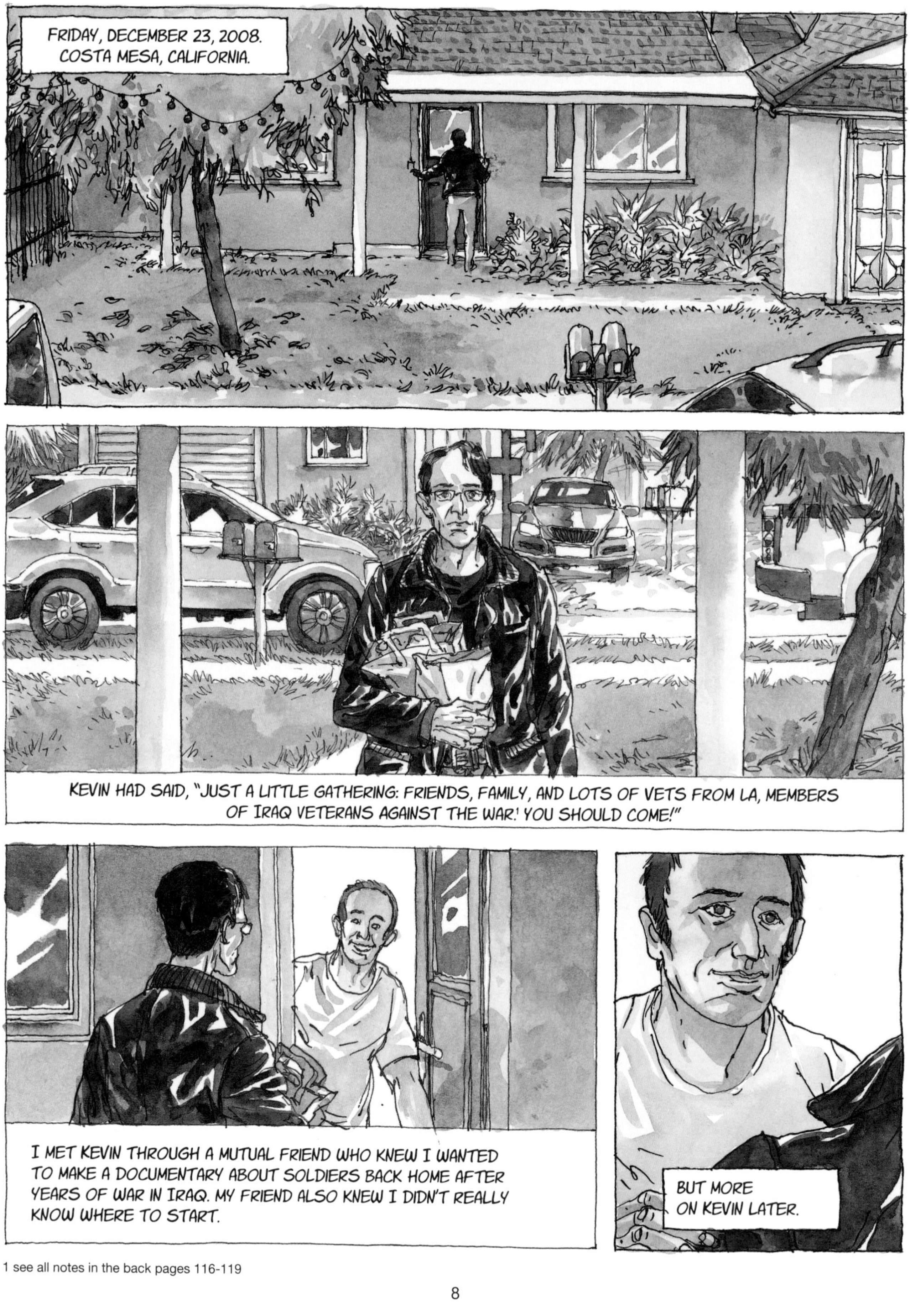
FRIDAY, DECEMBER 23, 2008. COSTA MESA, CALIFORNIA.
KEVIN HAD SAID, "JUST A LITTLE GATHERING: FRIENDS, FAMILY, AND LOTS OF VETS FROM LA, MEMBERS OF IRAQ VETERANS AGAINST THE WAR.[1] YOU SHOULD COME!"
I MET KEVIN THROUGH A MUTUAL FRIEND WHO KNEW I WANTED TO MAKE A DOCUMENTARY ABOUT SOLDIERS BACK HOME AFTER YEARS OF WAR IN IRAQ. MY FRIEND ALSO KNEW I DIDN'T REALLY KNOW WHERE TO START.
BUT MORE ON KEVIN LATER.

1 see all notes in the back pages 116-119

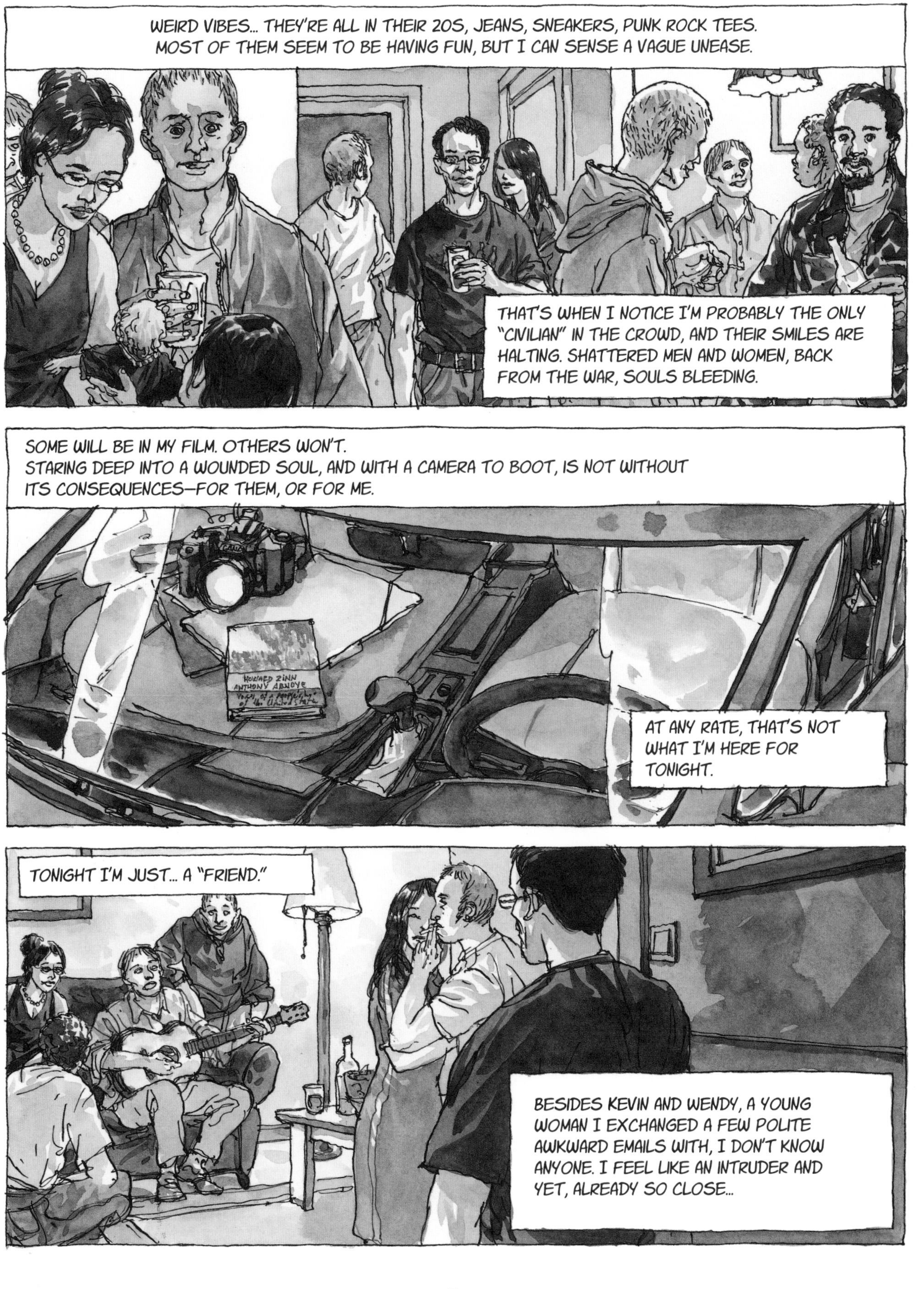
WEIRD VIBES... THEY'RE ALL IN THEIR 20S, JEANS, SNEAKERS, PUNK ROCK TEES.
MOST OF THEM SEEM TO BE HAVING FUN, BUT I CAN SENSE A VAGUE UNEASE.
THAT'S WHEN I NOTICE I'M PROBABLY THE ONLY "CIVILIAN" IN THE CROWD, AND THEIR SMILES ARE HALTING. SHATTERED MEN AND WOMEN, BACK FROM THE WAR, SOULS BLEEDING.
SOME WILL BE IN MY FILM. OTHERS WON'T.
STARING DEEP INTO A WOUNDED SOUL, AND WITH A CAMERA TO BOOT, IS NOT WITHOUT ITS CONSEQUENCES—FOR THEM, OR FOR ME.
HOWARD ZINN
AT ANY RATE, THAT'S NOT WHAT I'M HERE FOR TONIGHT.
TONIGHT I'M JUST... A "FRIEND."
BESIDES KEVIN AND WENDY, A YOUNG WOMAN I EXCHANGED A FEW POLITE AWKWARD EMAILS WITH, I DON'T KNOW ANYONE. I FEEL LIKE AN INTRUDER AND YET, ALREADY SO CLOSE...

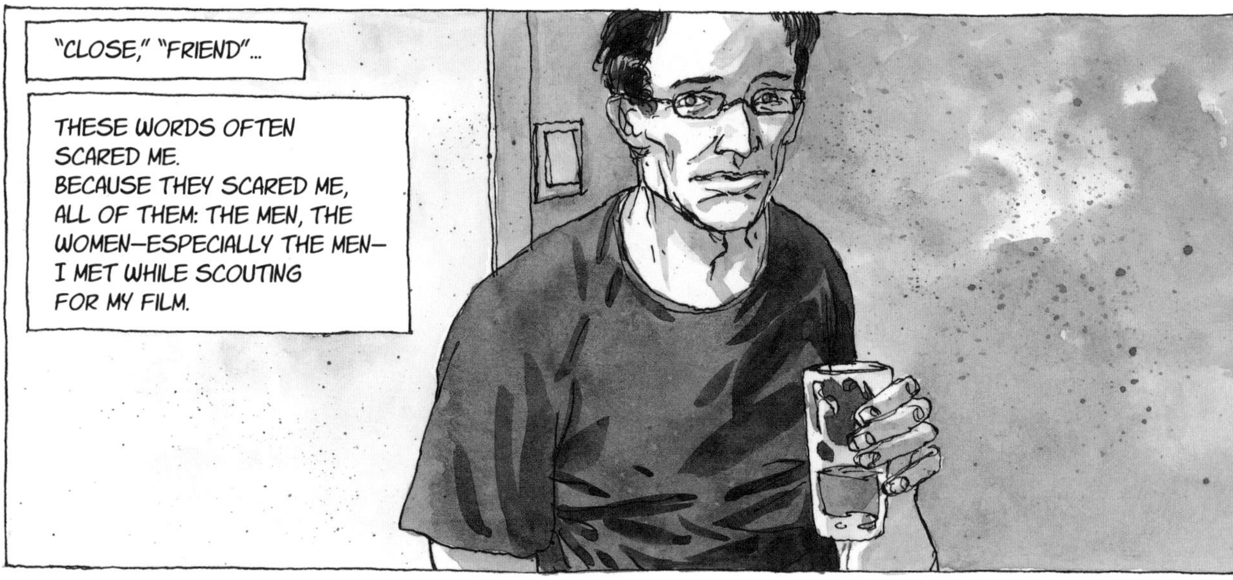
"CLOSE," "FRIEND"...
THESE WORDS OFTEN SCARED ME. BECAUSE THEY SCARED ME, ALL OF THEM: THE MEN, THE WOMEN—ESPECIALLY THE MEN—I MET WHILE SCOUTING FOR MY FILM.

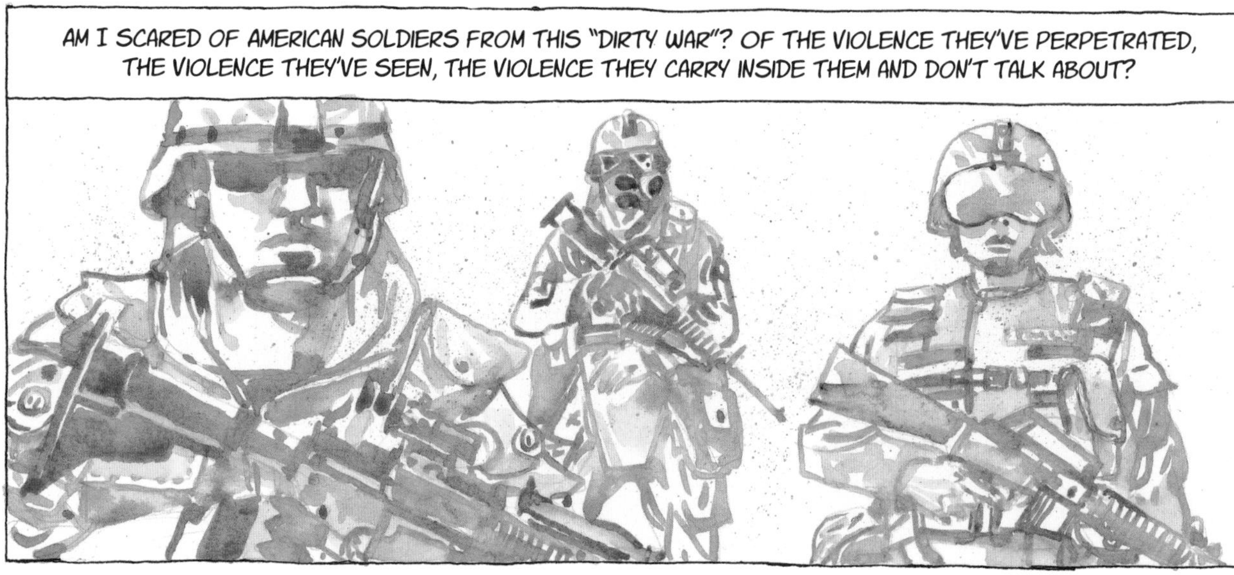
AM I SCARED OF AMERICAN SOLDIERS FROM THIS "DIRTY WAR"? OF THE VIOLENCE THEY'VE PERPETRATED, THE VIOLENCE THEY'VE SEEN, THE VIOLENCE THEY CARRY INSIDE THEM AND DON'T TALK ABOUT?

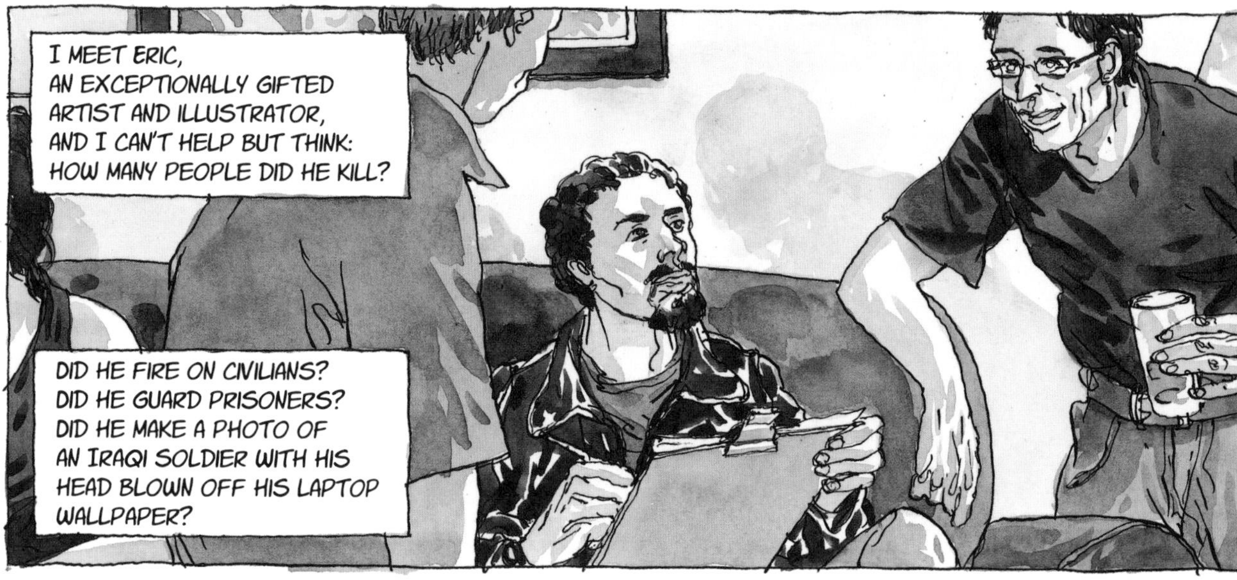
I MEET ERIC, AN EXCEPTIONALLY GIFTED ARTIST AND ILLUSTRATOR, AND I CAN'T HELP BUT THINK: HOW MANY PEOPLE DID HE KILL?
DID HE FIRE ON CIVILIANS? DID HE GUARD PRISONERS? DID HE MAKE A PHOTO OF AN IRAQI SOLDIER WITH HIS HEAD BLOWN OFF HIS LAPTOP WALLPAPER?

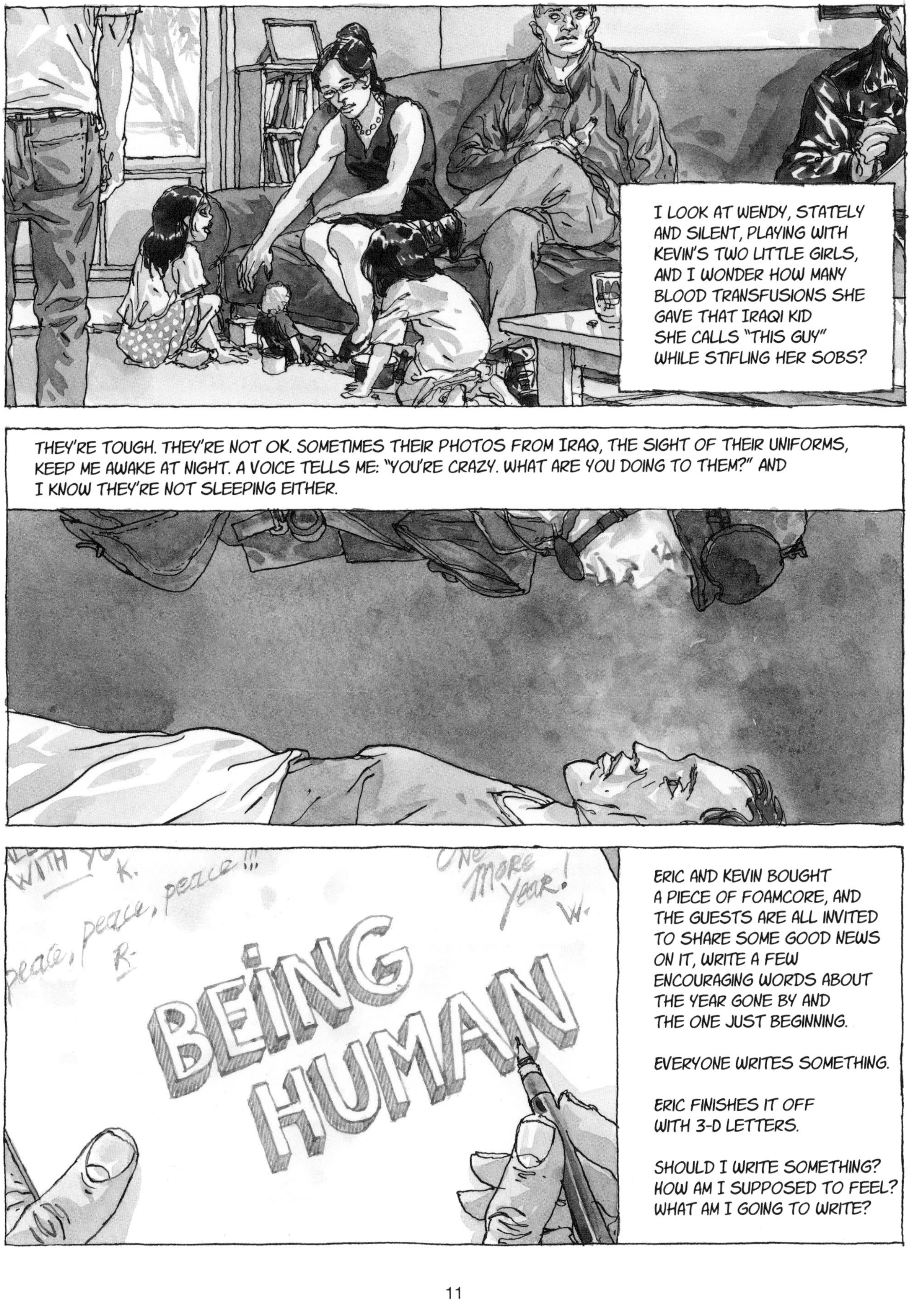
I LOOK AT WENDY, STATELY AND SILENT, PLAYING WITH KEVIN'S TWO LITTLE GIRLS, AND I WONDER HOW MANY BLOOD TRANSFUSIONS SHE GAVE THAT IRAQI KID SHE CALLS "THIS GUY" WHILE STIFLING HER SOBS?
THEY'RE TOUGH. THEY'RE NOT OK. SOMETIMES THEIR PHOTOS FROM IRAQ, THE SIGHT OF THEIR UNIFORMS, KEEP ME AWAKE AT NIGHT. A VOICE TELLS ME: "YOU'RE CRAZY. WHAT ARE YOU DOING TO THEM?" AND I KNOW THEY'RE NOT SLEEPING EITHER.
peace, peace, peace!!!
R.
One more year!
W.
BEING HUMAN
ERIC AND KEVIN BOUGHT A PIECE OF FOAMCORE, AND THE GUESTS ARE ALL INVITED TO SHARE SOME GOOD NEWS ON IT, WRITE A FEW ENCOURAGING WORDS ABOUT THE YEAR GONE BY AND THE ONE JUST BEGINNING.
EVERYONE WRITES SOMETHING.
ERIC FINISHES IT OFF WITH 3-D LETTERS.
SHOULD I WRITE SOMETHING? HOW AM I SUPPOSED TO FEEL? WHAT AM I GOING TO WRITE?

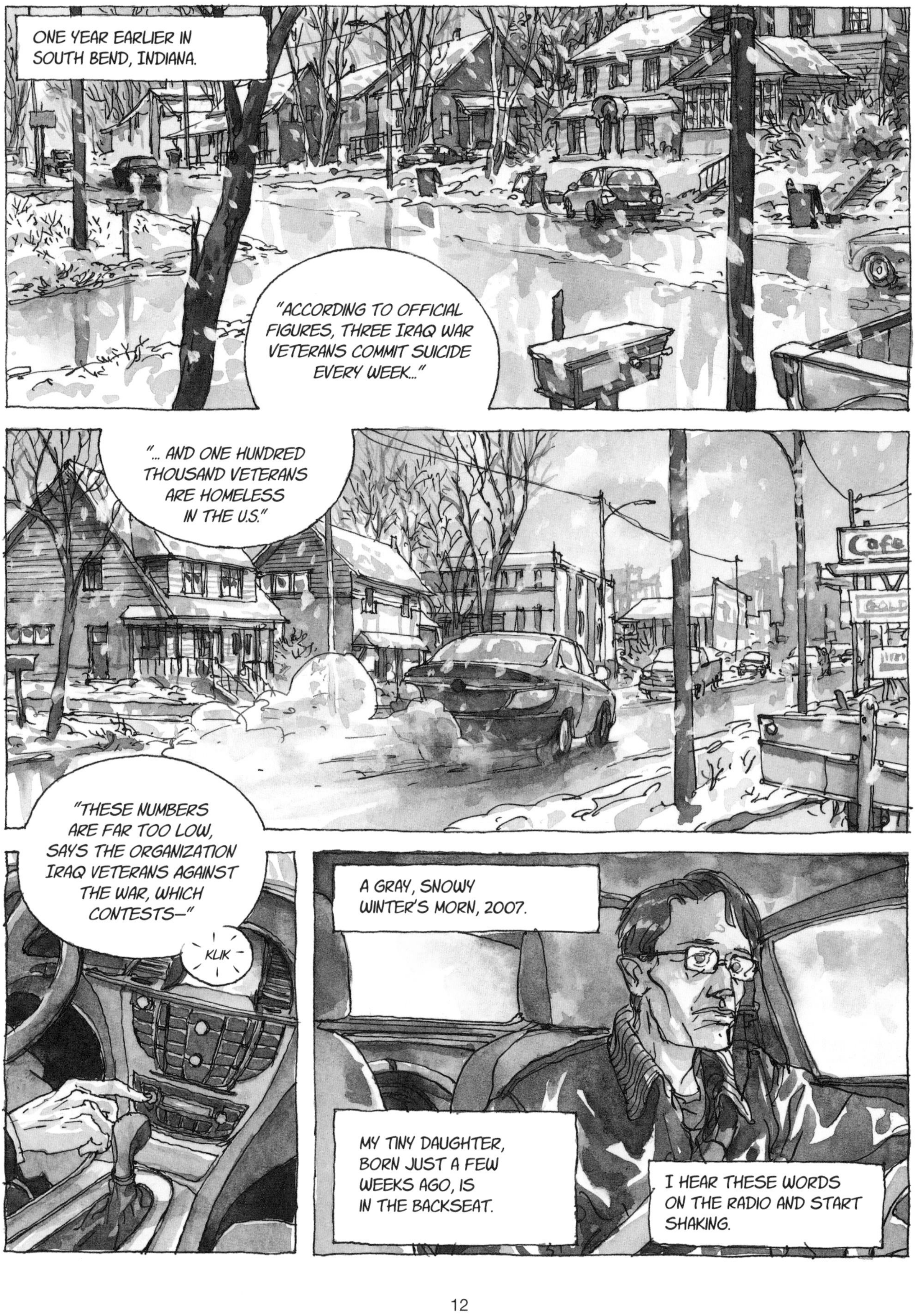
ONE YEAR EARLIER IN SOUTH BEND, INDIANA.
"ACCORDING TO OFFICIAL FIGURES, THREE IRAQ WAR VETERANS COMMIT SUICIDE EVERY WEEK..."
"... AND ONE HUNDRED THOUSAND VETERANS ARE HOMELESS IN THE U.S."
Cafe
"THESE NUMBERS ARE FAR TOO LOW, SAYS THE ORGANIZATION IRAQ VETERANS AGAINST THE WAR, WHICH CONTESTS–"
KLIK
A GRAY, SNOWY WINTER'S MORN, 2007.
MY TINY DAUGHTER, BORN JUST A FEW WEEKS AGO, IS IN THE BACKSEAT.
I HEAR THESE WORDS ON THE RADIO AND START SHAKING.

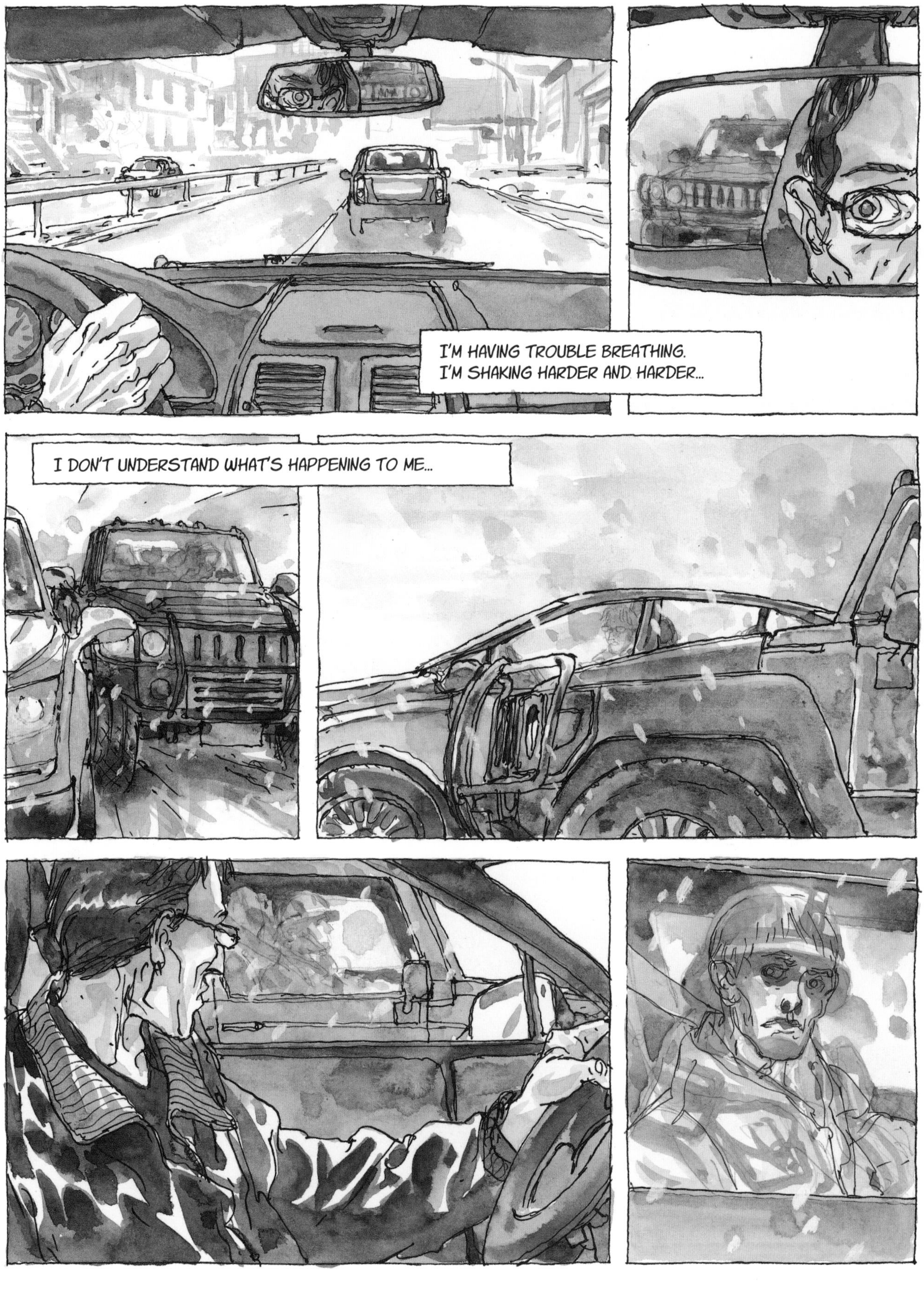
I'M HAVING TROUBLE BREATHING.
I'M SHAKING HARDER AND HARDER...
I DON'T UNDERSTAND WHAT'S HAPPENING TO ME...

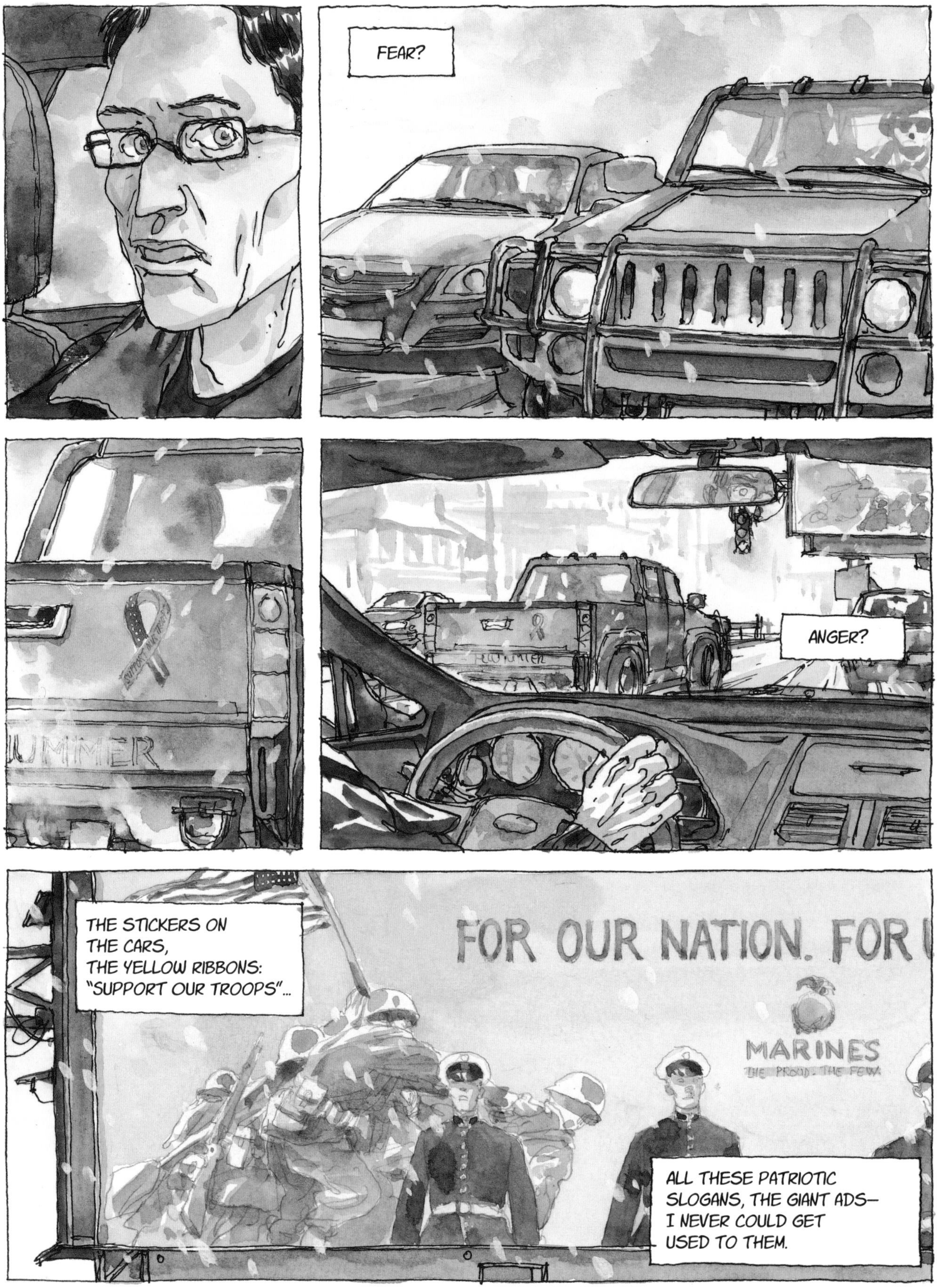
FEAR?
HUMMER
ANGER?
THE STICKERS ON THE CARS, THE YELLOW RIBBONS: "SUPPORT OUR TROOPS"...
FOR OUR NATION. FOR
MARINES
THE PROUD. THE FEW.
ALL THESE PATRIOTIC SLOGANS, THE GIANT ADS— I NEVER COULD GET USED TO THEM.

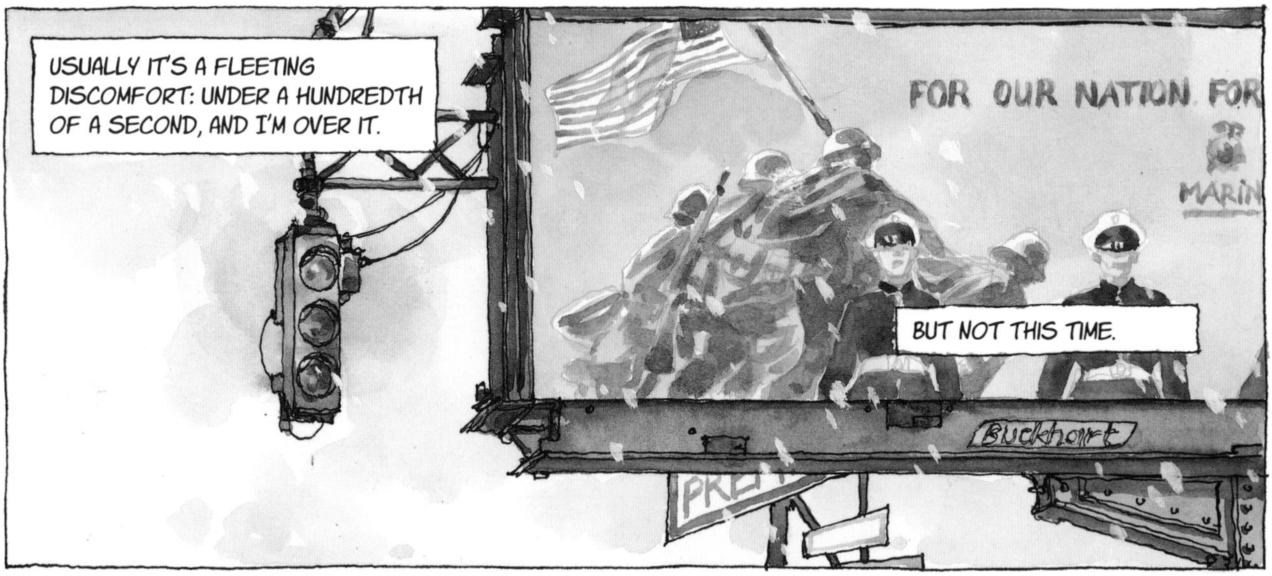
USUALLY IT'S A FLEETING DISCOMFORT: UNDER A HUNDREDTH OF A SECOND, AND I'M OVER IT.
FOR OUR NATION FOR
MARIN
BUT NOT THIS TIME.
Buckhort

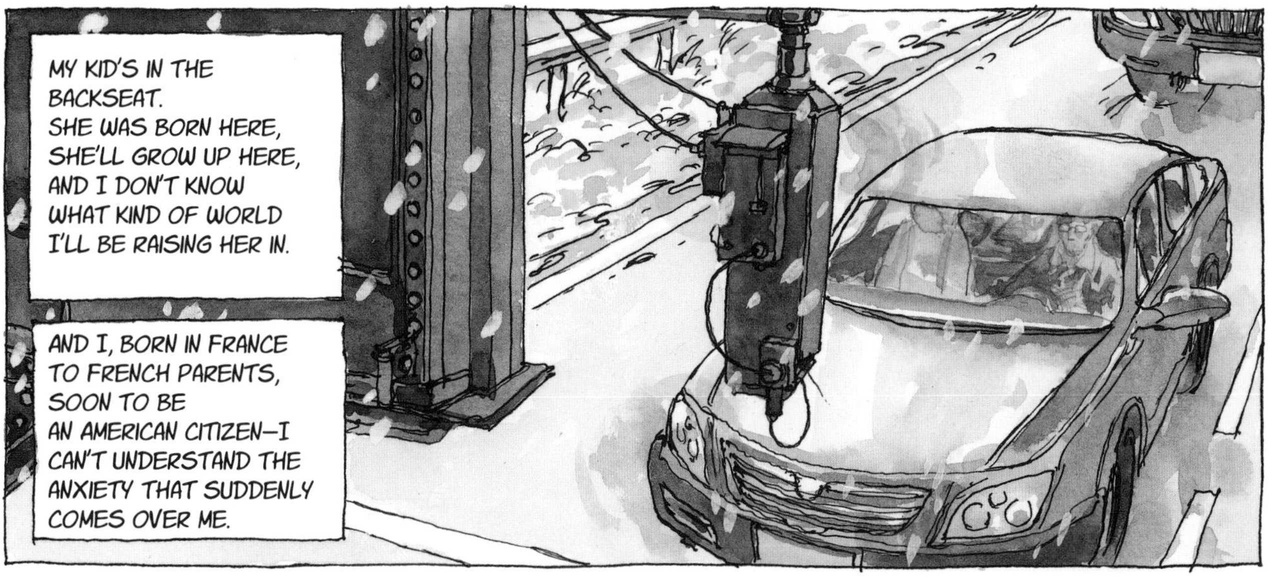
MY KID'S IN THE BACKSEAT.
SHE WAS BORN HERE, SHE'LL GROW UP HERE, AND I DON'T KNOW WHAT KIND OF WORLD I'LL BE RAISING HER IN.
AND I, BORN IN FRANCE TO FRENCH PARENTS, SOON TO BE AN AMERICAN CITIZEN—I CAN'T UNDERSTAND THE ANXIETY THAT SUDDENLY COMES OVER ME.

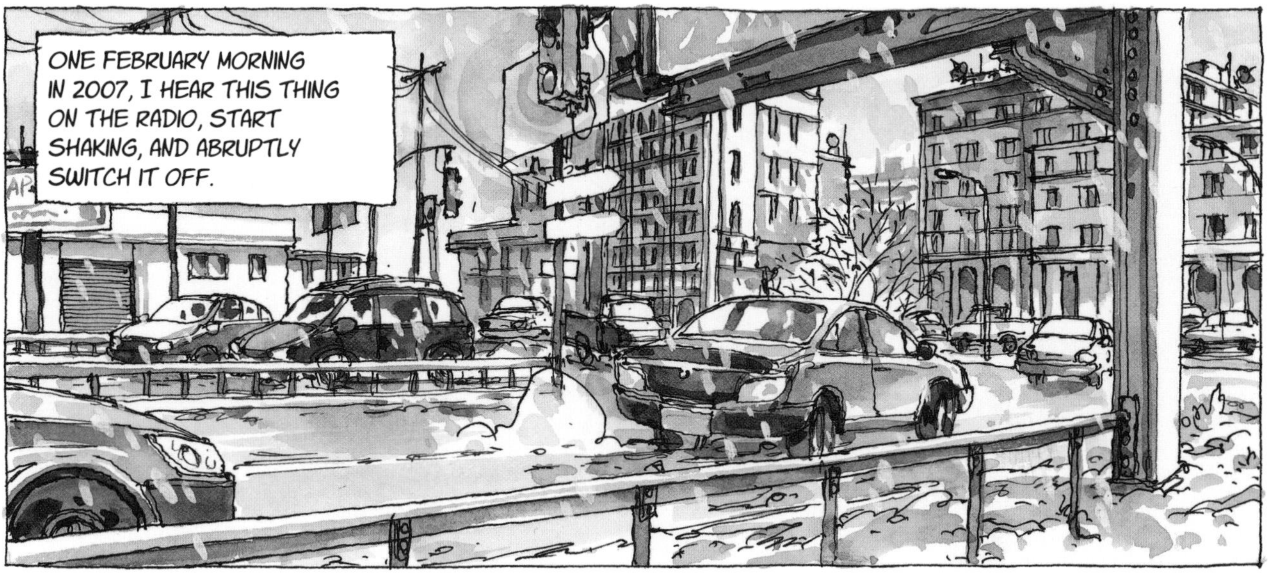
ONE FEBRUARY MORNING IN 2007, I HEAR THIS THING ON THE RADIO, START SHAKING, AND ABRUPTLY SWITCH IT OFF.

N. FOR US ALL.
MARINES
THE FEW. THE PROUD.
I REMEMBER AN AFTERNOON IN JULY 1997, IN THE LITTLE HOUSE OF MARIUS ESTRATAT IN PROVENCE.
IT WAS A HOT DAY.
VOS
Adieu to life, adieu to death, to all the women too
This wretched war has torn us from everything we knew
VOS
It's in Craonne we'll meet our end, our bodies in the mud...
I'VE KNOWN THAT SONG FOR EIGHTY YEARS!
WE NEVER SANG IT IN FRONT OF THE OFFICERS, MIND YOU![2]

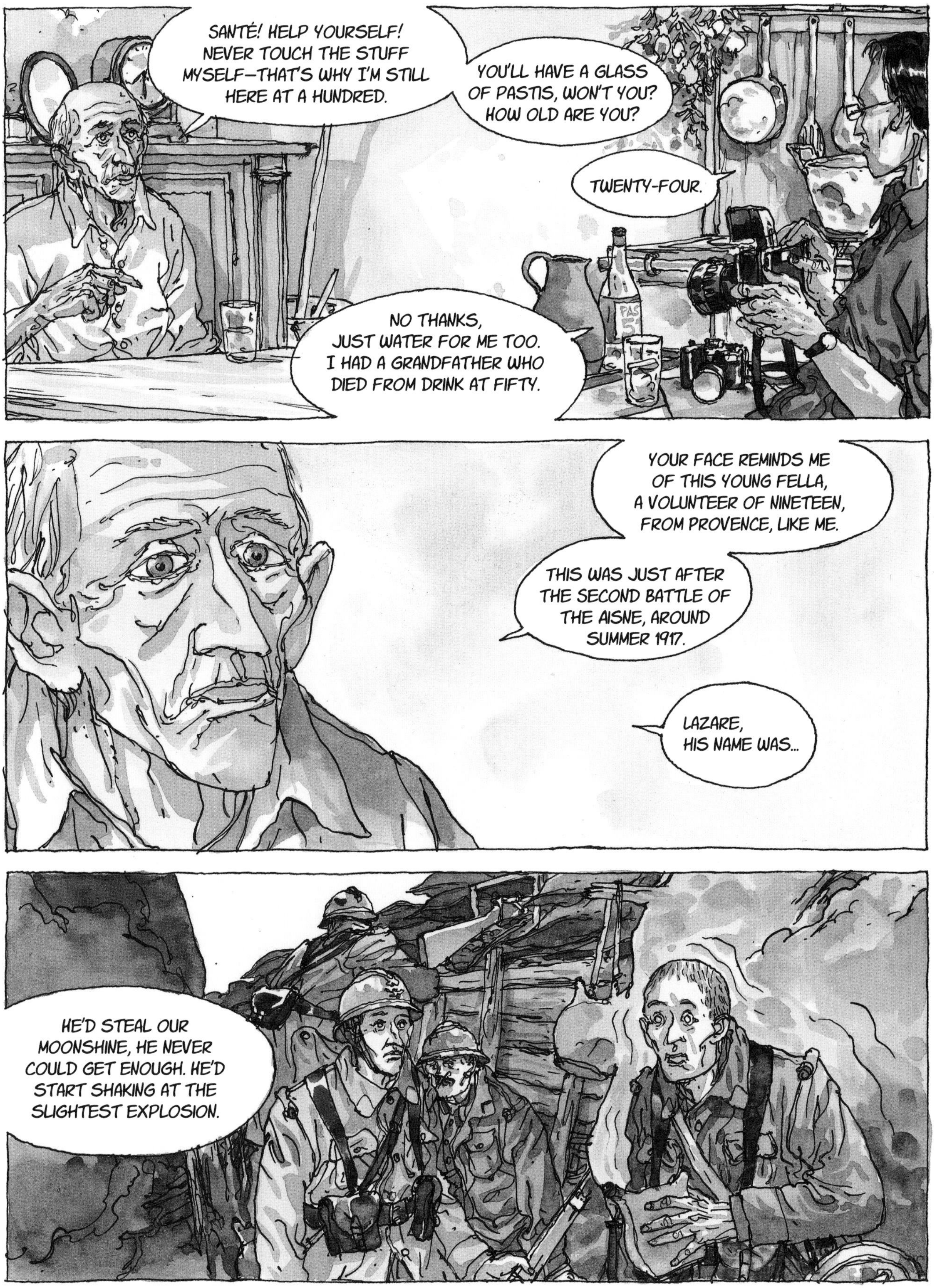
SANTÉ! HELP YOURSELF! NEVER TOUCH THE STUFF MYSELF—THAT'S WHY I'M STILL HERE AT A HUNDRED.
YOU'LL HAVE A GLASS OF PASTIS, WON'T YOU? HOW OLD ARE YOU?
TWENTY-FOUR.
NO THANKS, JUST WATER FOR ME TOO. I HAD A GRANDFATHER WHO DIED FROM DRINK AT FIFTY.
YOUR FACE REMINDS ME OF THIS YOUNG FELLA, A VOLUNTEER OF NINETEEN, FROM PROVENCE, LIKE ME.
THIS WAS JUST AFTER THE SECOND BATTLE OF THE AISNE, AROUND SUMMER 1917.
LAZARE, HIS NAME WAS...
HE'D STEAL OUR MOONSHINE, HE NEVER COULD GET ENOUGH. HE'D START SHAKING AT THE SLIGHTEST EXPLOSION.

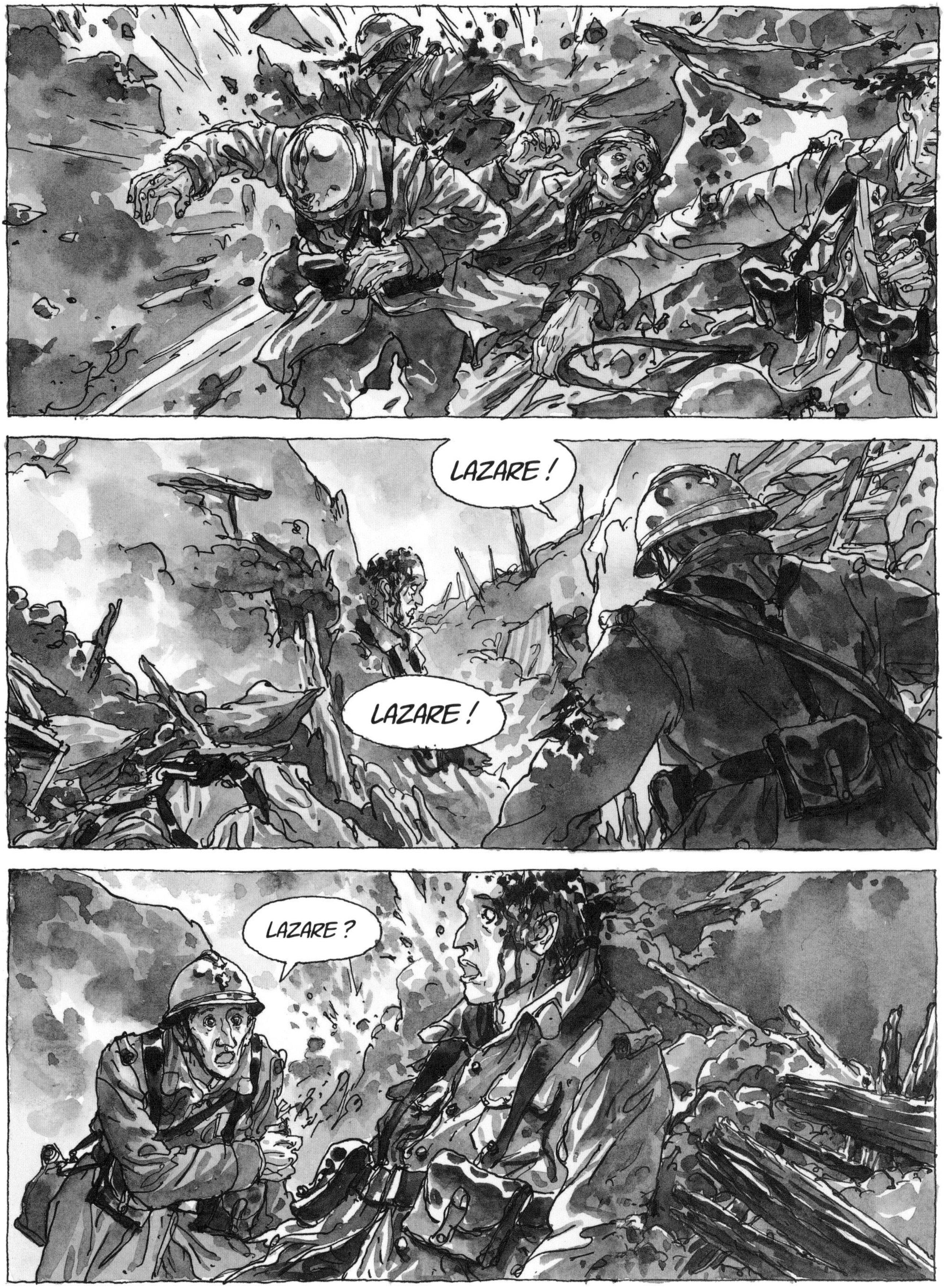
LAZARE !
LAZARE !
LAZARE ?

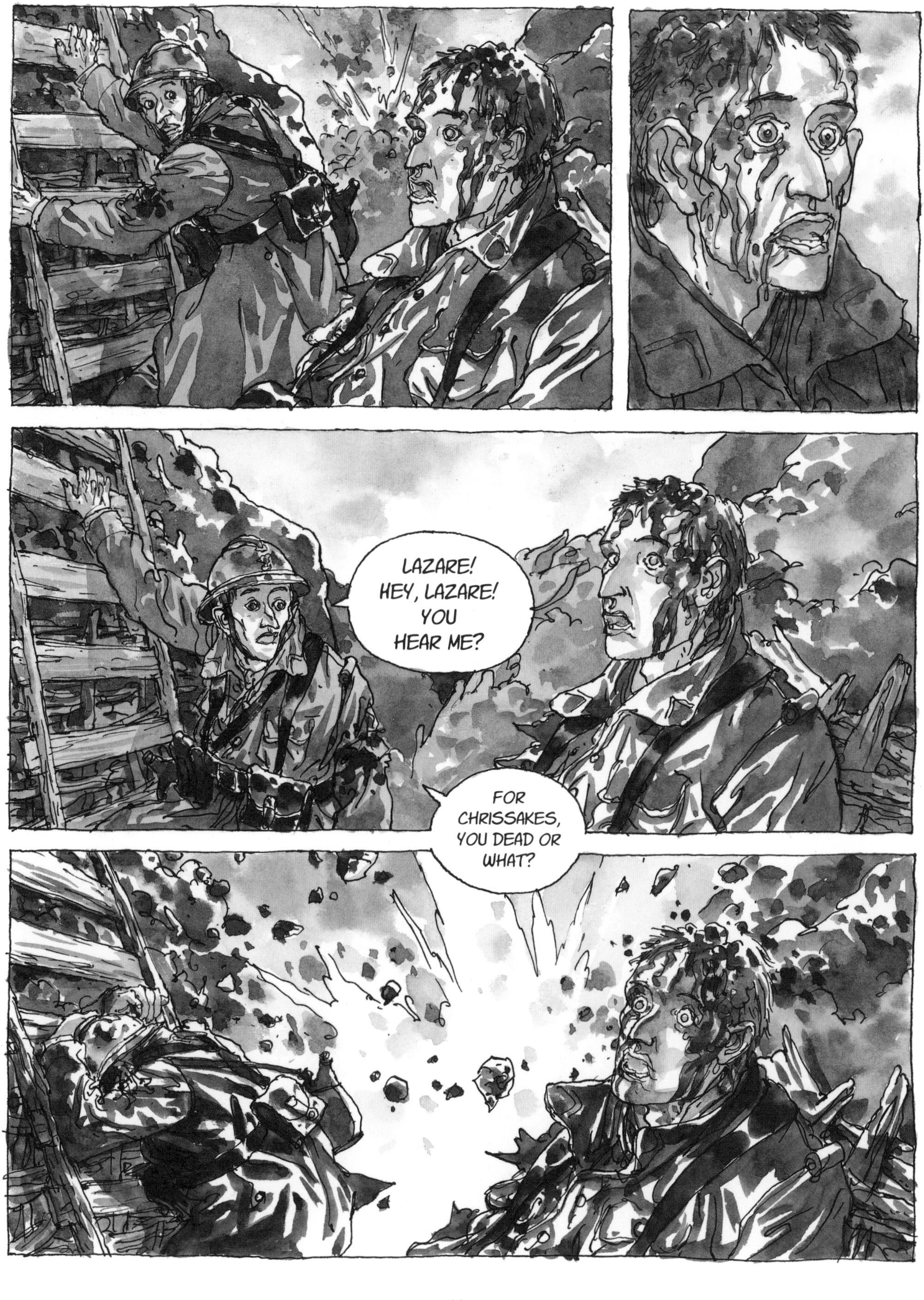
LAZARE! HEY, LAZARE! YOU HEAR ME?
FOR CHRISSAKES, YOU DEAD OR WHAT?

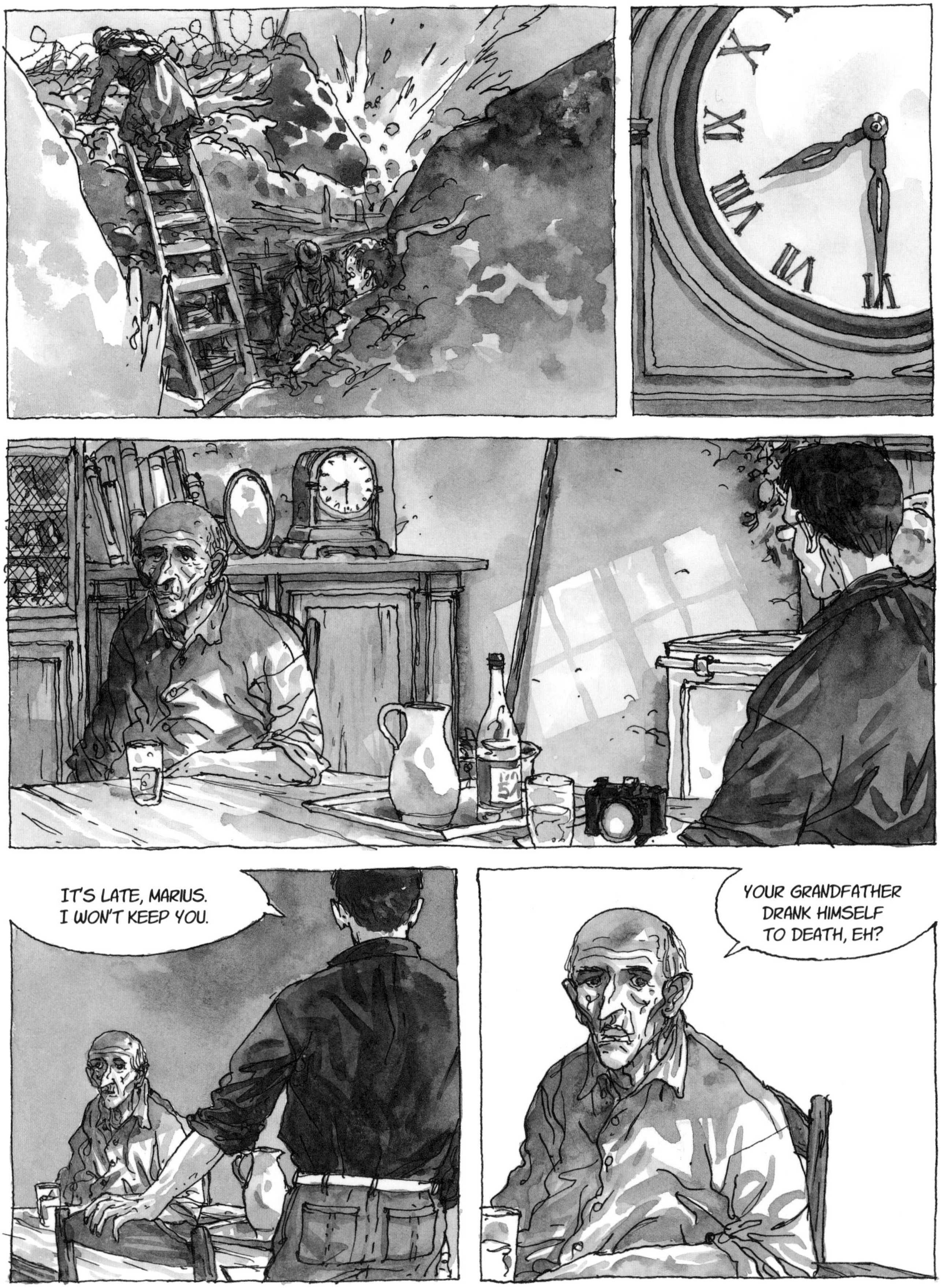
IT'S LATE, MARIUS.
I WON'T KEEP YOU.
YOUR GRANDFATHER
DRANK HIMSELF
TO DEATH, EH?

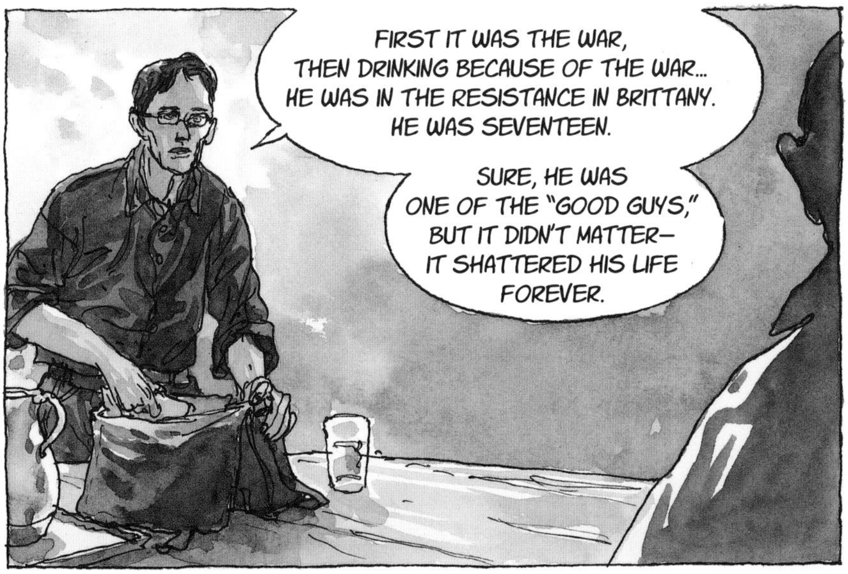
FIRST IT WAS THE WAR, THEN DRINKING BECAUSE OF THE WAR... HE WAS IN THE RESISTANCE IN BRITTANY. HE WAS SEVENTEEN.
SURE, HE WAS ONE OF THE "GOOD GUYS," BUT IT DIDN'T MATTER— IT SHATTERED HIS LIFE FOREVER.

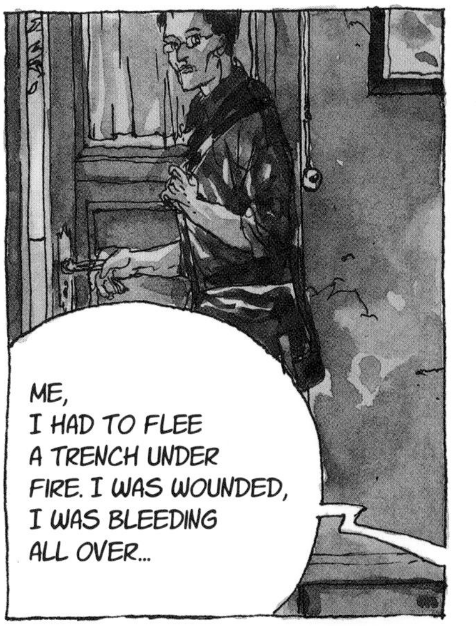
ME, I HAD TO FLEE A TRENCH UNDER FIRE. I WAS WOUNDED, I WAS BLEEDING ALL OVER...

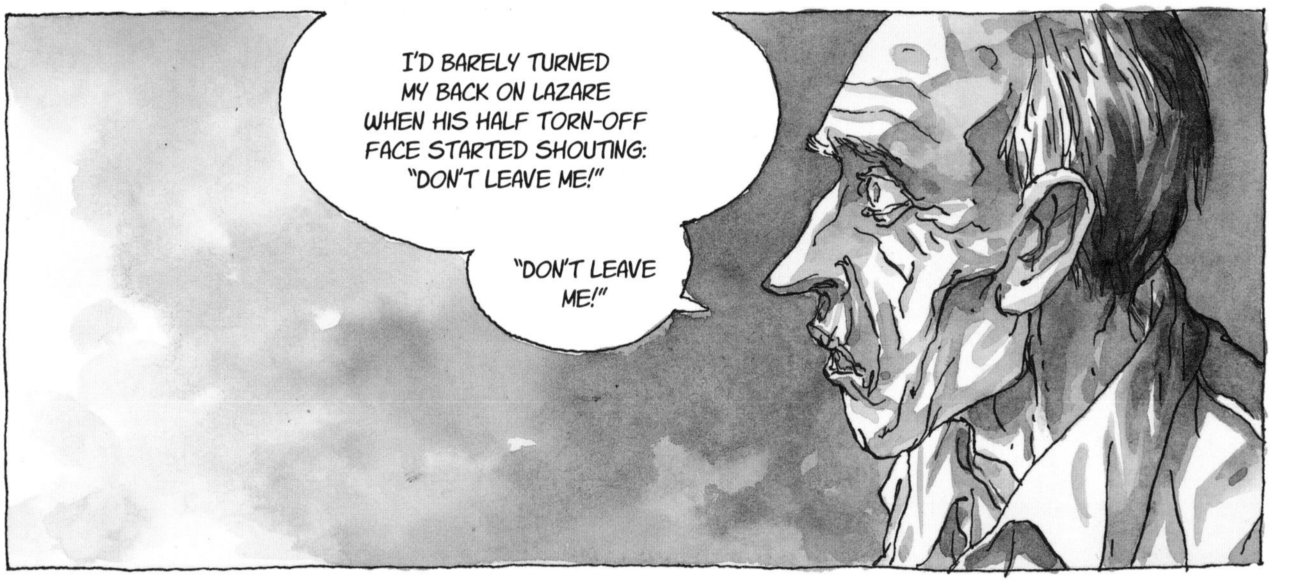
I'D BARELY TURNED MY BACK ON LAZARE WHEN HIS HALF TORN-OFF FACE STARTED SHOUTING: "DON'T LEAVE ME!"
"DON'T LEAVE ME!"

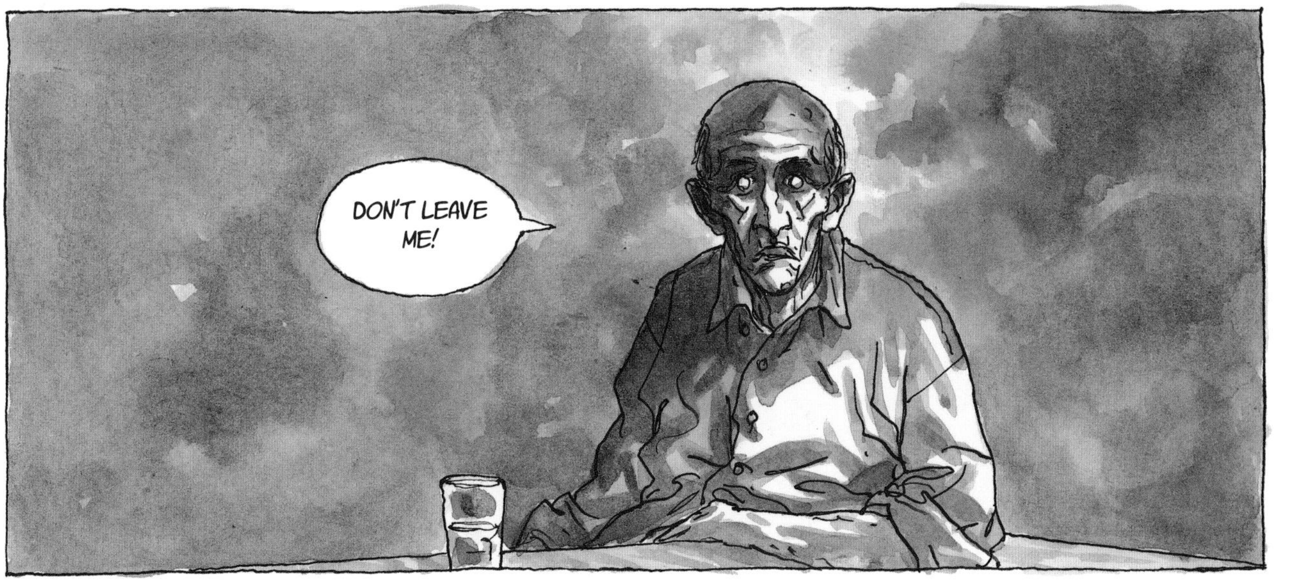
DON'T LEAVE ME!

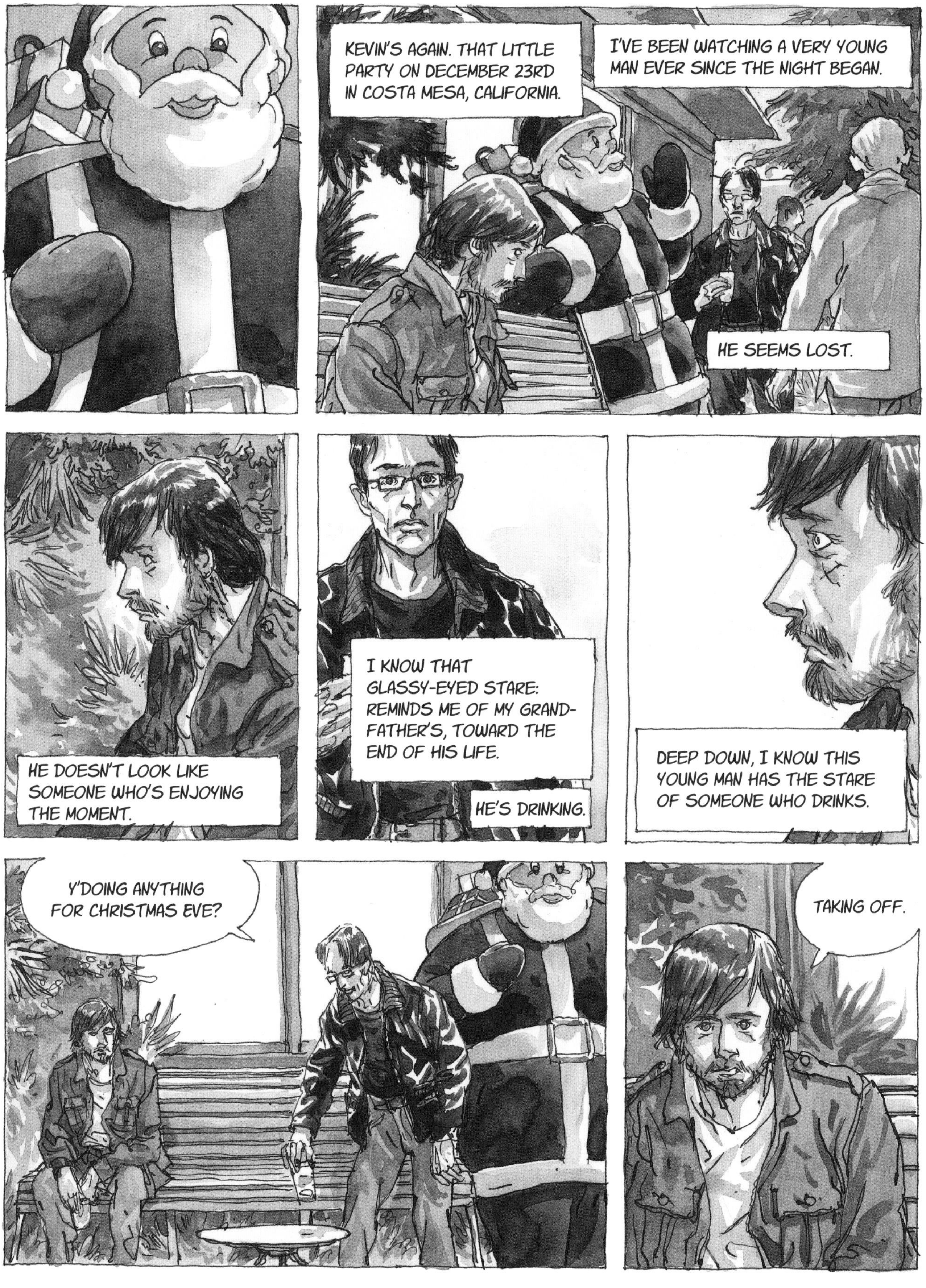
KEVIN'S AGAIN. THAT LITTLE PARTY ON DECEMBER 23RD IN COSTA MESA, CALIFORNIA.
I'VE BEEN WATCHING A VERY YOUNG MAN EVER SINCE THE NIGHT BEGAN.
HE SEEMS LOST.
HE DOESN'T LOOK LIKE SOMEONE WHO'S ENJOYING THE MOMENT.
I KNOW THAT GLASSY-EYED STARE: REMINDS ME OF MY GRAND-FATHER'S, TOWARD THE END OF HIS LIFE.
HE'S DRINKING.
DEEP DOWN, I KNOW THIS YOUNG MAN HAS THE STARE OF SOMEONE WHO DRINKS.
Y'DOING ANYTHING FOR CHRISTMAS EVE?
TAKING OFF.

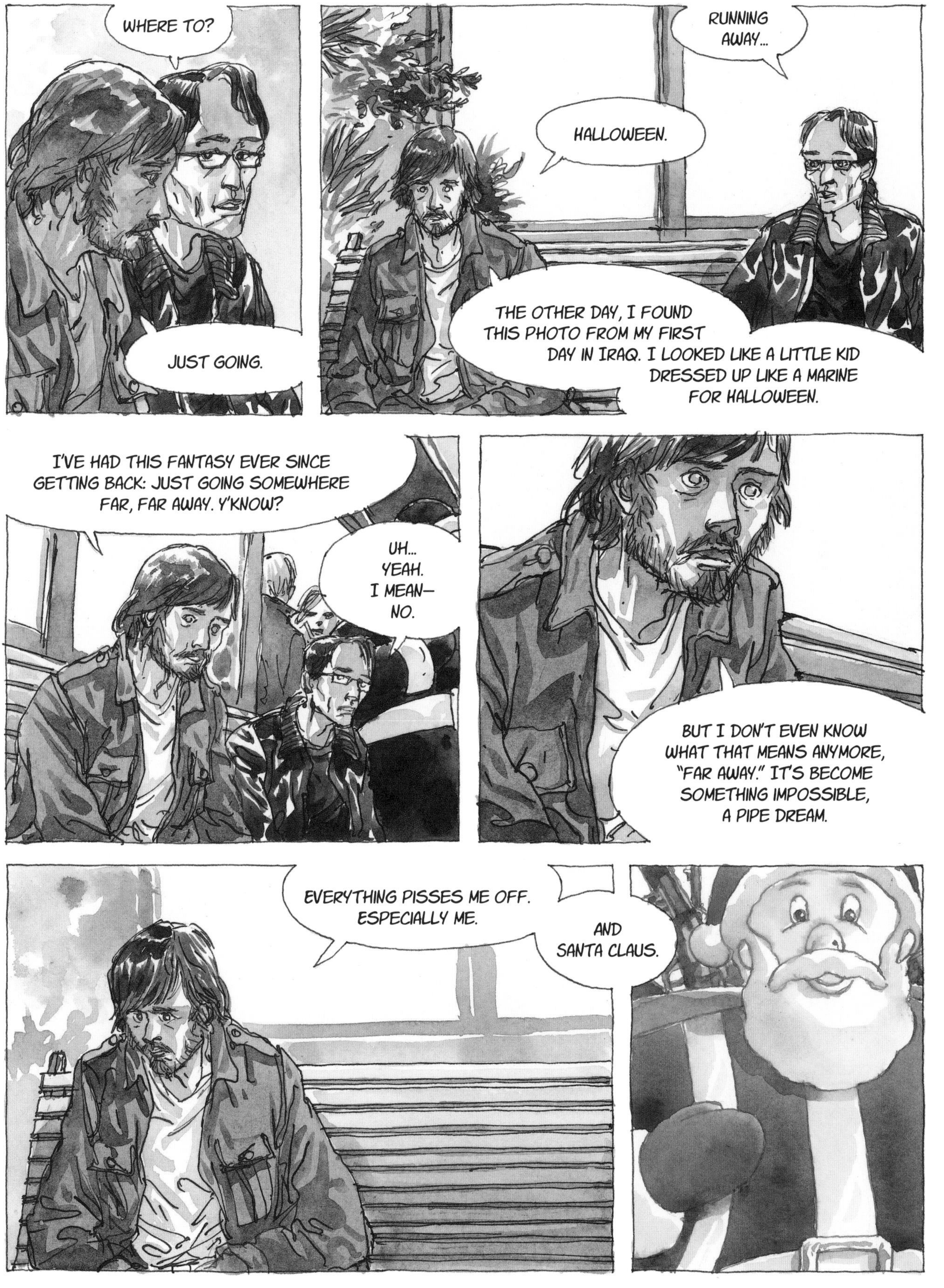
WHERE TO?
JUST GOING.
RUNNING AWAY...
HALLOWEEN.
THE OTHER DAY, I FOUND THIS PHOTO FROM MY FIRST DAY IN IRAQ. I LOOKED LIKE A LITTLE KID DRESSED UP LIKE A MARINE FOR HALLOWEEN.
I'VE HAD THIS FANTASY EVER SINCE GETTING BACK: JUST GOING SOMEWHERE FAR, FAR AWAY. Y'KNOW?
UH... YEAH. I MEAN— NO.
BUT I DON'T EVEN KNOW WHAT THAT MEANS ANYMORE, "FAR AWAY." IT'S BECOME SOMETHING IMPOSSIBLE, A PIPE DREAM.
EVERYTHING PISSES ME OFF. ESPECIALLY ME.
AND SANTA CLAUS.

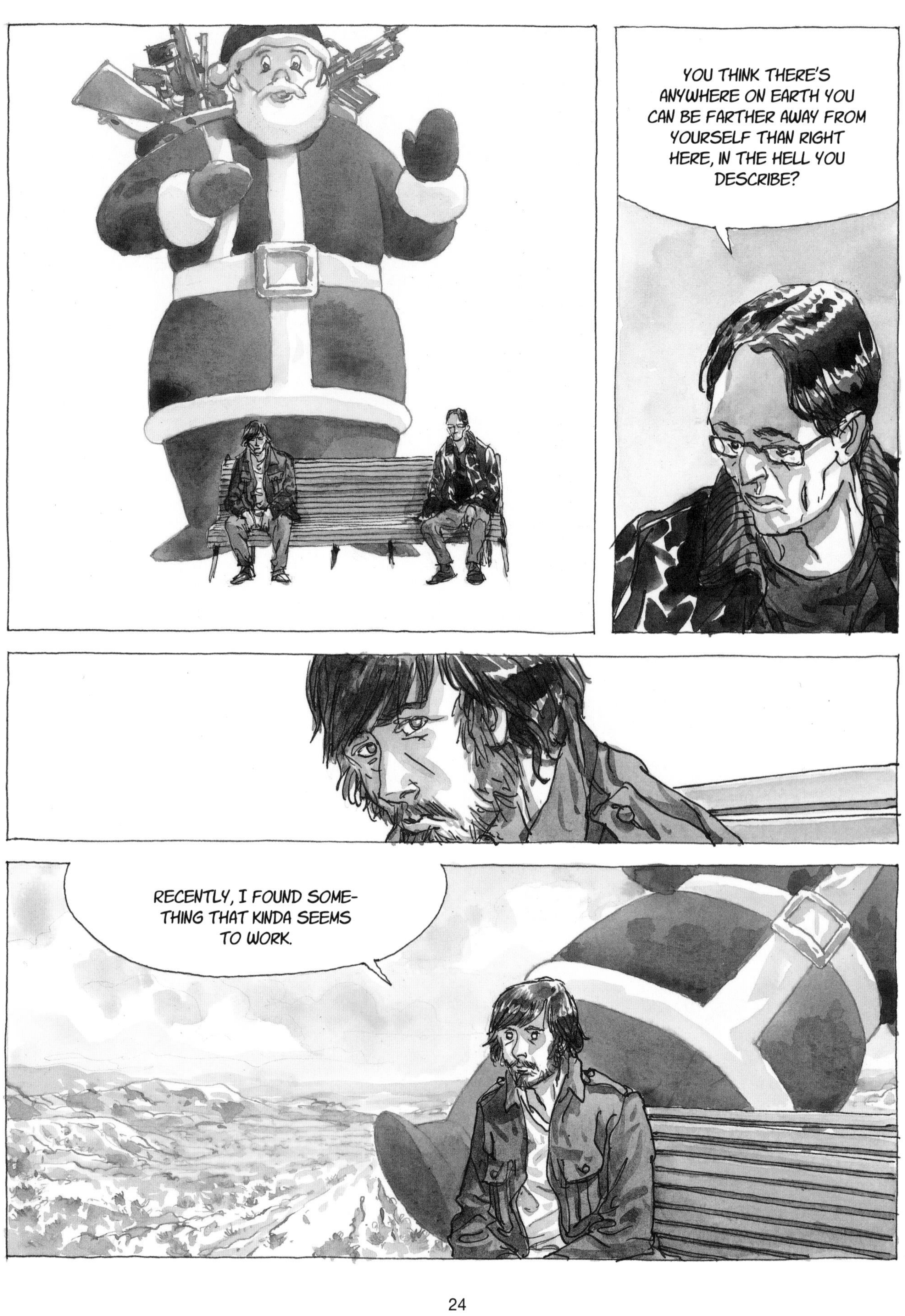
YOU THINK THERE'S ANYWHERE ON EARTH YOU CAN BE FARTHER AWAY FROM YOURSELF THAN RIGHT HERE, IN THE HELL YOU DESCRIBE?
RECENTLY, I FOUND SOMETHING THAT KINDA SEEMS TO WORK.

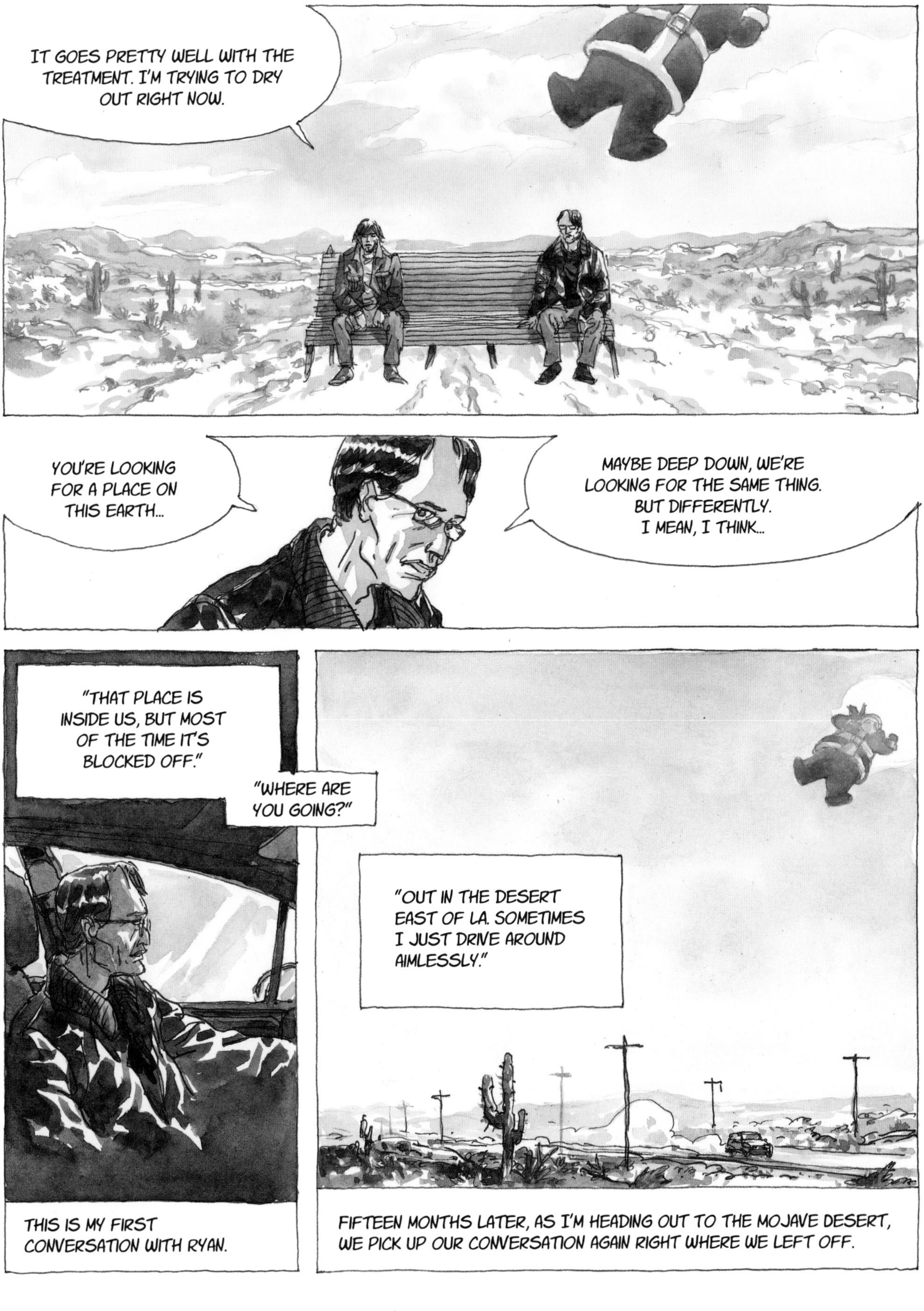
IT GOES PRETTY WELL WITH THE TREATMENT. I'M TRYING TO DRY OUT RIGHT NOW.
YOU'RE LOOKING FOR A PLACE ON THIS EARTH...
MAYBE DEEP DOWN, WE'RE LOOKING FOR THE SAME THING. BUT DIFFERENTLY. I MEAN, I THINK...
"THAT PLACE IS INSIDE US, BUT MOST OF THE TIME IT'S BLOCKED OFF."
"WHERE ARE YOU GOING?"
THIS IS MY FIRST CONVERSATION WITH RYAN.
"OUT IN THE DESERT EAST OF LA. SOMETIMES I JUST DRIVE AROUND AIMLESSLY."
FIFTEEN MONTHS LATER, AS I'M HEADING OUT TO THE MOJAVE DESERT, WE PICK UP OUR CONVERSATION AGAIN RIGHT WHERE WE LEFT OFF.

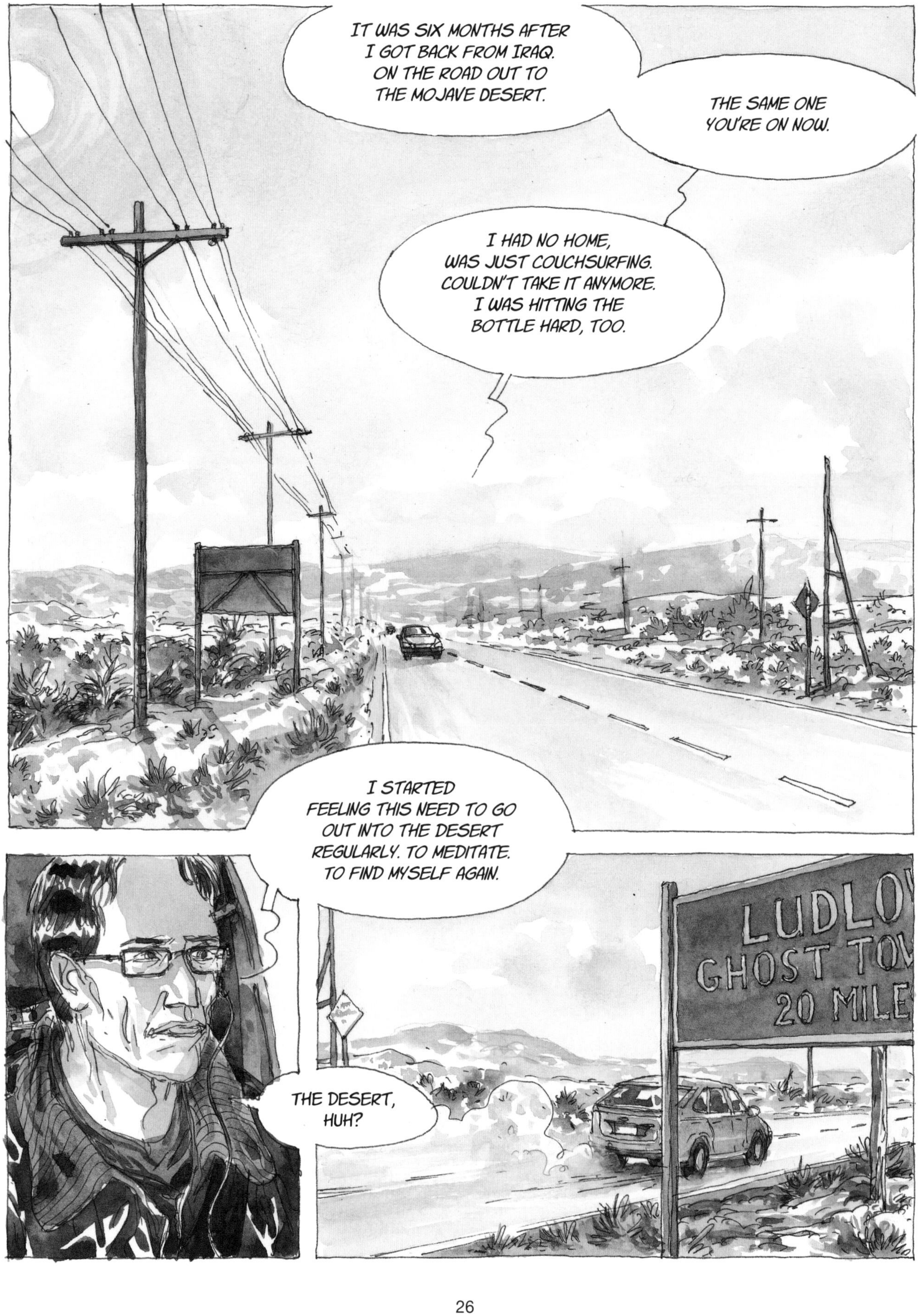
IT WAS SIX MONTHS AFTER I GOT BACK FROM IRAQ. ON THE ROAD OUT TO THE MOJAVE DESERT.
THE SAME ONE YOU'RE ON NOW.
I HAD NO HOME, WAS JUST COUCHSURFING. COULDN'T TAKE IT ANYMORE. I WAS HITTING THE BOTTLE HARD, TOO.
I STARTED FEELING THIS NEED TO GO OUT INTO THE DESERT REGULARLY. TO MEDITATE. TO FIND MYSELF AGAIN.
THE DESERT, HUH?
LUDLO
GHOST TOV
20 MILE

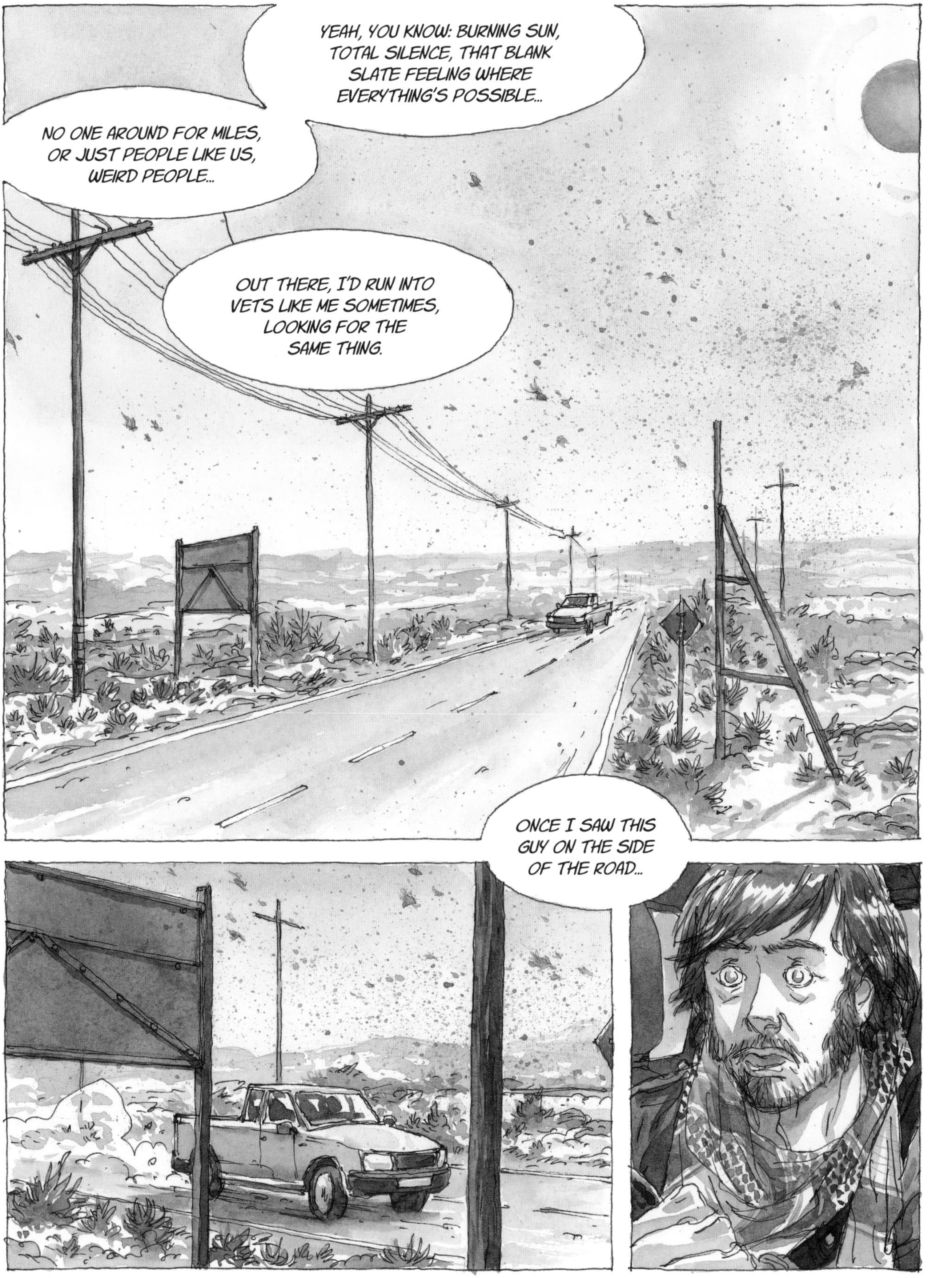
NO ONE AROUND FOR MILES, OR JUST PEOPLE LIKE US, WEIRD PEOPLE...
YEAH, YOU KNOW: BURNING SUN, TOTAL SILENCE, THAT BLANK SLATE FEELING WHERE EVERYTHING'S POSSIBLE...
OUT THERE, I'D RUN INTO VETS LIKE ME SOMETIMES, LOOKING FOR THE SAME THING.
ONCE I SAW THIS GUY ON THE SIDE OF THE ROAD...

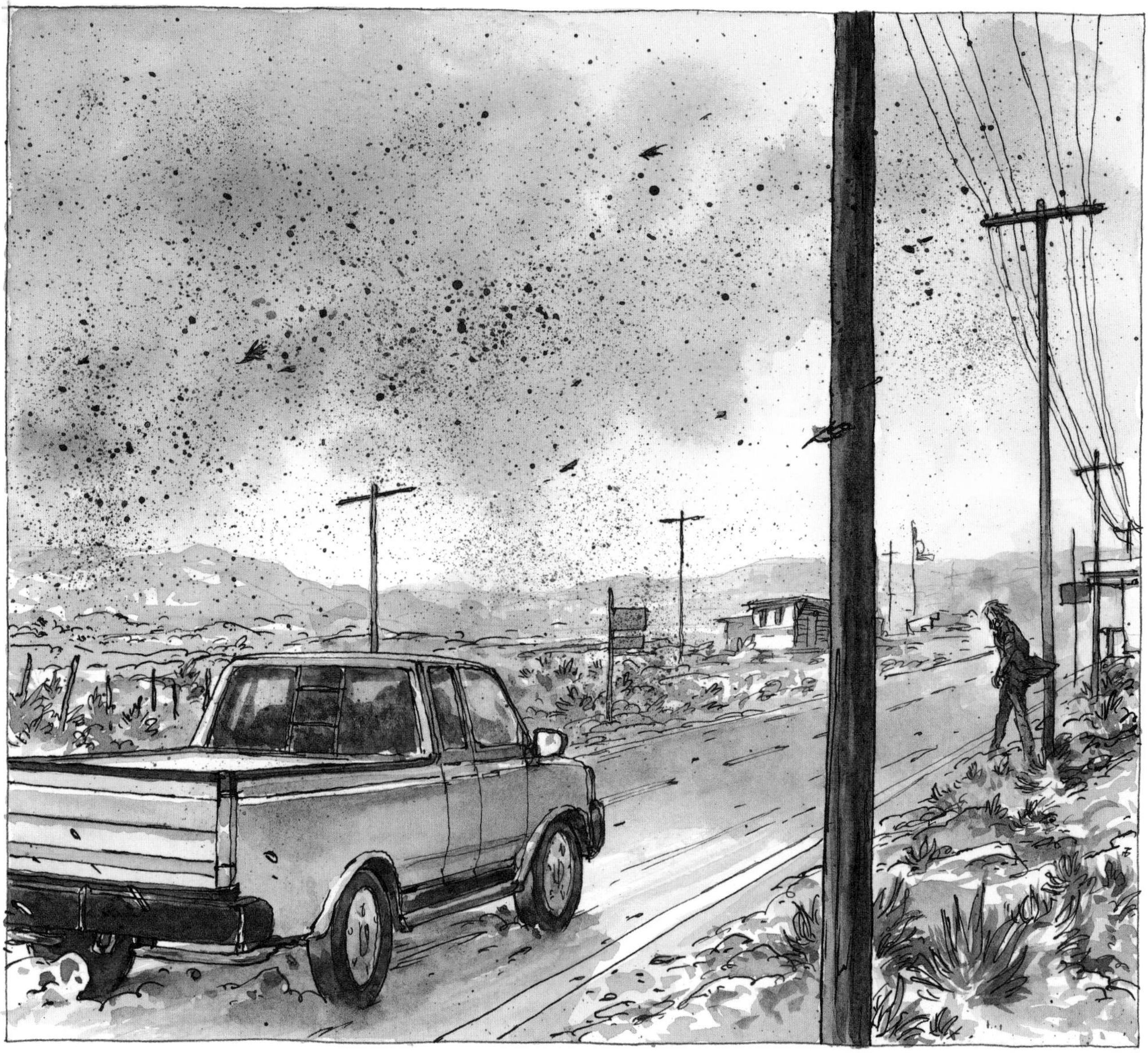

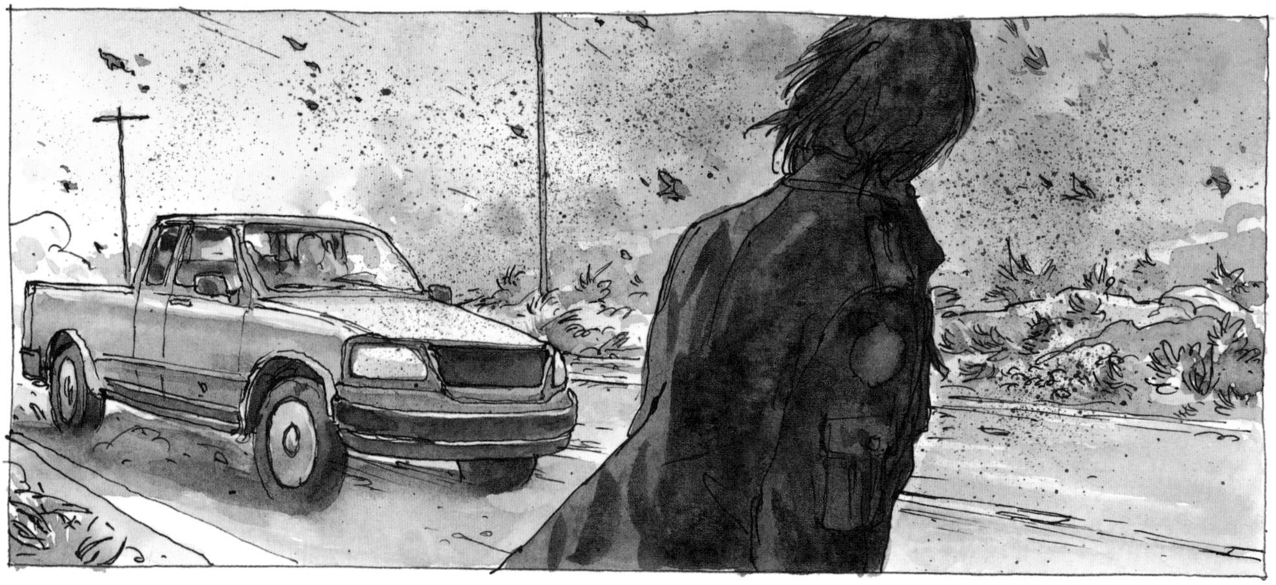

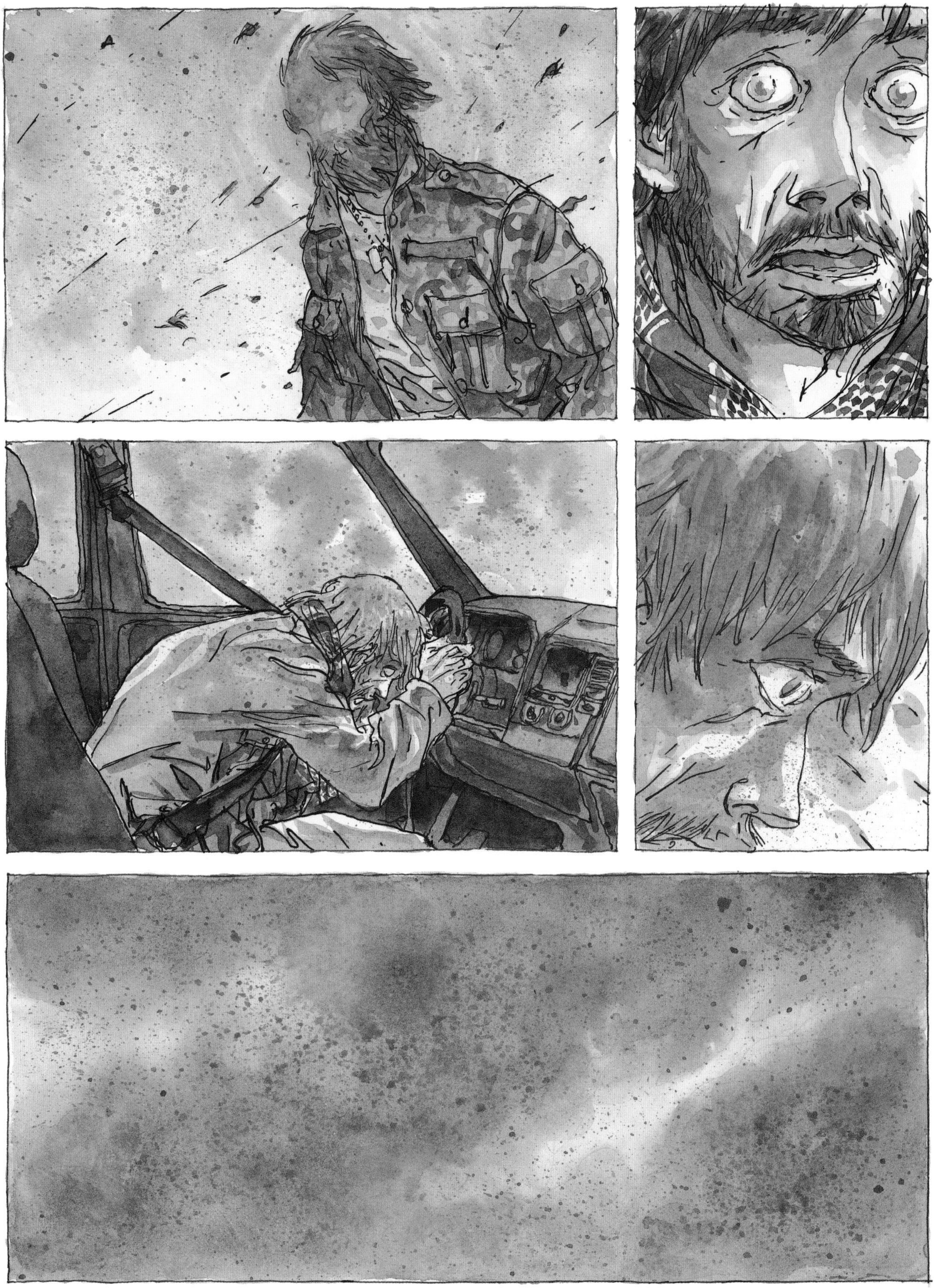

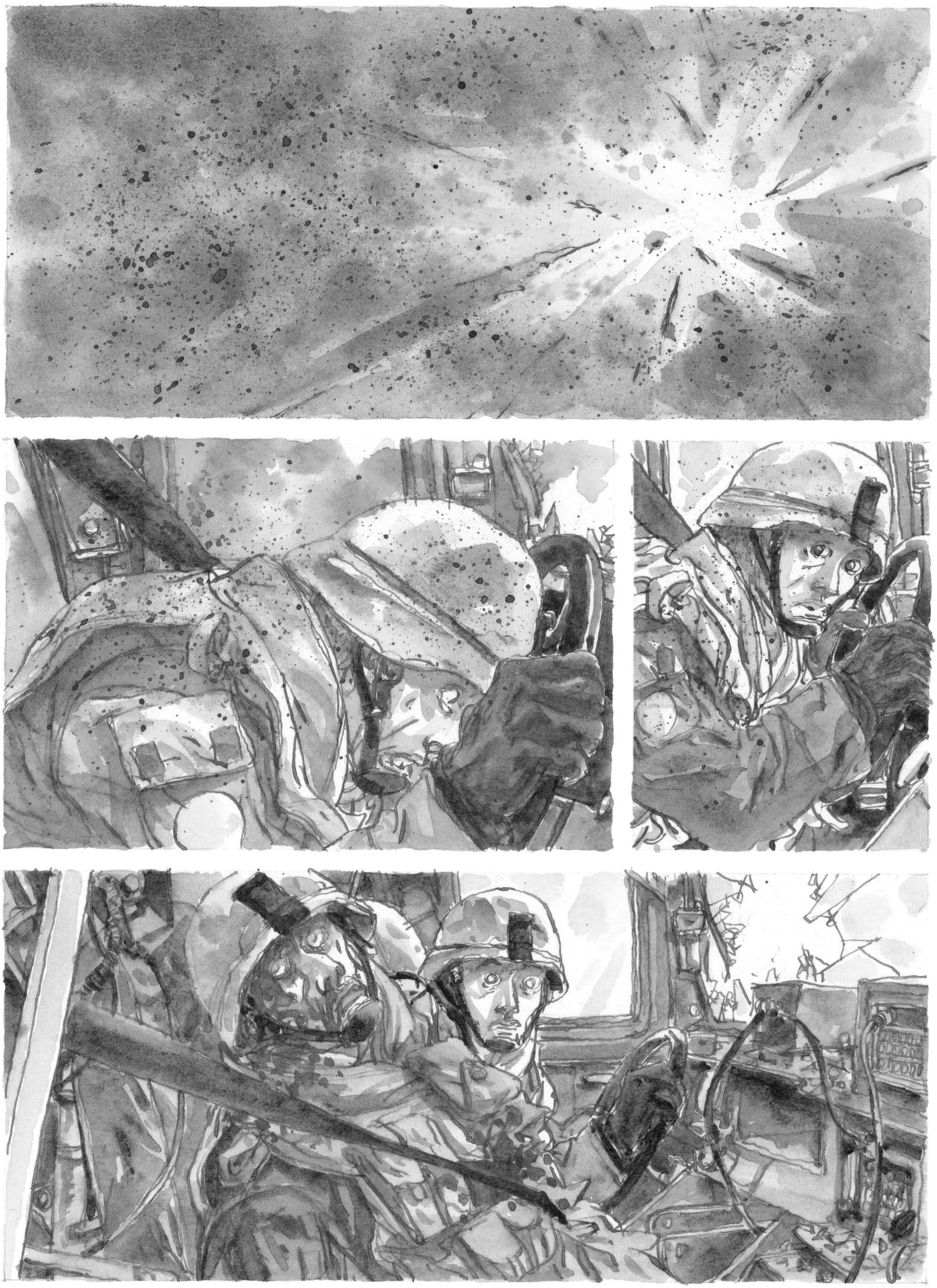

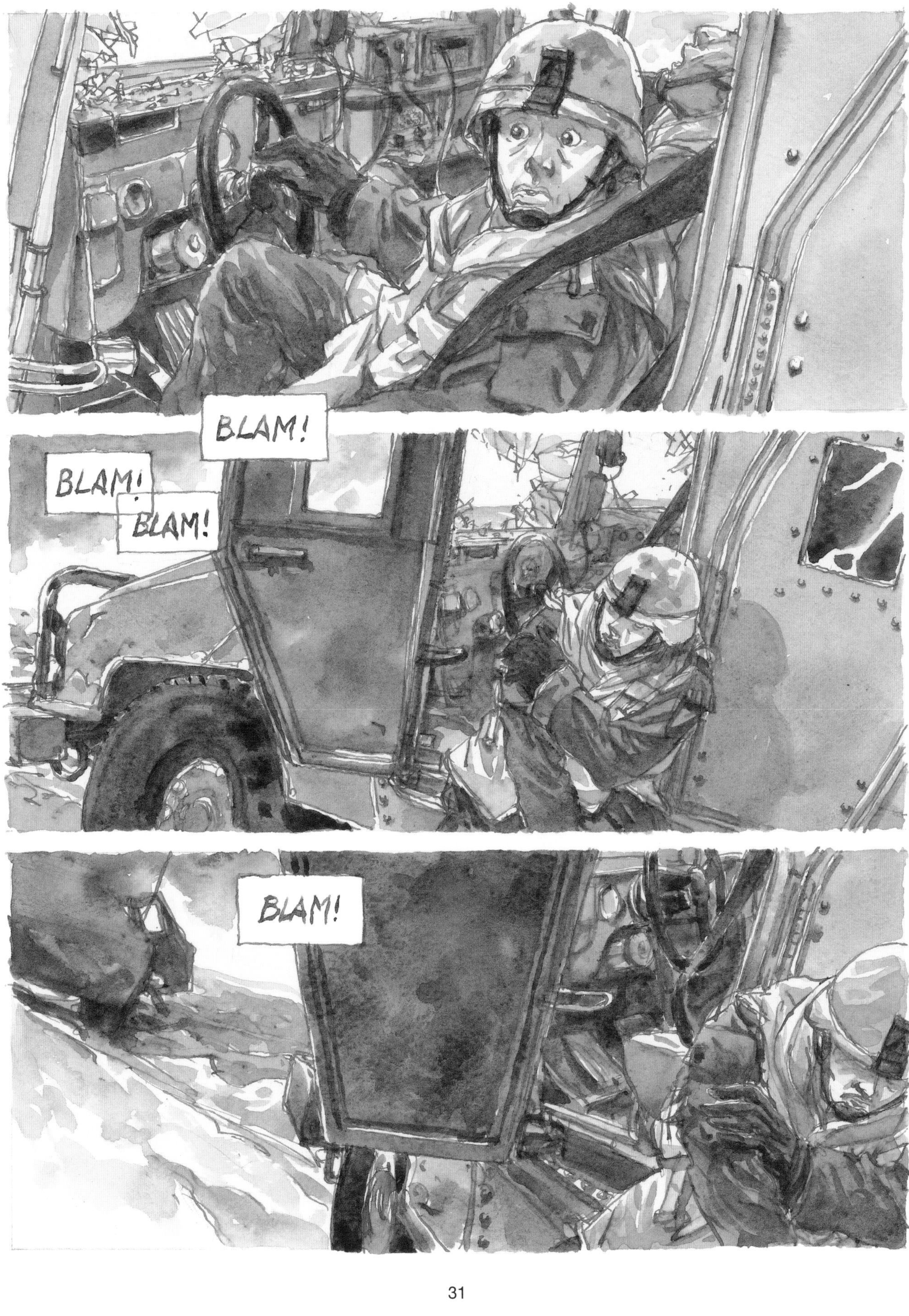
BLAM!
BLAM!
BLAM!
BLAM!

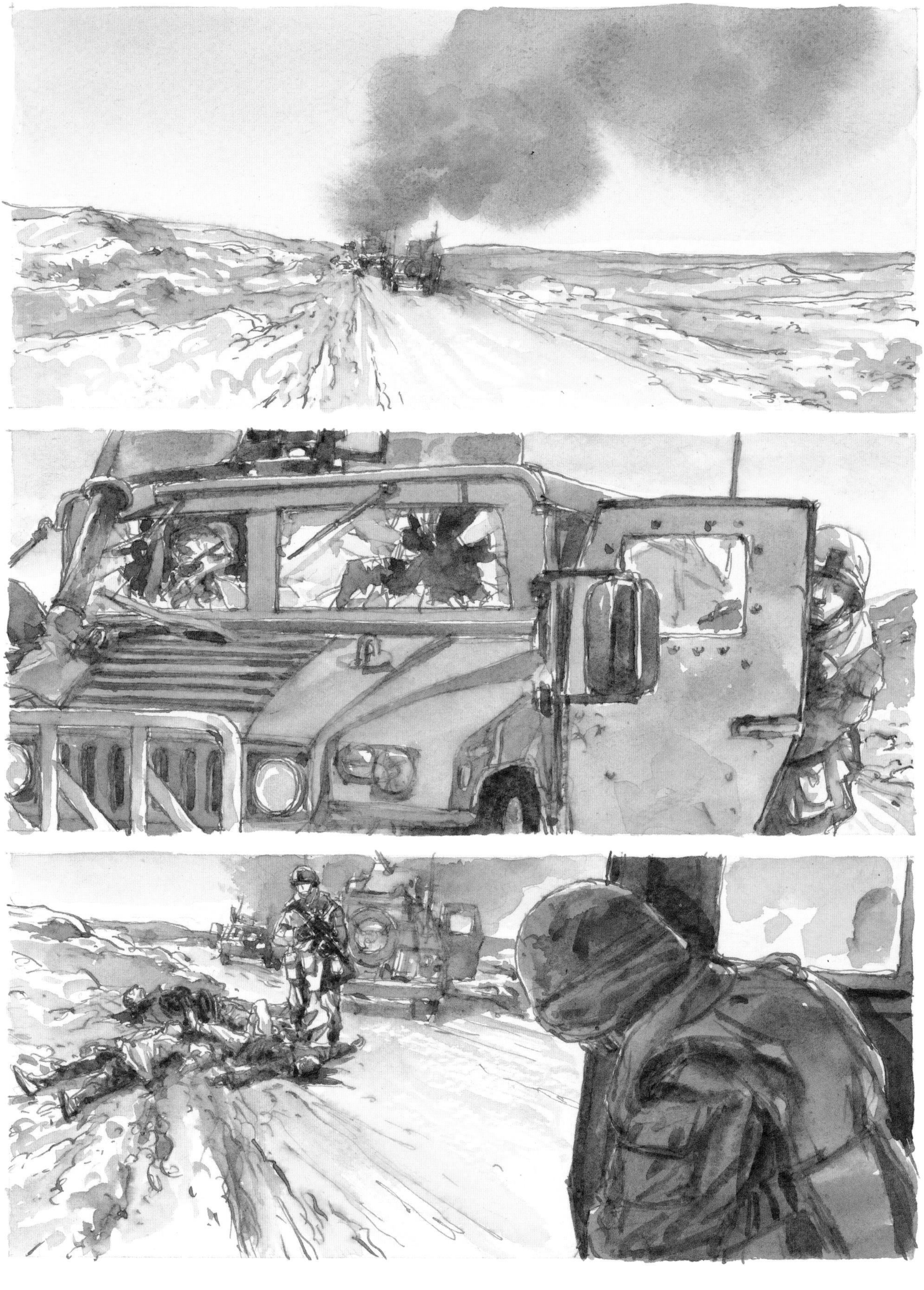

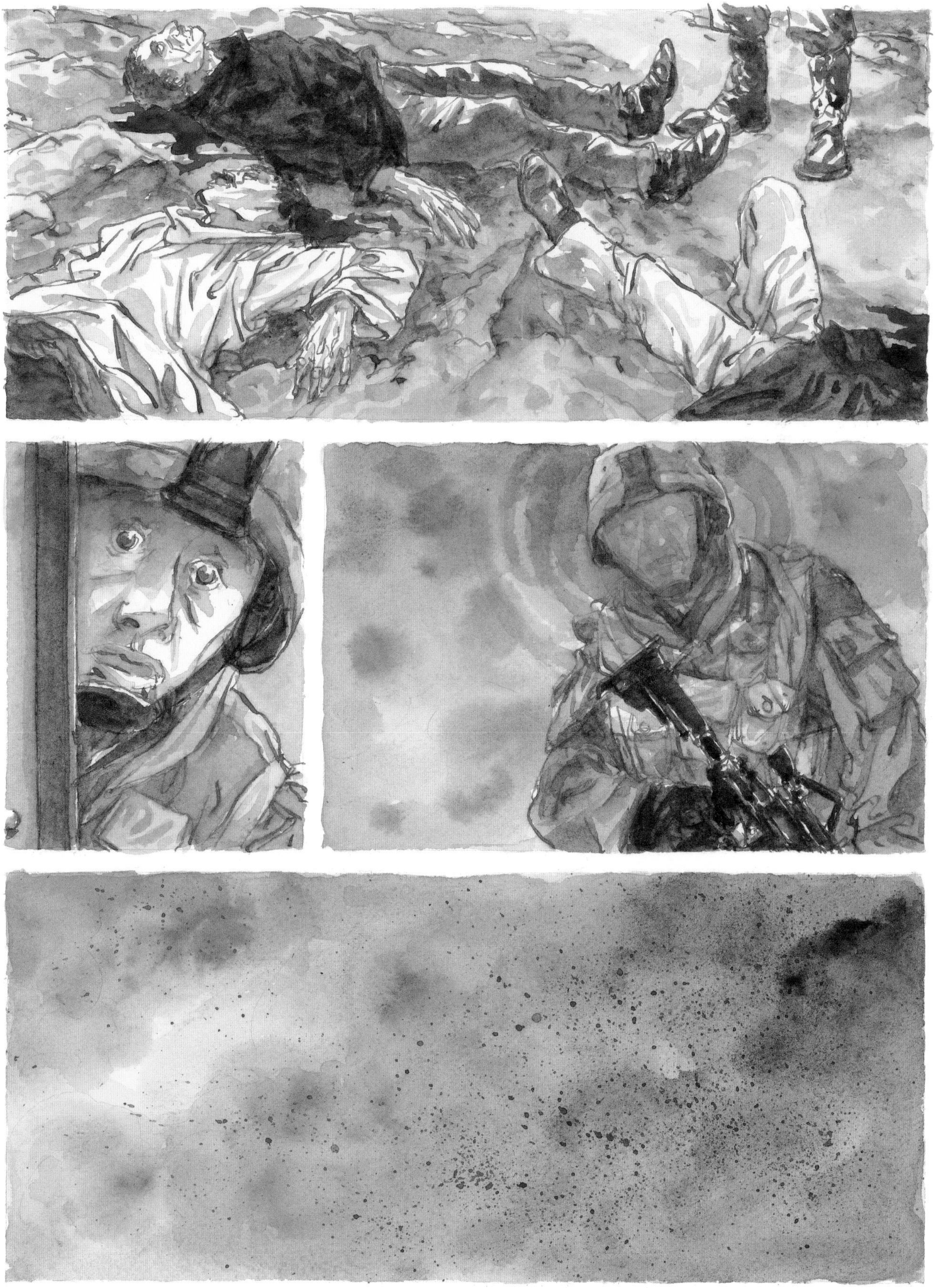

AND I
MADE IT...
Cafe
SINCE THEN,
I'VE OFTEN WONDERED
IF THE FACE OF THE
YOUNG MARINE WHO
KILLED THE THREE IRAQI
CIVILIANS WAS A GHOST
MY TRAUMA HAD MADE UP,
OR IF HE'D BEEN REAL.

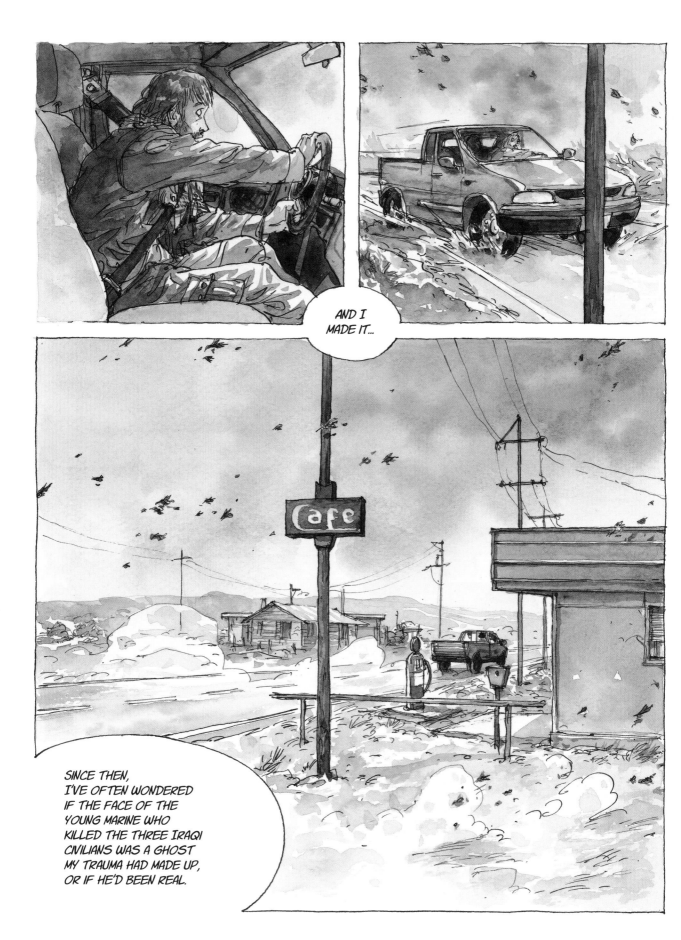

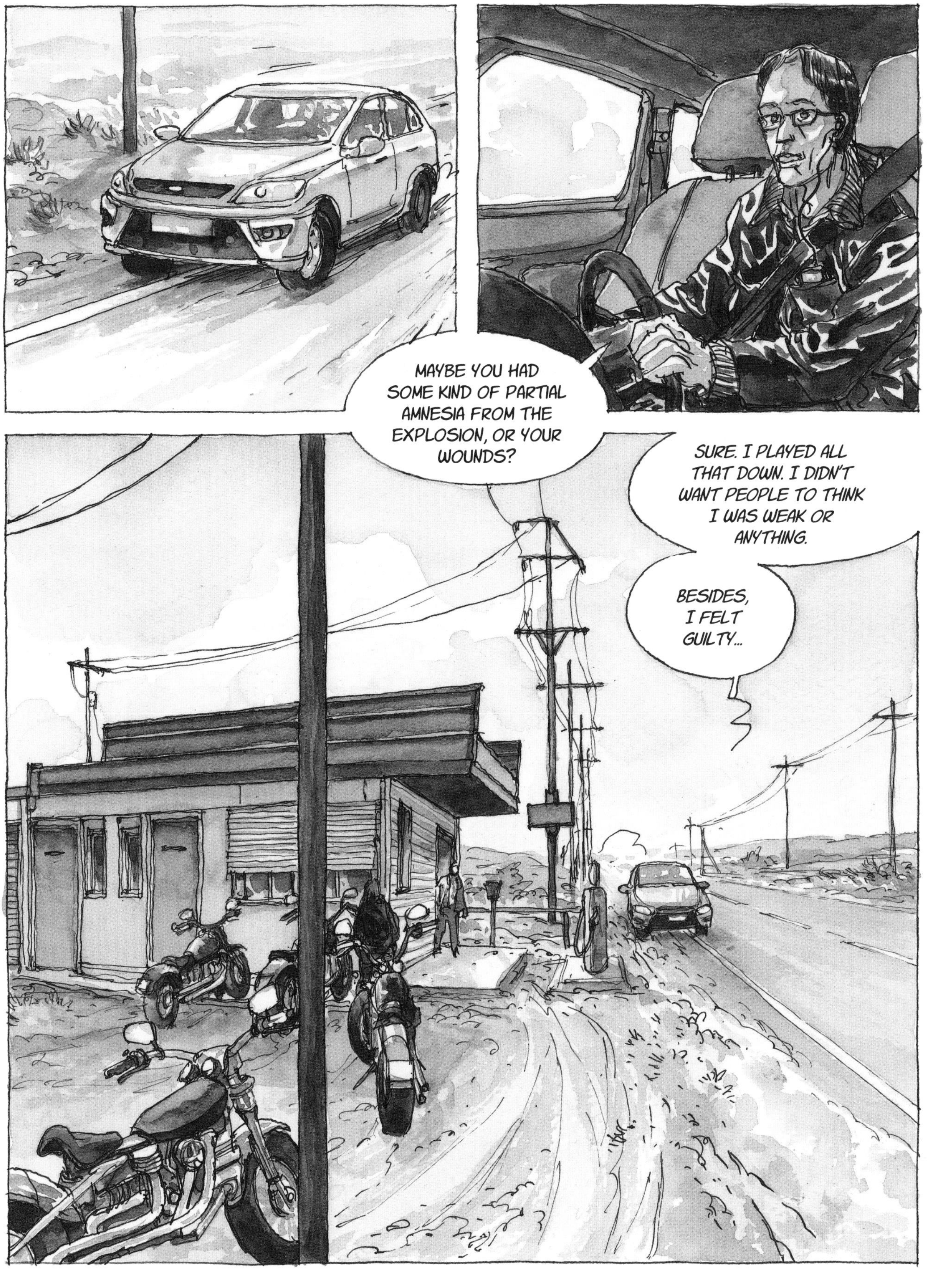
MAYBE YOU HAD SOME KIND OF PARTIAL AMNESIA FROM THE EXPLOSION, OR YOUR WOUNDS?
SURE. I PLAYED ALL THAT DOWN. I DIDN'T WANT PEOPLE TO THINK I WAS WEAK OR ANYTHING.
BESIDES, I FELT GUILTY...

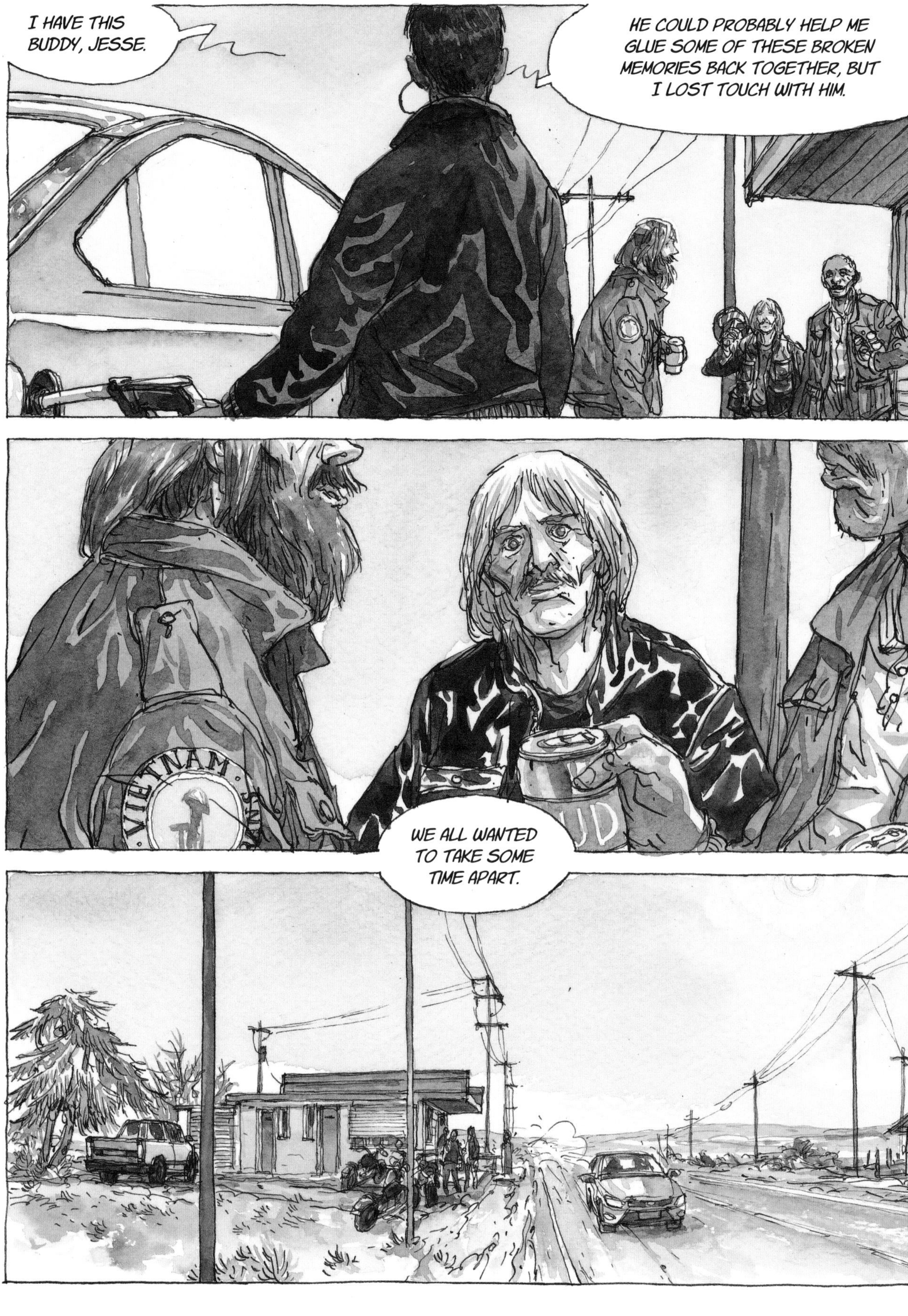
I HAVE THIS BUDDY, JESSE.
HE COULD PROBABLY HELP ME GLUE SOME OF THESE BROKEN MEMORIES BACK TOGETHER, BUT I LOST TOUCH WITH HIM.
VIETNAM
WE ALL WANTED TO TAKE SOME TIME APART.

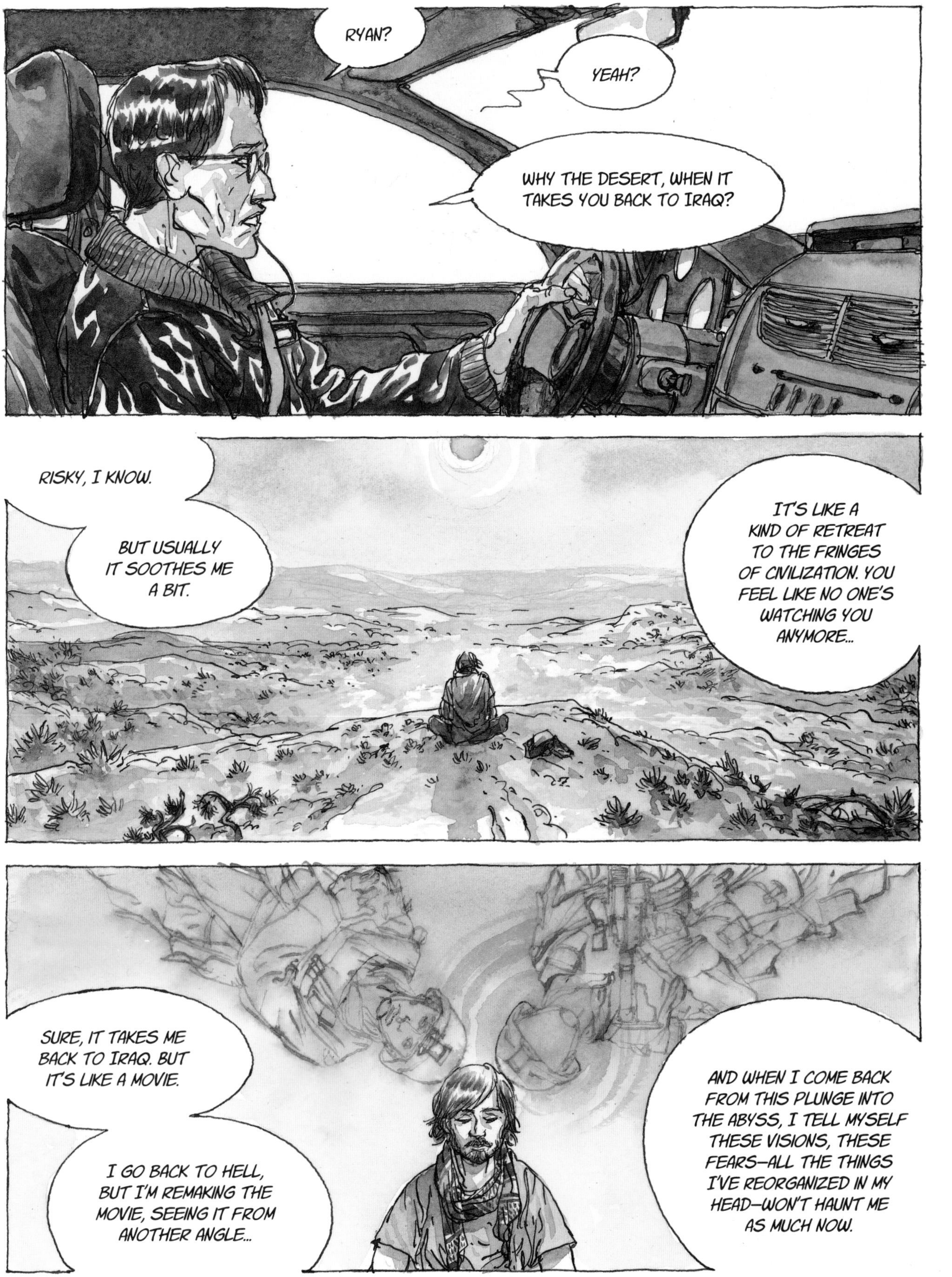
RYAN?
YEAH?
WHY THE DESERT, WHEN IT TAKES YOU BACK TO IRAQ?
RISKY, I KNOW.
BUT USUALLY IT SOOTHES ME A BIT.
IT'S LIKE A KIND OF RETREAT TO THE FRINGES OF CIVILIZATION. YOU FEEL LIKE NO ONE'S WATCHING YOU ANYMORE...
SURE, IT TAKES ME BACK TO IRAQ. BUT IT'S LIKE A MOVIE.
I GO BACK TO HELL, BUT I'M REMAKING THE MOVIE, SEEING IT FROM ANOTHER ANGLE...
AND WHEN I COME BACK FROM THIS PLUNGE INTO THE ABYSS, I TELL MYSELF THESE VISIONS, THESE FEARS—ALL THE THINGS I'VE REORGANIZED IN MY HEAD—WON'T HAUNT ME AS MUCH NOW.

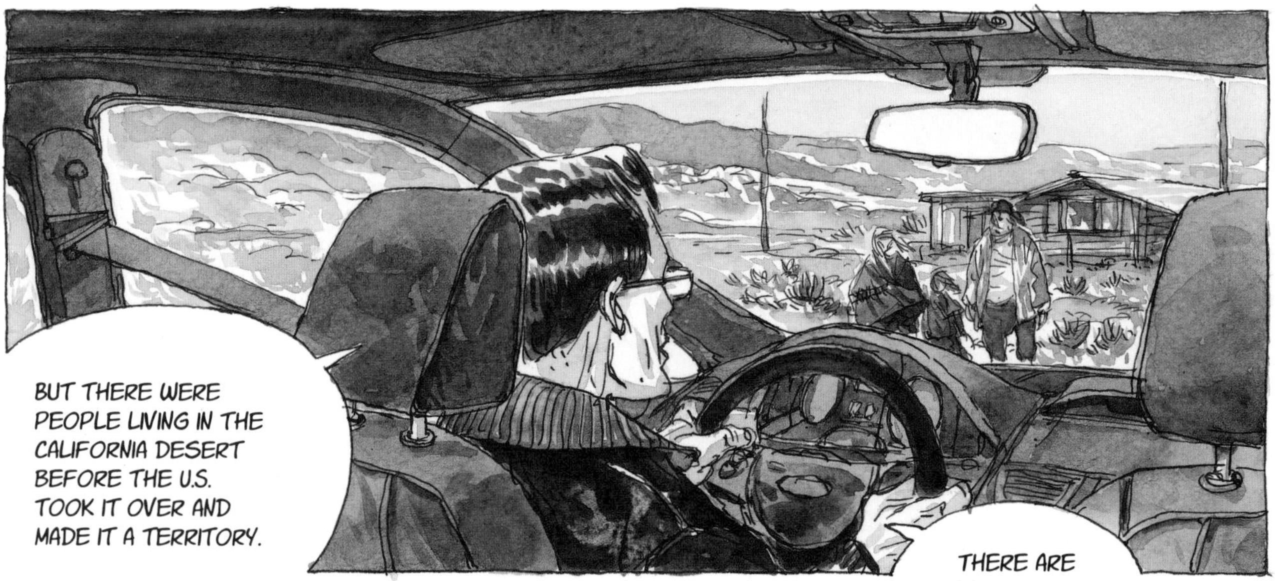
BUT THERE WERE PEOPLE LIVING IN THE CALIFORNIA DESERT BEFORE THE U.S. TOOK IT OVER AND MADE IT A TERRITORY.
THERE ARE OTHER GHOSTS HERE...

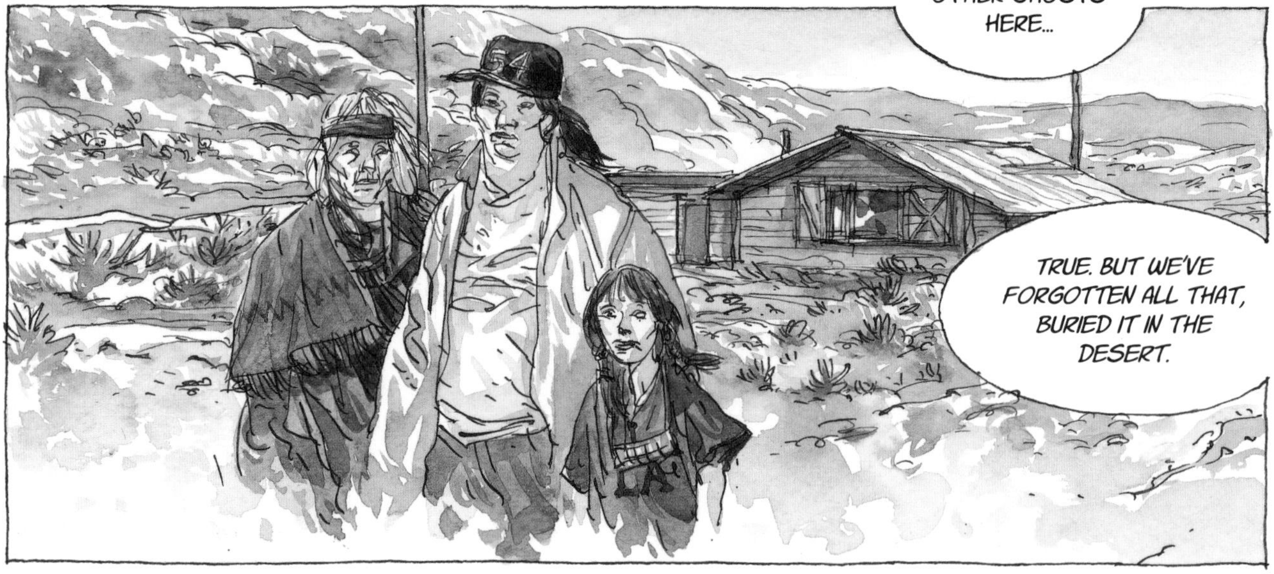
TRUE. BUT WE'VE FORGOTTEN ALL THAT, BURIED IT IN THE DESERT.

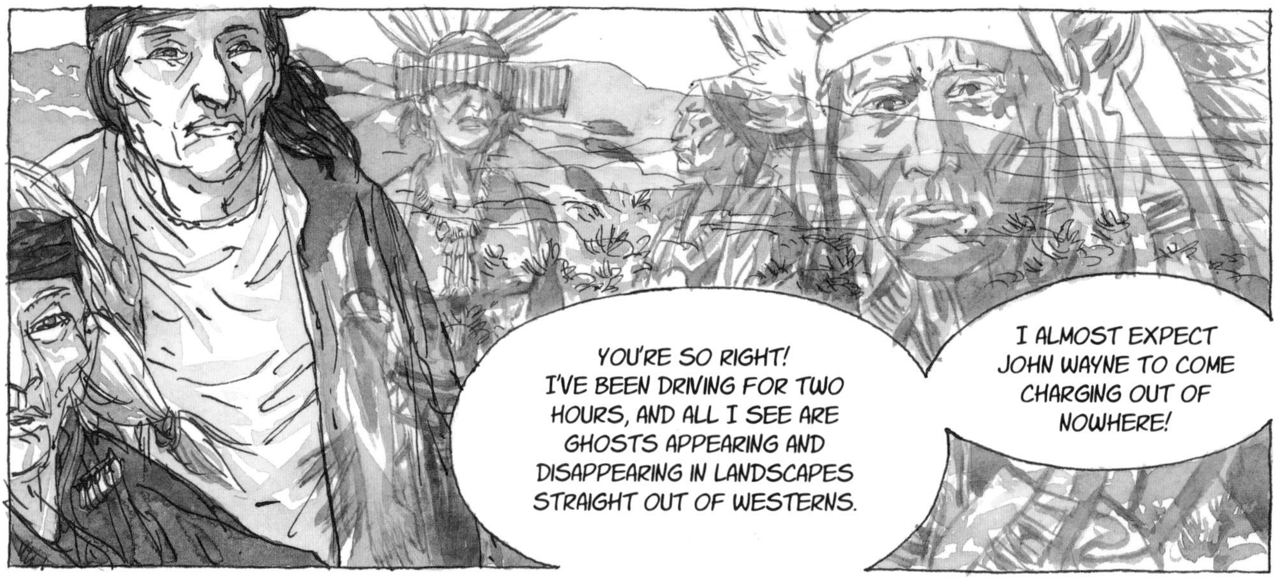
YOU'RE SO RIGHT! I'VE BEEN DRIVING FOR TWO HOURS, AND ALL I SEE ARE GHOSTS APPEARING AND DISAPPEARING IN LANDSCAPES STRAIGHT OUT OF WESTERNS.
I ALMOST EXPECT JOHN WAYNE TO COME CHARGING OUT OF NOWHERE!

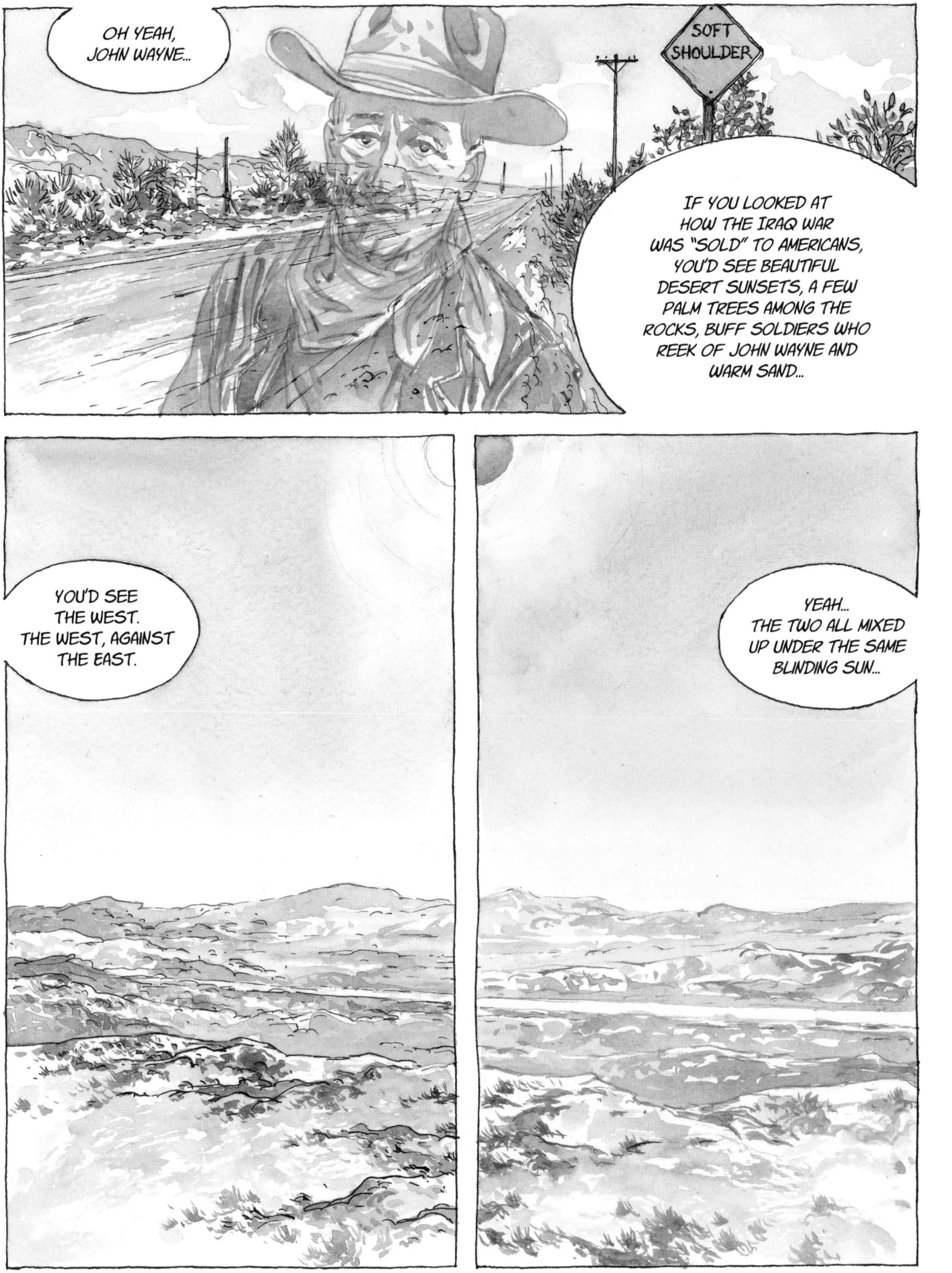
OH YEAH, JOHN WAYNE...
SOFT SHOULDER
IF YOU LOOKED AT HOW THE IRAQ WAR WAS "SOLD" TO AMERICANS, YOU'D SEE BEAUTIFUL DESERT SUNSETS, A FEW PALM TREES AMONG THE ROCKS, BUFF SOLDIERS WHO REEK OF JOHN WAYNE AND WARM SAND...
YOU'D SEE THE WEST. THE WEST, AGAINST THE EAST.
YEAH... THE TWO ALL MIXED UP UNDER THE SAME BLINDING SUN...

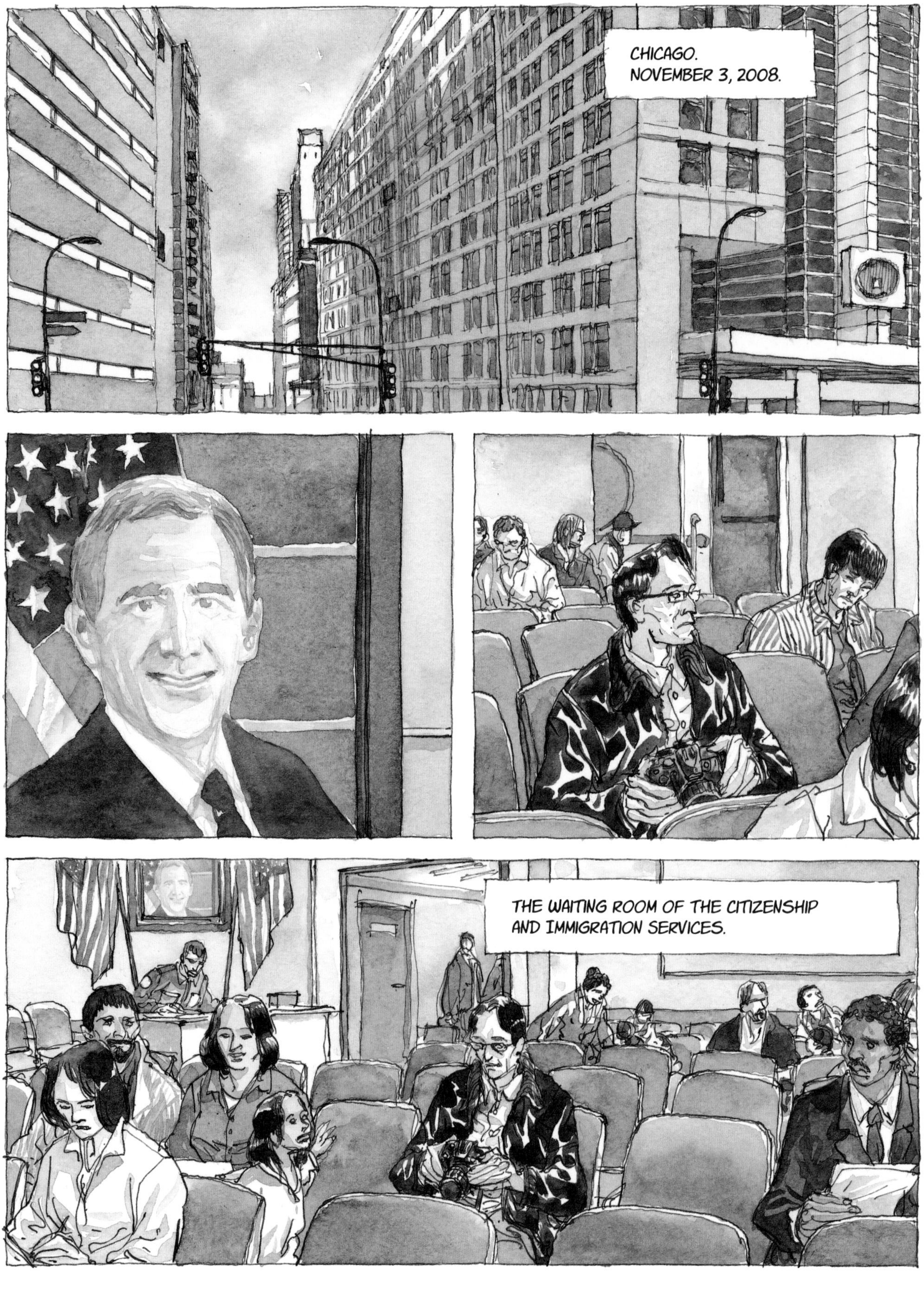
CHICAGO.
NOVEMBER 3, 2008.
THE WAITING ROOM OF THE CITIZENSHIP AND IMMIGRATION SERVICES.

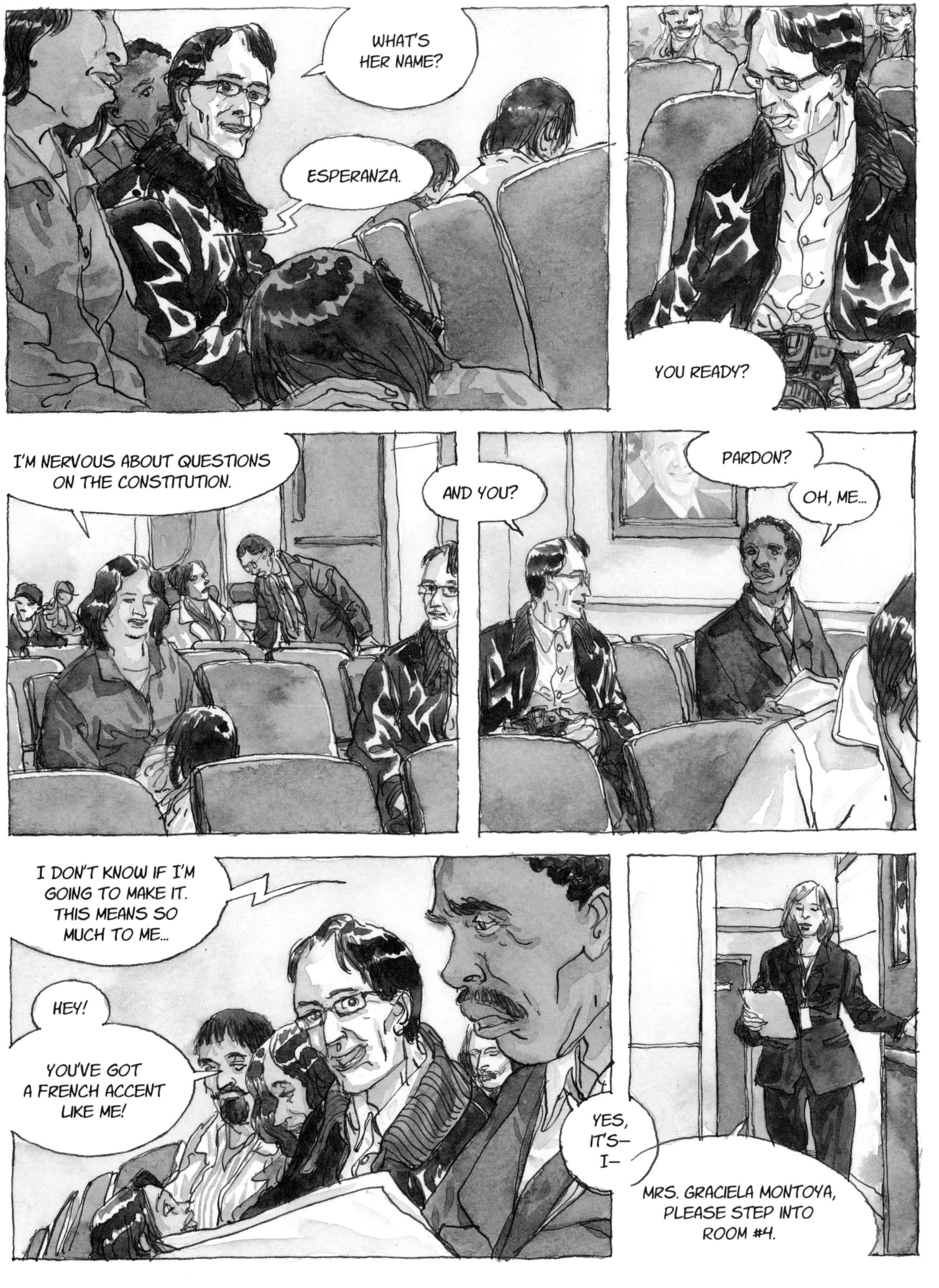
WHAT'S HER NAME?
ESPERANZA.
YOU READY?
I'M NERVOUS ABOUT QUESTIONS ON THE CONSTITUTION.
AND YOU?
PARDON?
OH, ME...
I DON'T KNOW IF I'M GOING TO MAKE IT. THIS MEANS SO MUCH TO ME...
HEY!
YOU'VE GOT A FRENCH ACCENT LIKE ME!
YES, IT'S— I—
MRS. GRACIELA MONTOYA, PLEASE STEP INTO ROOM #4.

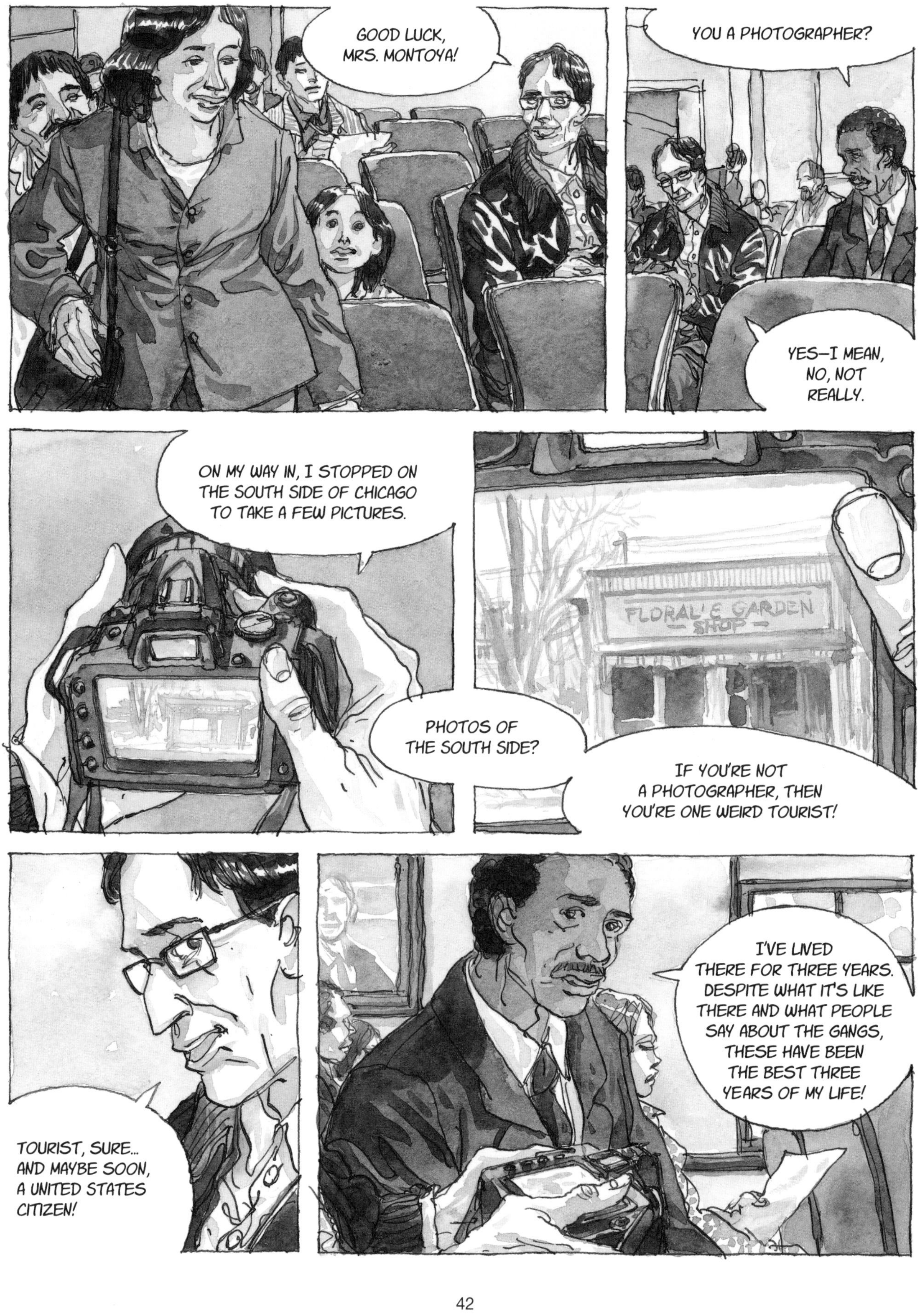
GOOD LUCK, MRS. MONTOYA!
YOU A PHOTOGRAPHER?
YES—I MEAN, NO, NOT REALLY.
ON MY WAY IN, I STOPPED ON THE SOUTH SIDE OF CHICAGO TO TAKE A FEW PICTURES.
FLORAL & GARDEN SHOP
PHOTOS OF THE SOUTH SIDE?
IF YOU'RE NOT A PHOTOGRAPHER, THEN YOU'RE ONE WEIRD TOURIST!
TOURIST, SURE... AND MAYBE SOON, A UNITED STATES CITIZEN!
I'VE LIVED THERE FOR THREE YEARS. DESPITE WHAT IT'S LIKE THERE AND WHAT PEOPLE SAY ABOUT THE GANGS, THESE HAVE BEEN THE BEST THREE YEARS OF MY LIFE!

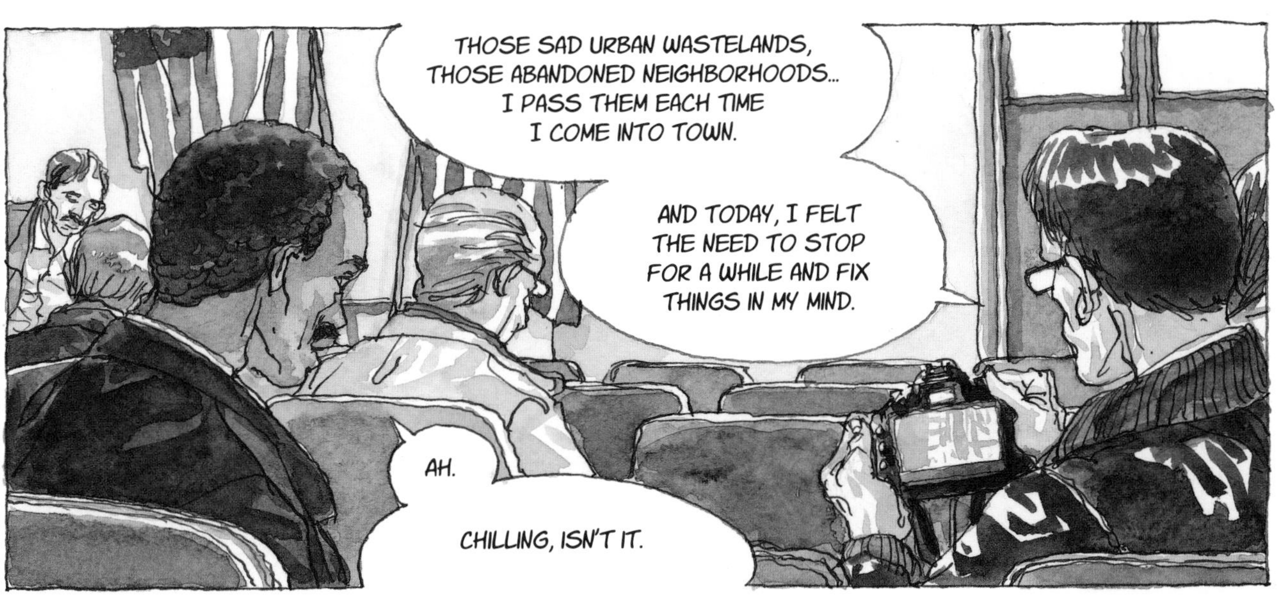
THOSE SAD URBAN WASTELANDS, THOSE ABANDONED NEIGHBORHOODS... I PASS THEM EACH TIME I COME INTO TOWN.
AND TODAY, I FELT THE NEED TO STOP FOR A WHILE AND FIX THINGS IN MY MIND.
AH.
CHILLING, ISN'T IT.

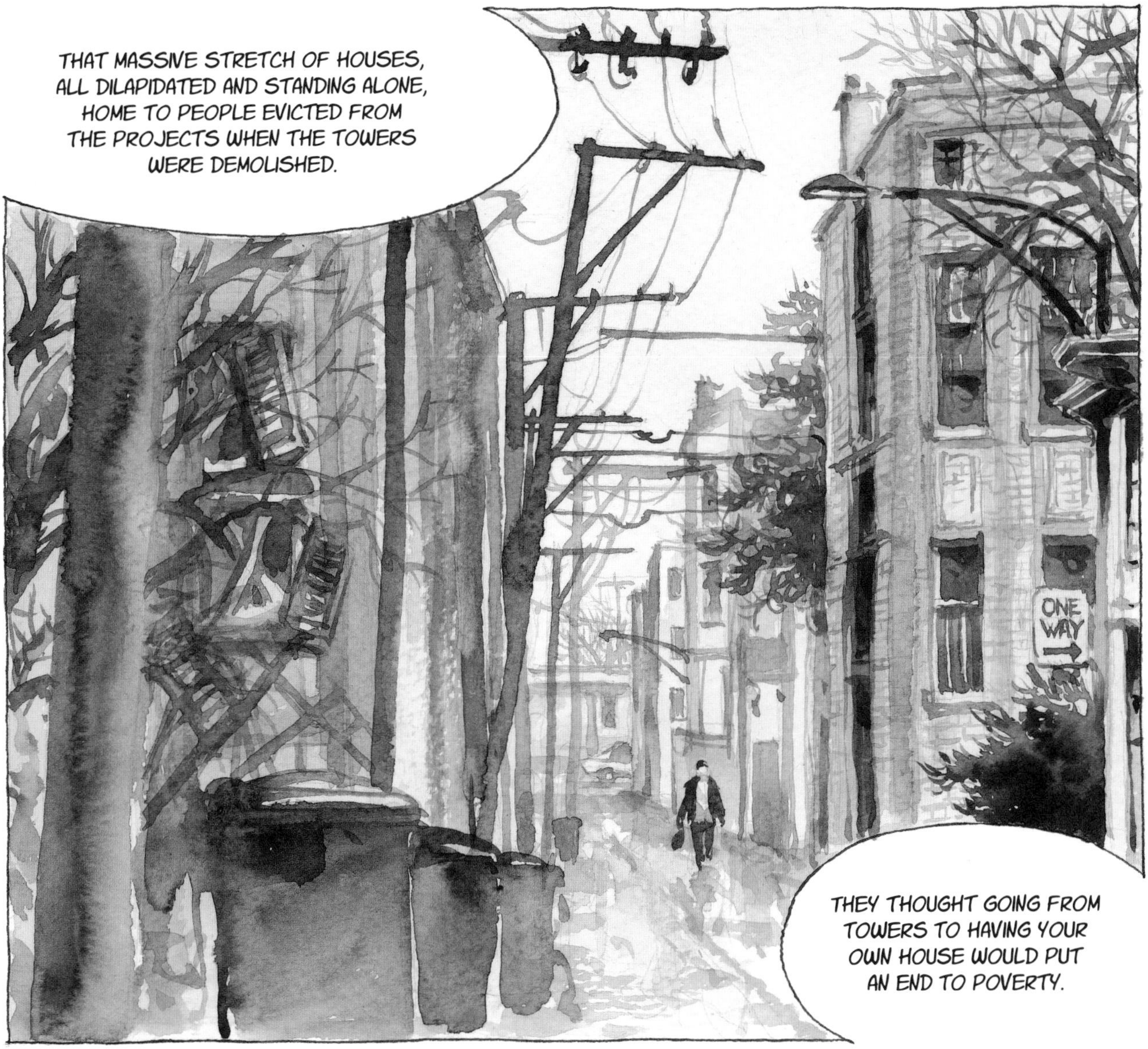
THAT MASSIVE STRETCH OF HOUSES, ALL DILAPIDATED AND STANDING ALONE, HOME TO PEOPLE EVICTED FROM THE PROJECTS WHEN THE TOWERS WERE DEMOLISHED.
ONE WAY
THEY THOUGHT GOING FROM TOWERS TO HAVING YOUR OWN HOUSE WOULD PUT AN END TO POVERTY.

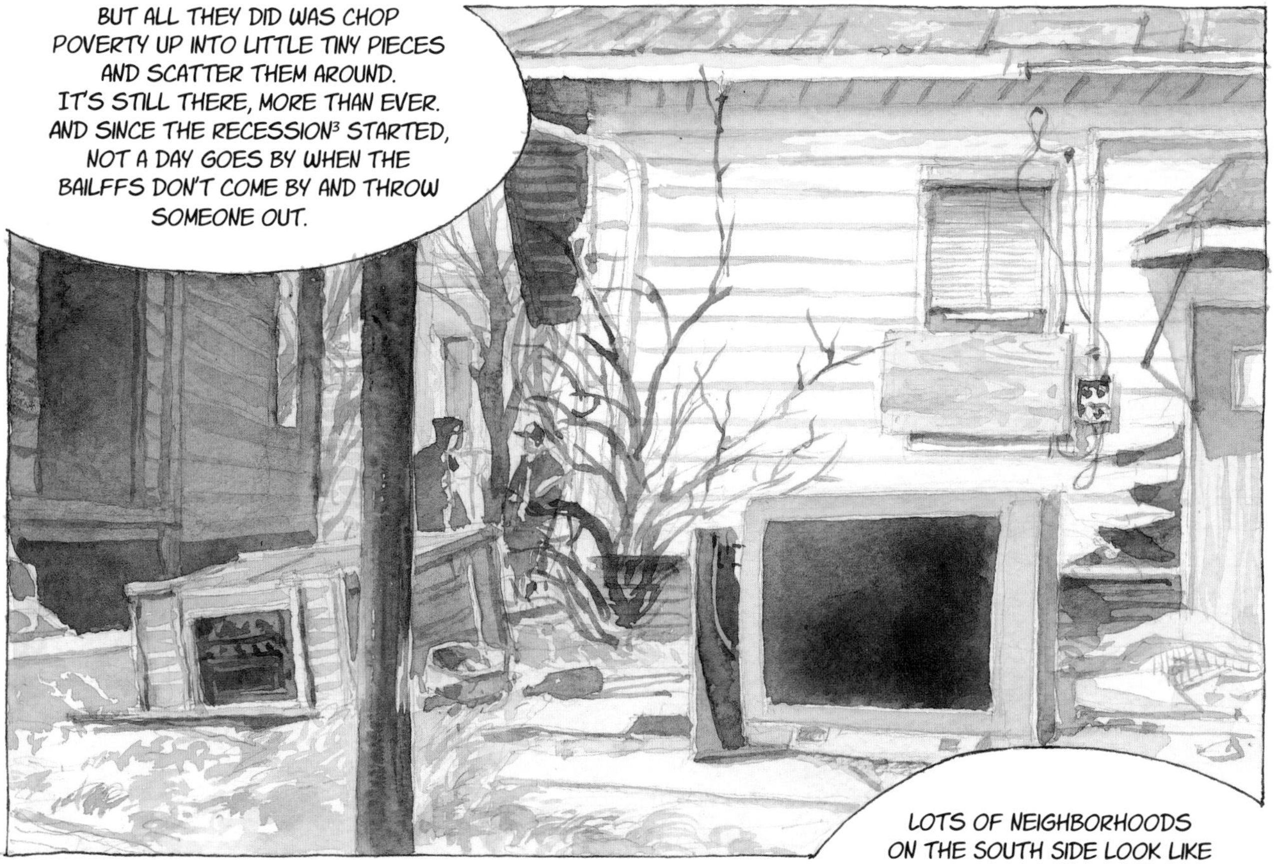
BUT ALL THEY DID WAS CHOP POVERTY UP INTO LITTLE TINY PIECES AND SCATTER THEM AROUND. IT'S STILL THERE, MORE THAN EVER. AND SINCE THE RECESSION[3] STARTED, NOT A DAY GOES BY WHEN THE BAILFFS DON'T COME BY AND THROW SOMEONE OUT.
LOTS OF NEIGHBORHOODS ON THE SOUTH SIDE LOOK LIKE GHOST TOWNS. BUT THE GHOSTS ARE VERY REAL, THE WALKING WOUNDED: THE HOMELESS, THE UNEMPLOYED, RAGGEDY OLD PEOPLE AND YOUNG ONES ALL HUNCHED OVER.

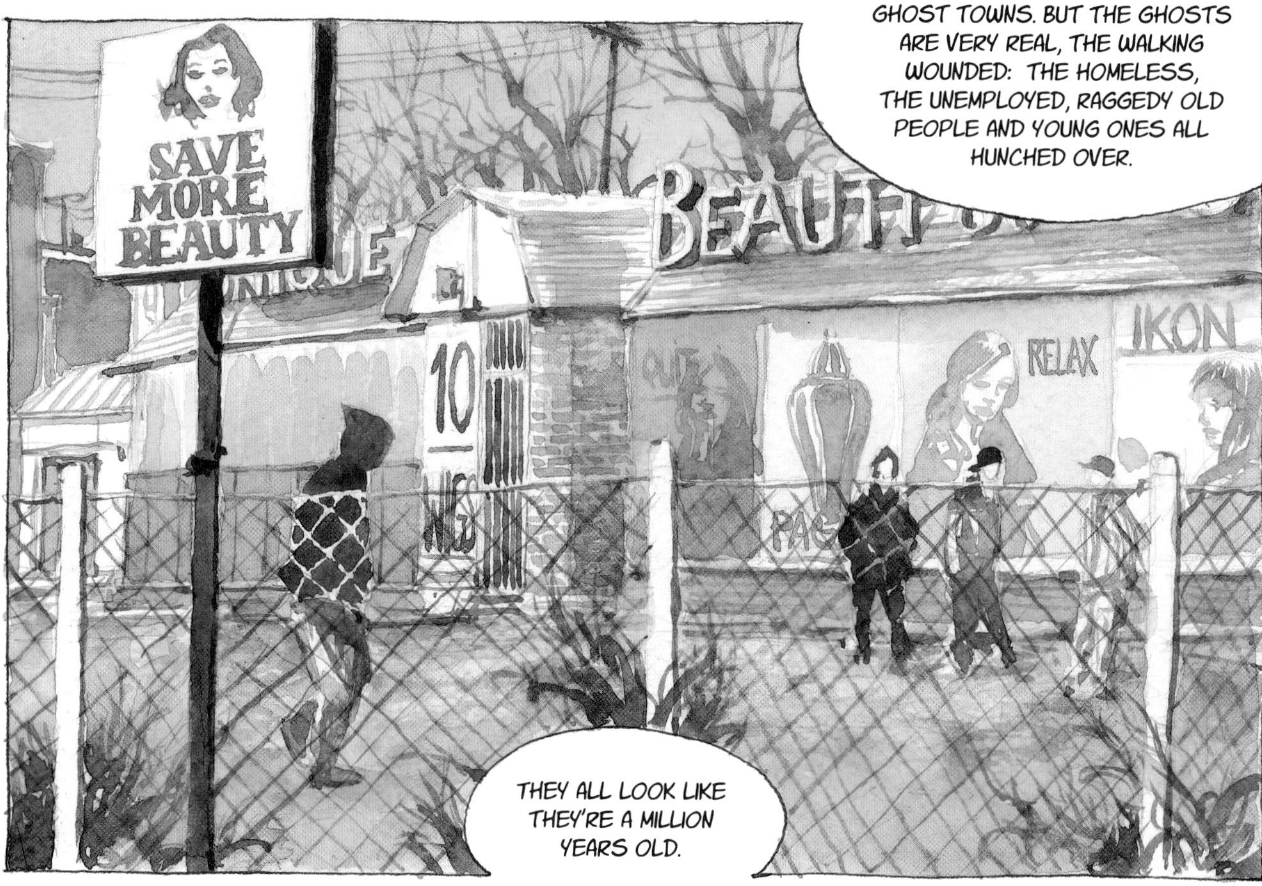
SAVE MORE BEAUTY
10
RELAX
IKON
THEY ALL LOOK LIKE THEY'RE A MILLION YEARS OLD.

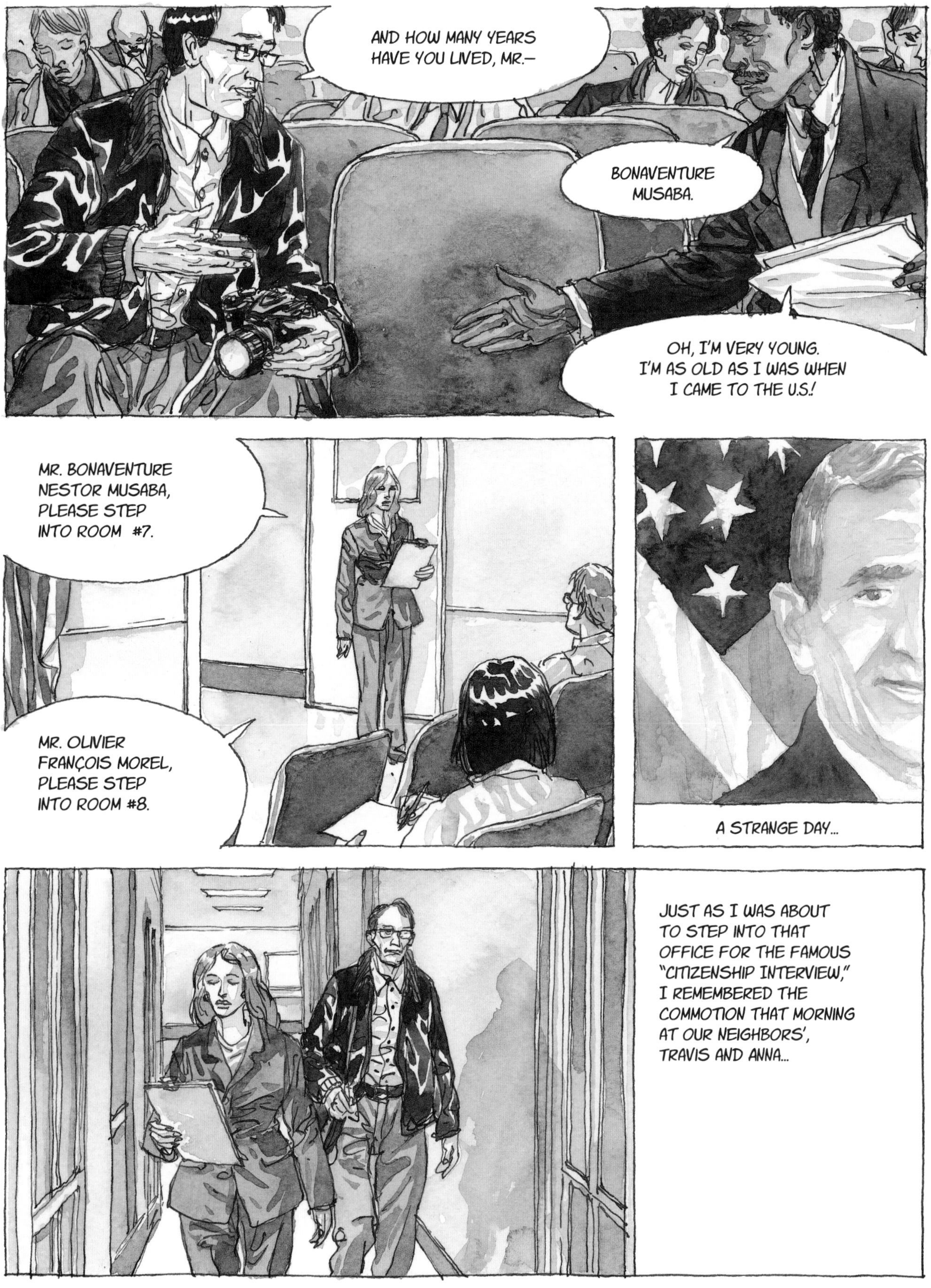
AND HOW MANY YEARS HAVE YOU LIVED, MR.–
BONAVENTURE MUSABA.
OH, I'M VERY YOUNG. I'M AS OLD AS I WAS WHEN I CAME TO THE U.S.!
MR. BONAVENTURE NESTOR MUSABA, PLEASE STEP INTO ROOM #7.
MR. OLIVIER FRANÇOIS MOREL, PLEASE STEP INTO ROOM #8.
A STRANGE DAY...
JUST AS I WAS ABOUT TO STEP INTO THAT OFFICE FOR THE FAMOUS "CITIZENSHIP INTERVIEW," I REMEMBERED THE COMMOTION THAT MORNING AT OUR NEIGHBORS', TRAVIS AND ANNA...

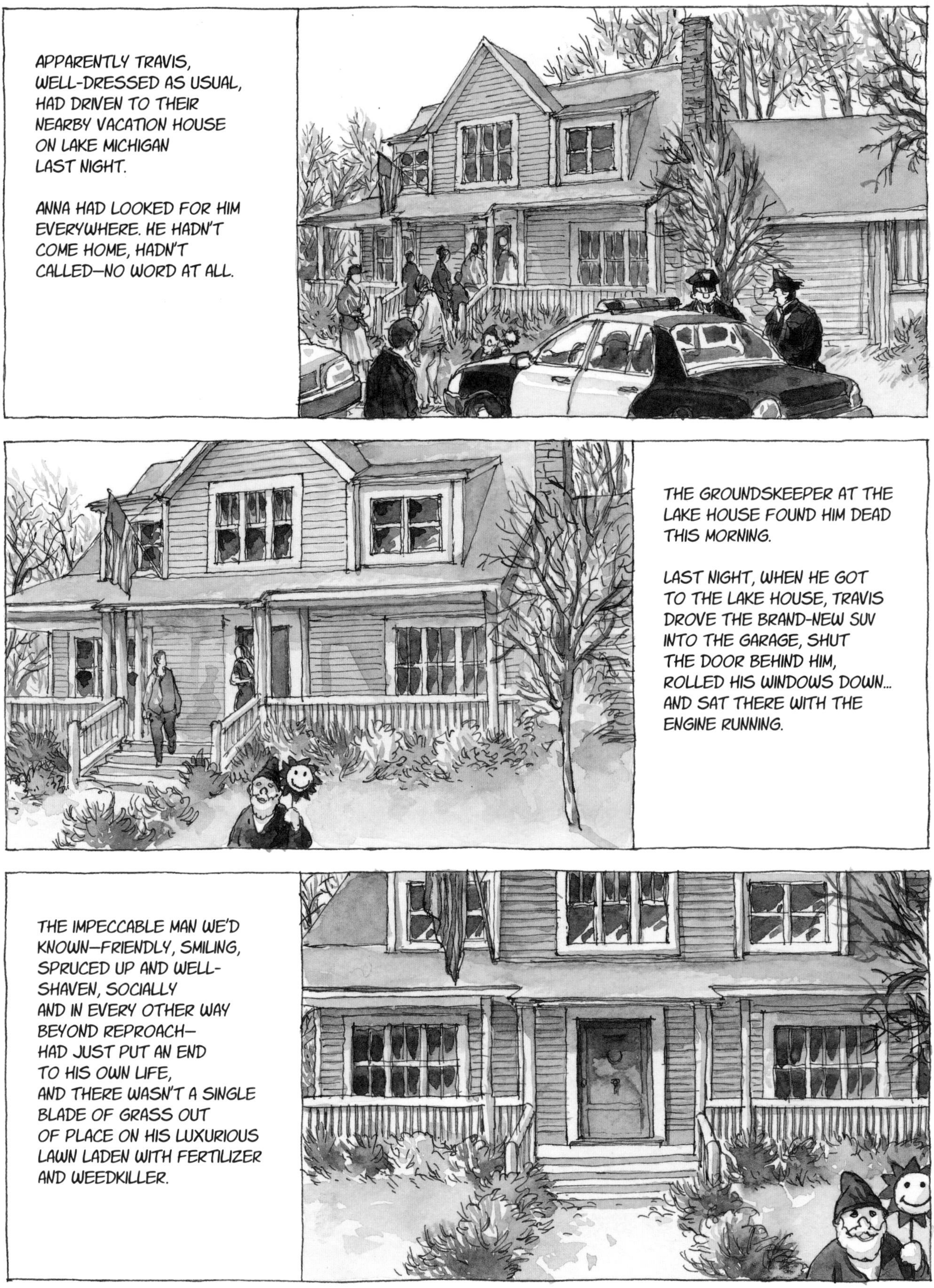
APPARENTLY TRAVIS, WELL-DRESSED AS USUAL, HAD DRIVEN TO THEIR NEARBY VACATION HOUSE ON LAKE MICHIGAN LAST NIGHT.
ANNA HAD LOOKED FOR HIM EVERYWHERE. HE HADN'T COME HOME, HADN'T CALLED—NO WORD AT ALL.
THE GROUNDSKEEPER AT THE LAKE HOUSE FOUND HIM DEAD THIS MORNING.
LAST NIGHT, WHEN HE GOT TO THE LAKE HOUSE, TRAVIS DROVE THE BRAND-NEW SUV INTO THE GARAGE, SHUT THE DOOR BEHIND HIM, ROLLED HIS WINDOWS DOWN... AND SAT THERE WITH THE ENGINE RUNNING.
THE IMPECCABLE MAN WE'D KNOWN—FRIENDLY, SMILING, SPRUCED UP AND WELL-SHAVEN, SOCIALLY AND IN EVERY OTHER WAY BEYOND REPROACH—HAD JUST PUT AN END TO HIS OWN LIFE, AND THERE WASN'T A SINGLE BLADE OF GRASS OUT OF PLACE ON HIS LUXURIOUS LAWN LADEN WITH FERTILIZER AND WEEDKILLER.

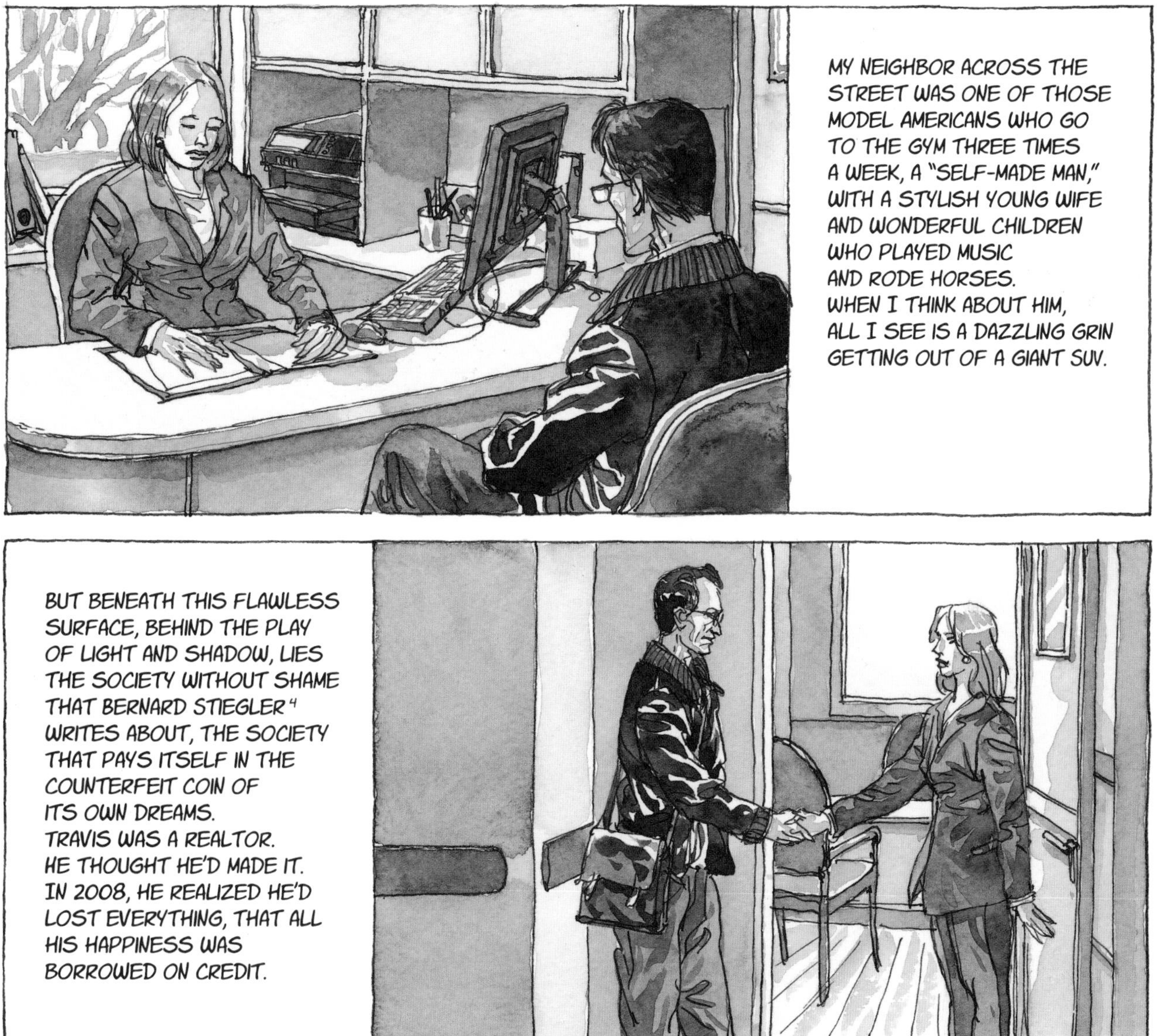
MY NEIGHBOR ACROSS THE STREET WAS ONE OF THOSE MODEL AMERICANS WHO GO TO THE GYM THREE TIMES A WEEK, A "SELF-MADE MAN," WITH A STYLISH YOUNG WIFE AND WONDERFUL CHILDREN WHO PLAYED MUSIC AND RODE HORSES.
WHEN I THINK ABOUT HIM, ALL I SEE IS A DAZZLING GRIN GETTING OUT OF A GIANT SUV.
BUT BENEATH THIS FLAWLESS SURFACE, BEHIND THE PLAY OF LIGHT AND SHADOW, LIES THE SOCIETY WITHOUT SHAME THAT BERNARD STIEGLER[4] WRITES ABOUT, THE SOCIETY THAT PAYS ITSELF IN THE COUNTERFEIT COIN OF ITS OWN DREAMS.
TRAVIS WAS A REALTOR. HE THOUGHT HE'D MADE IT. IN 2008, HE REALIZED HE'D LOST EVERYTHING, THAT ALL HIS HAPPINESS WAS BORROWED ON CREDIT.
THE FAMOUS AMERICAN DREAM, THAT FOUNDING ILLUSION... AND YET, I CAN'T QUITE LOSE SIGHT OF WHAT HAPPENED TO BONAVENTURE OR GRACIELA. TO THEM, THE MAGICAL PROCESS OF NATURALIZATION MEANS "FREEDOM," "INDEPENDENCE," A "FRESH START." "PURSUIT OF HAPPINESS," AND THEY'VE GOT GOOD REASON TO BELIEVE IN IT.

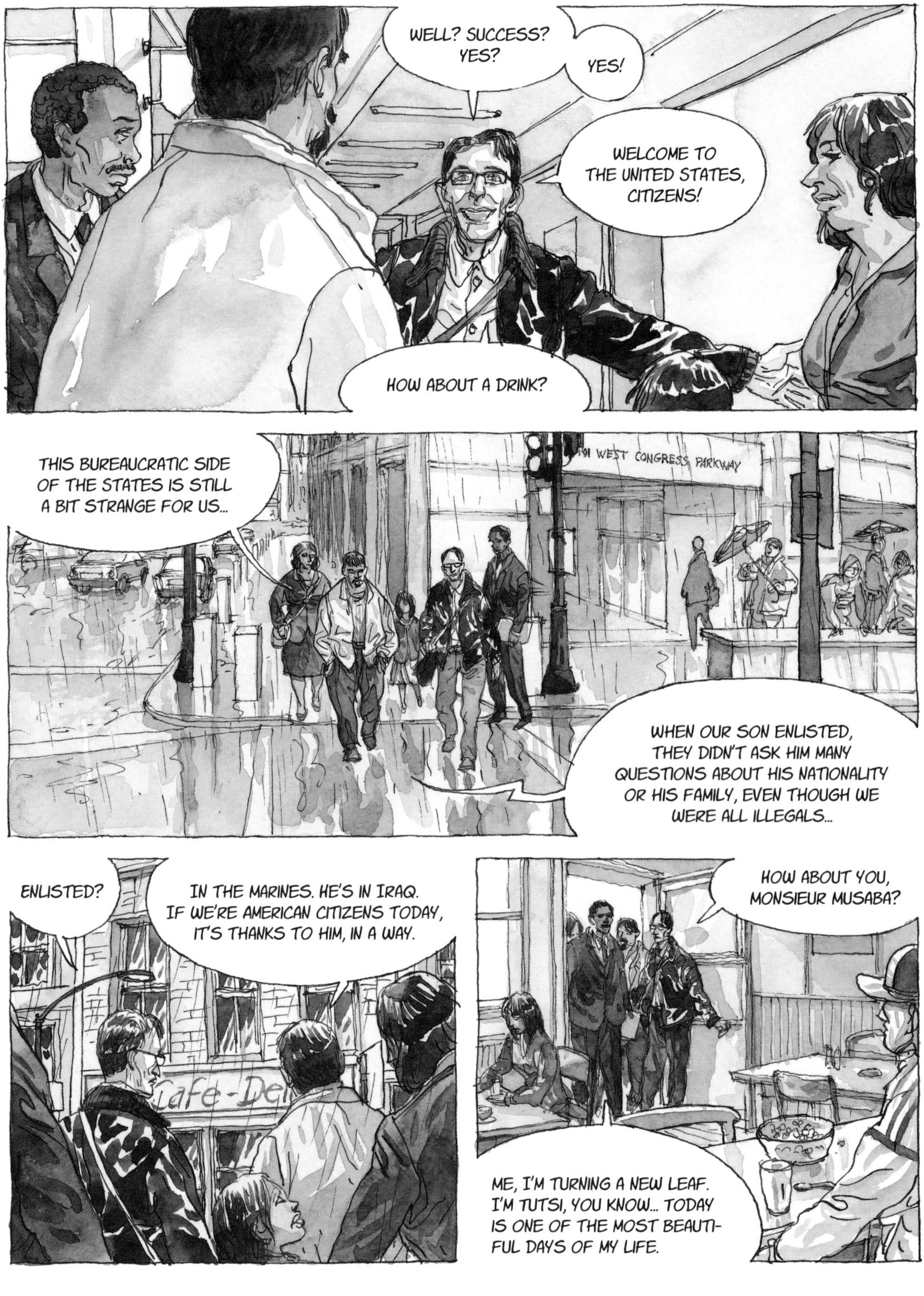
WELL? SUCCESS? YES?
YES!
WELCOME TO THE UNITED STATES, CITIZENS!
HOW ABOUT A DRINK?
THIS BUREAUCRATIC SIDE OF THE STATES IS STILL A BIT STRANGE FOR US...
WEST CONGRESS PARKWAY
WHEN OUR SON ENLISTED, THEY DIDN'T ASK HIM MANY QUESTIONS ABOUT HIS NATIONALITY OR HIS FAMILY, EVEN THOUGH WE WERE ALL ILLEGALS...
ENLISTED?
IN THE MARINES. HE'S IN IRAQ. IF WE'RE AMERICAN CITIZENS TODAY, IT'S THANKS TO HIM, IN A WAY.
HOW ABOUT YOU, MONSIEUR MUSABA?
ME, I'M TURNING A NEW LEAF. I'M TUTSI, YOU KNOW... TODAY IS ONE OF THE MOST BEAUTI-FUL DAYS OF MY LIFE.

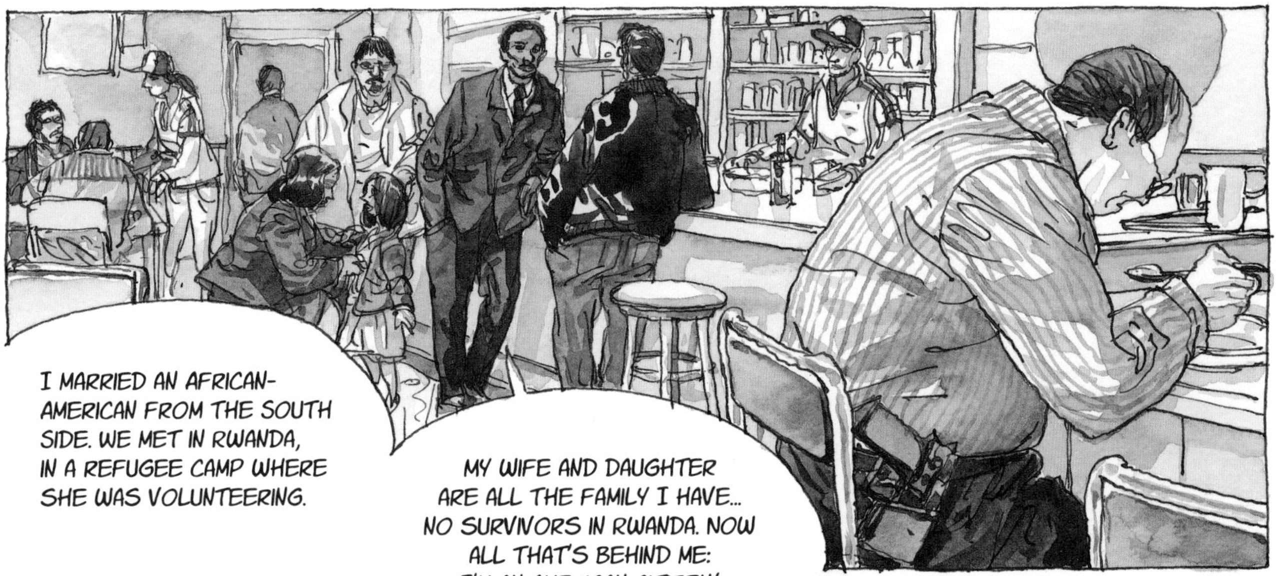
I MARRIED AN AFRICAN-AMERICAN FROM THE SOUTH SIDE. WE MET IN RWANDA, IN A REFUGEE CAMP WHERE SHE WAS VOLUNTEERING.
MY WIFE AND DAUGHTER ARE ALL THE FAMILY I HAVE... NO SURVIVORS IN RWANDA. NOW ALL THAT'S BEHIND ME: I'M AN AMERICAN CITIZEN! THIS IS A DAY OF BIRTH: "PURSUIT OF HAPPINESS"...

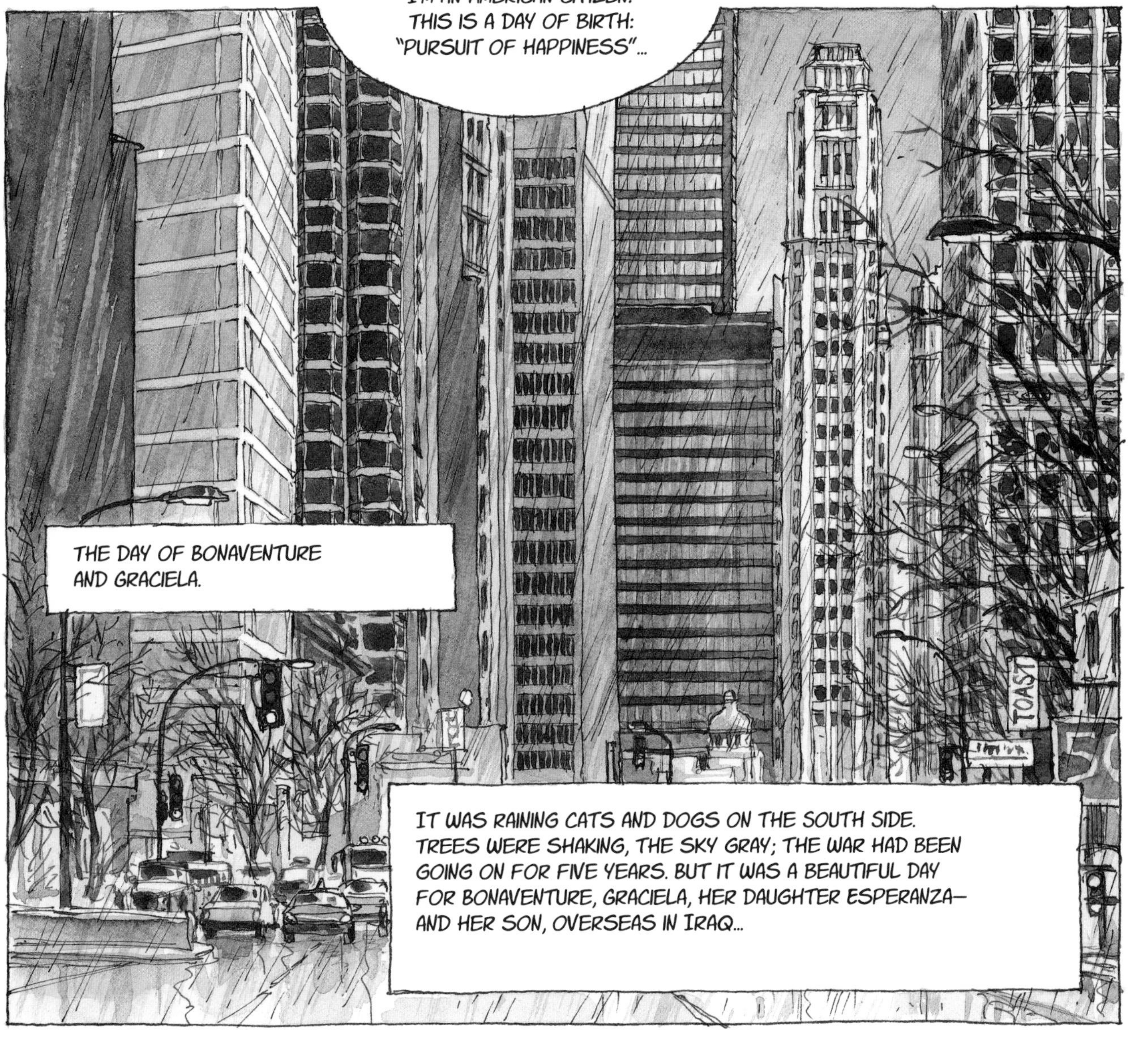
THE DAY OF BONAVENTURE AND GRACIELA.
TOAST
IT WAS RAINING CATS AND DOGS ON THE SOUTH SIDE. TREES WERE SHAKING, THE SKY GRAY; THE WAR HAD BEEN GOING ON FOR FIVE YEARS. BUT IT WAS A BEAUTIFUL DAY FOR BONAVENTURE, GRACIELA, HER DAUGHTER ESPERANZA—AND HER SON, OVERSEAS IN IRAQ...

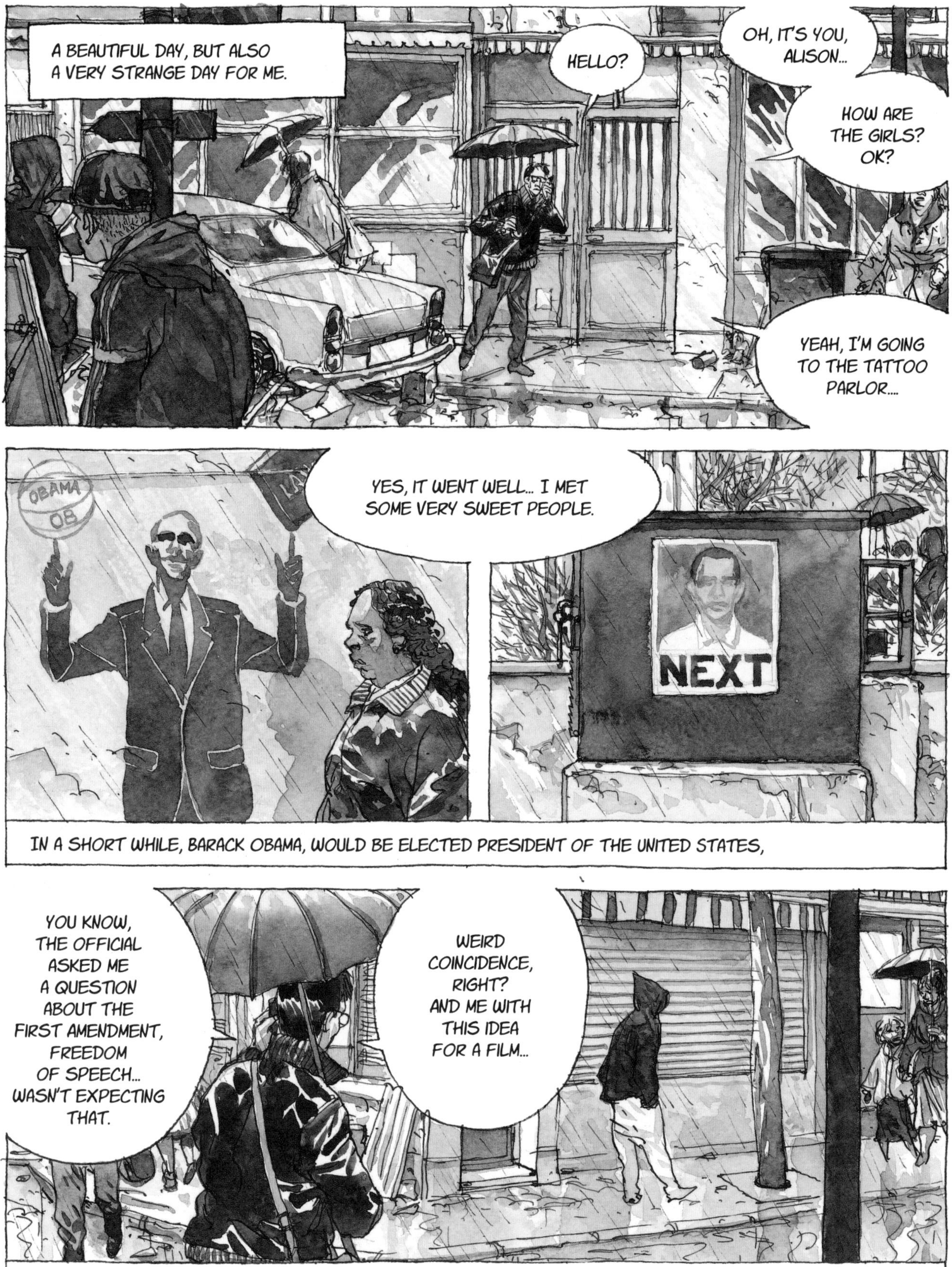
A BEAUTIFUL DAY, BUT ALSO A VERY STRANGE DAY FOR ME.
HELLO?
OH, IT'S YOU, ALISON...
HOW ARE THE GIRLS? OK?
YEAH, I'M GOING TO THE TATTOO PARLOR....
OBAMA 08
YES, IT WENT WELL... I MET SOME VERY SWEET PEOPLE.
NEXT
IN A SHORT WHILE, BARACK OBAMA, WOULD BE ELECTED PRESIDENT OF THE UNITED STATES,
YOU KNOW, THE OFFICIAL ASKED ME A QUESTION ABOUT THE FIRST AMENDMENT, FREEDOM OF SPEECH... WASN'T EXPECTING THAT.
WEIRD COINCIDENCE, RIGHT? AND ME WITH THIS IDEA FOR A FILM...
THE AMERICA I WAS GOING TO LIVE IN, THE ONE I WAS GOING TO STARE IN THE WHITES OF ITS EYES.

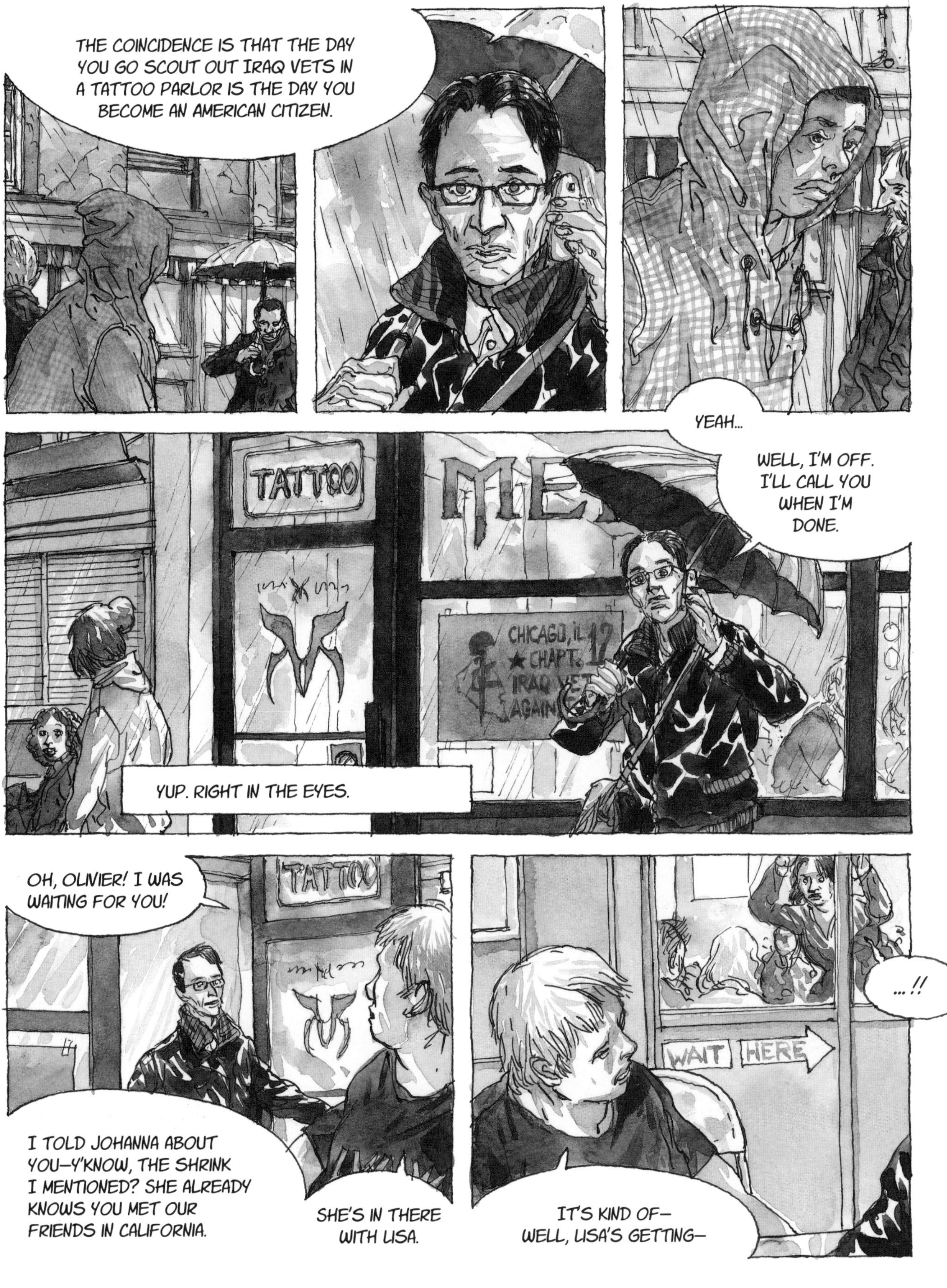
THE COINCIDENCE IS THAT THE DAY YOU GO SCOUT OUT IRAQ VETS IN A TATTOO PARLOR IS THE DAY YOU BECOME AN AMERICAN CITIZEN.
YEAH...
WELL, I'M OFF. I'LL CALL YOU WHEN I'M DONE.
TATTOO
CHICAGO, IL CHAPT. 12 IRAQ VETS AGAIN
YUP. RIGHT IN THE EYES.
OH, OLIVIER! I WAS WAITING FOR YOU!
TATTOO
I TOLD JOHANNA ABOUT YOU—Y'KNOW, THE SHRINK I MENTIONED? SHE ALREADY KNOWS YOU MET OUR FRIENDS IN CALIFORNIA.
SHE'S IN THERE WITH LISA.
...!!
WAIT HERE
IT'S KIND OF— WELL, LISA'S GETTING—

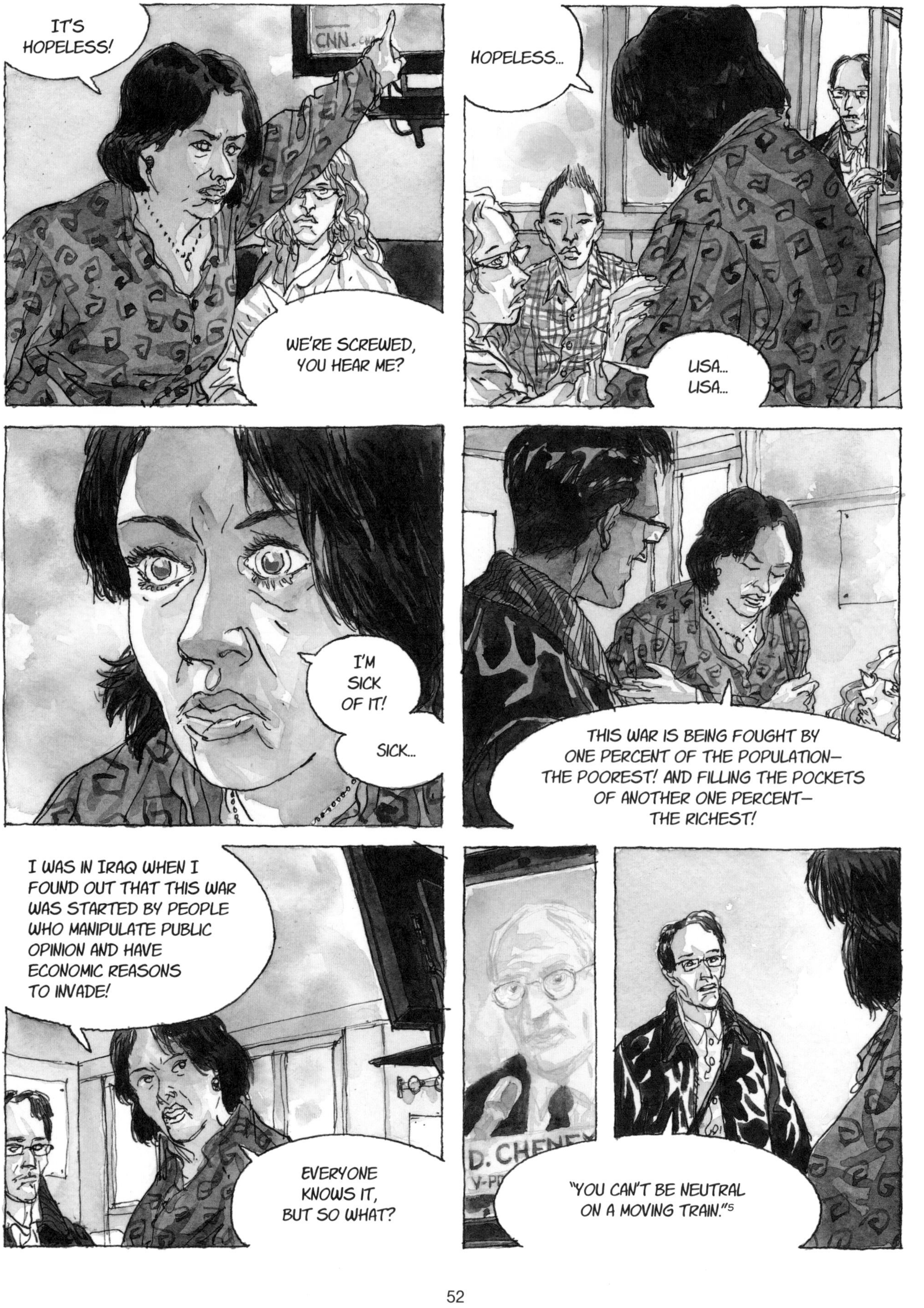
IT'S HOPELESS!
CNN.
WE'RE SCREWED, YOU HEAR ME?
HOPELESS...
LISA... LISA...
I'M SICK OF IT!
SICK...
THIS WAR IS BEING FOUGHT BY ONE PERCENT OF THE POPULATION— THE POOREST! AND FILLING THE POCKETS OF ANOTHER ONE PERCENT— THE RICHEST!
I WAS IN IRAQ WHEN I FOUND OUT THAT THIS WAR WAS STARTED BY PEOPLE WHO MANIPULATE PUBLIC OPINION AND HAVE ECONOMIC REASONS TO INVADE!
EVERYONE KNOWS IT, BUT SO WHAT?
"YOU CAN'T BE NEUTRAL ON A MOVING TRAIN."[5]

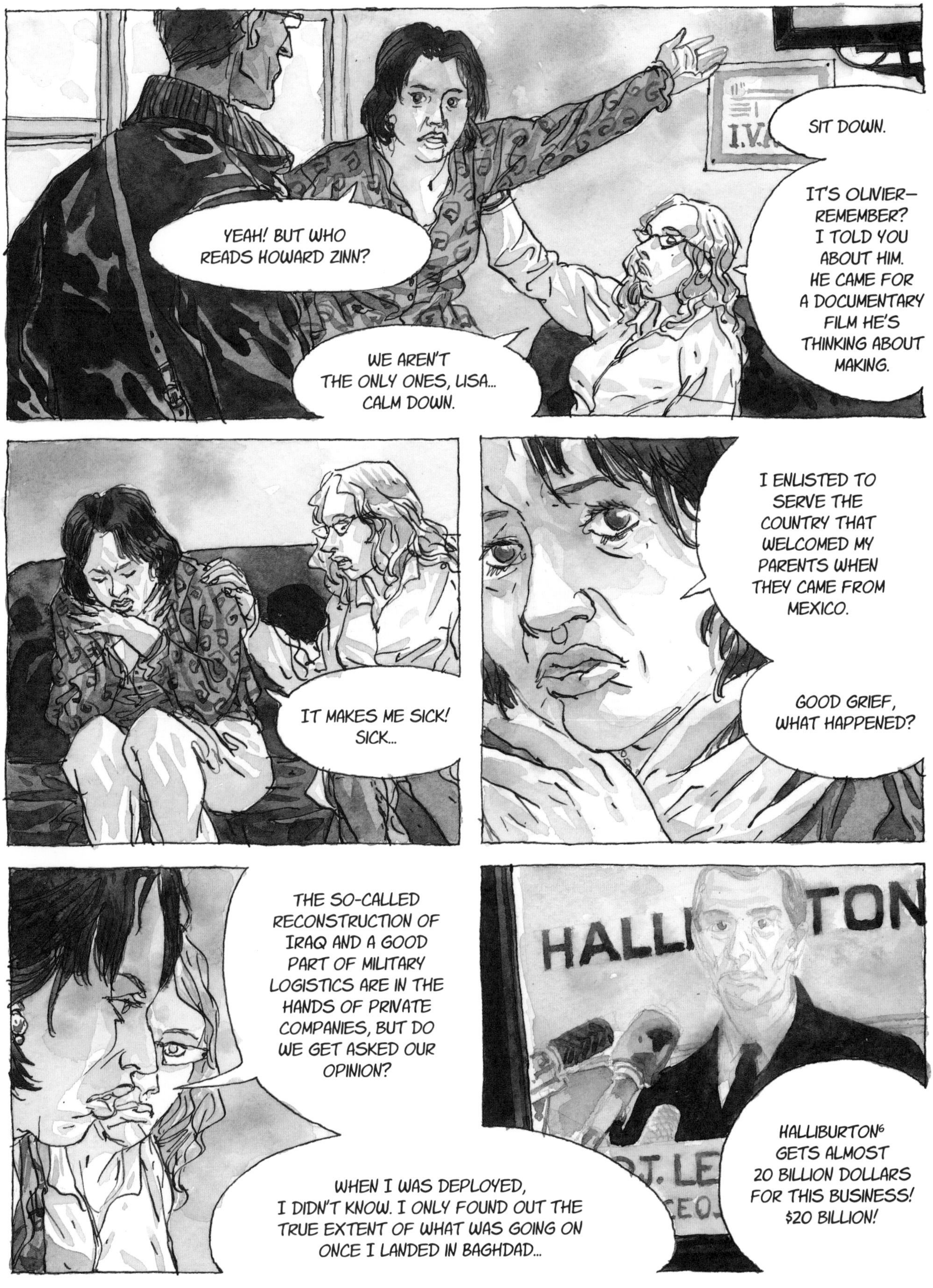
YEAH! BUT WHO READS HOWARD ZINN?
SIT DOWN.
WE AREN'T THE ONLY ONES, LISA... CALM DOWN.
IT'S OLIVIER—REMEMBER? I TOLD YOU ABOUT HIM. HE CAME FOR A DOCUMENTARY FILM HE'S THINKING ABOUT MAKING.
IT MAKES ME SICK! SICK...
I ENLISTED TO SERVE THE COUNTRY THAT WELCOMED MY PARENTS WHEN THEY CAME FROM MEXICO.
GOOD GRIEF, WHAT HAPPENED?
THE SO-CALLED RECONSTRUCTION OF IRAQ AND A GOOD PART OF MILITARY LOGISTICS ARE IN THE HANDS OF PRIVATE COMPANIES, BUT DO WE GET ASKED OUR OPINION?
WHEN I WAS DEPLOYED, I DIDN'T KNOW. I ONLY FOUND OUT THE TRUE EXTENT OF WHAT WAS GOING ON ONCE I LANDED IN BAGHDAD...
HALLIBURTON[6] GETS ALMOST 20 BILLION DOLLARS FOR THIS BUSINESS! $20 BILLION!

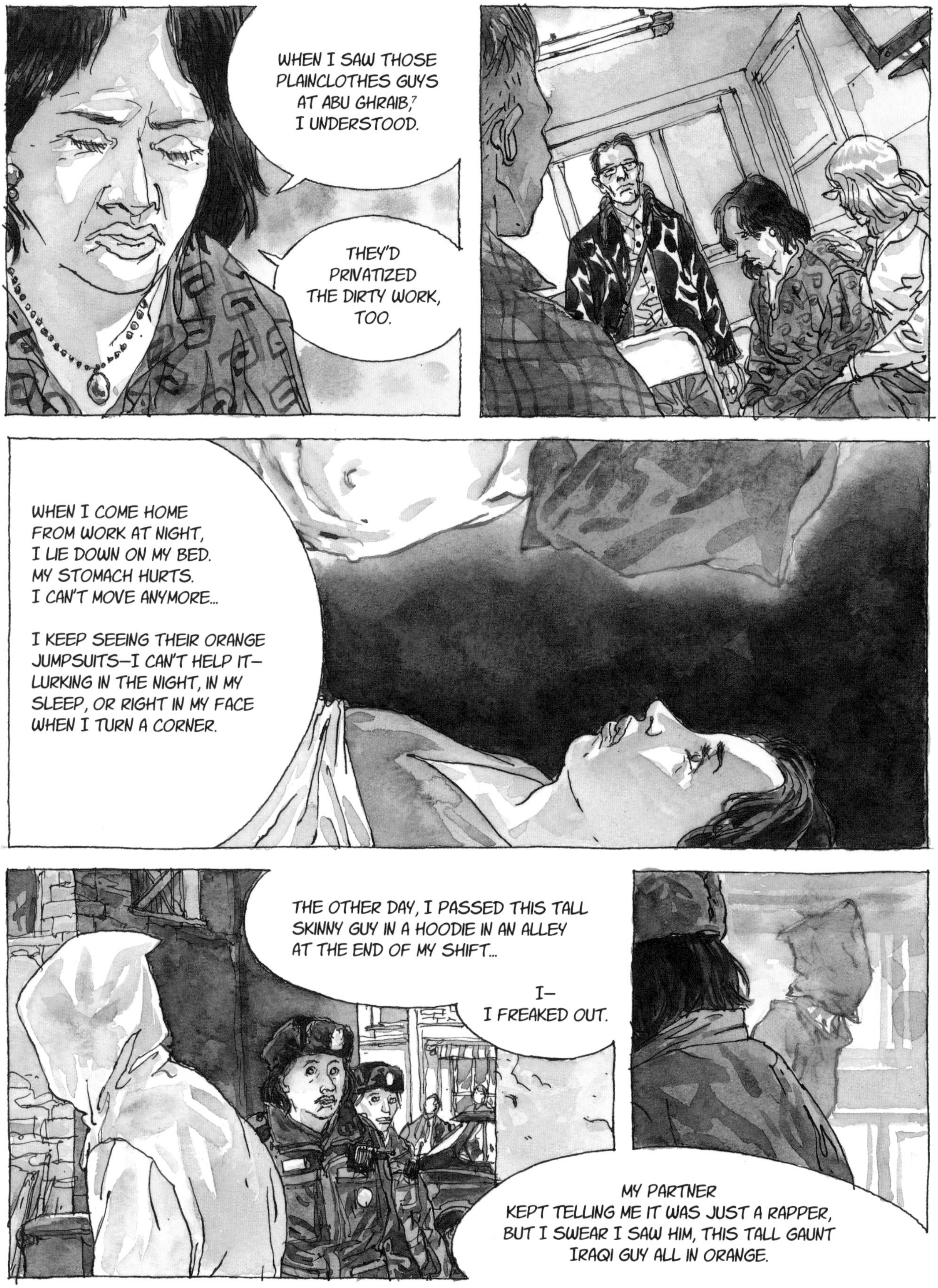
WHEN I SAW THOSE PLAINCLOTHES GUYS AT ABU GHRAIB,[7] I UNDERSTOOD.
THEY'D PRIVATIZED THE DIRTY WORK, TOO.
WHEN I COME HOME FROM WORK AT NIGHT, I LIE DOWN ON MY BED. MY STOMACH HURTS. I CAN'T MOVE ANYMORE...
I KEEP SEEING THEIR ORANGE JUMPSUITS—I CAN'T HELP IT—LURKING IN THE NIGHT, IN MY SLEEP, OR RIGHT IN MY FACE WHEN I TURN A CORNER.
THE OTHER DAY, I PASSED THIS TALL SKINNY GUY IN A HOODIE IN AN ALLEY AT THE END OF MY SHIFT...
I— I FREAKED OUT.
MY PARTNER KEPT TELLING ME IT WAS JUST A RAPPER, BUT I SWEAR I SAW HIM, THIS TALL GAUNT IRAQI GUY ALL IN ORANGE.

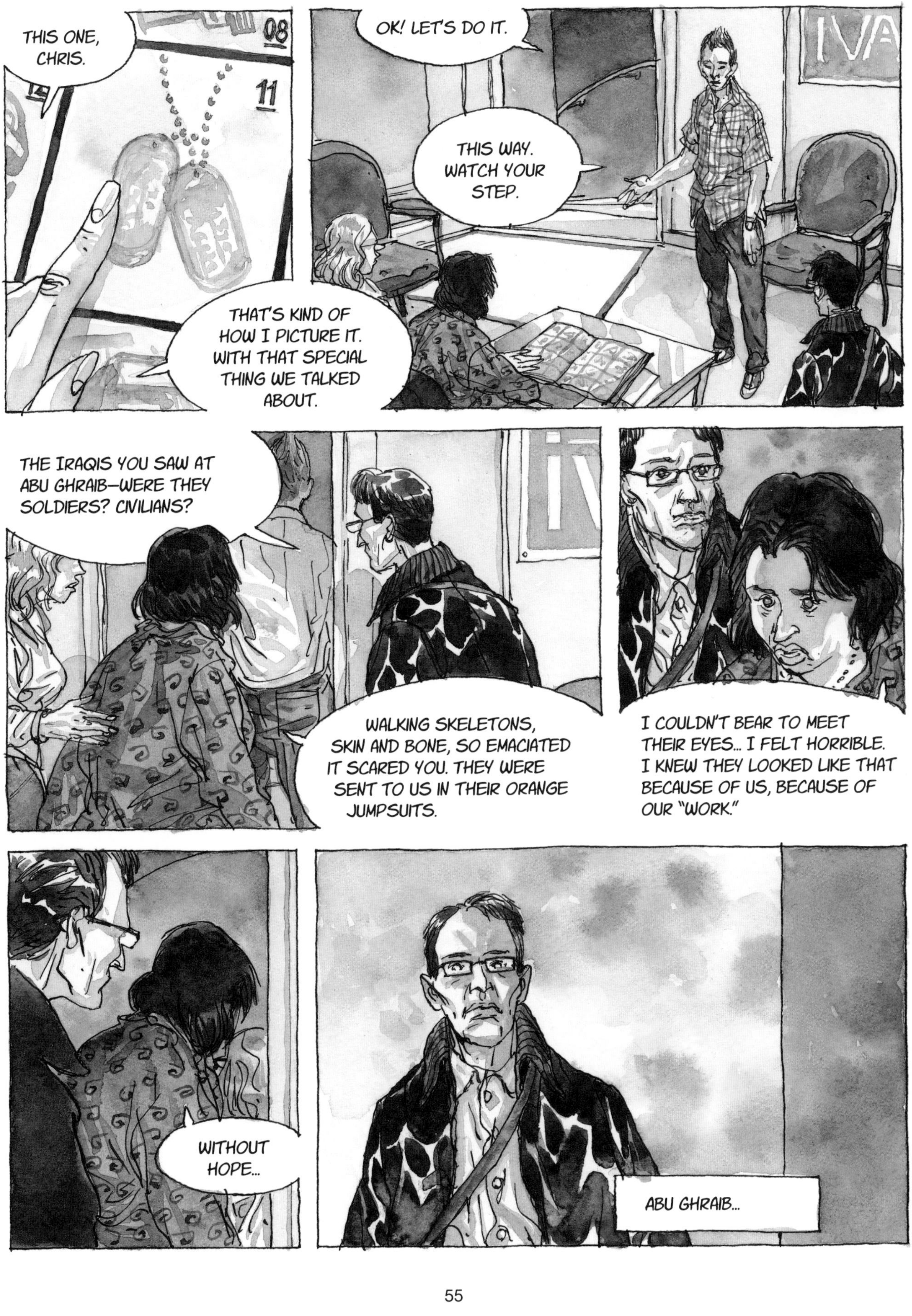
THIS ONE, CHRIS.
OK! LET'S DO IT.
THIS WAY. WATCH YOUR STEP.
THAT'S KIND OF HOW I PICTURE IT. WITH THAT SPECIAL THING WE TALKED ABOUT.
THE IRAQIS YOU SAW AT ABU GHRAIB—WERE THEY SOLDIERS? CIVILIANS?
WALKING SKELETONS, SKIN AND BONE, SO EMACIATED IT SCARED YOU. THEY WERE SENT TO US IN THEIR ORANGE JUMPSUITS.
I COULDN'T BEAR TO MEET THEIR EYES... I FELT HORRIBLE. I KNEW THEY LOOKED LIKE THAT BECAUSE OF US, BECAUSE OF OUR "WORK."
WITHOUT HOPE...
ABU GHRAIB...

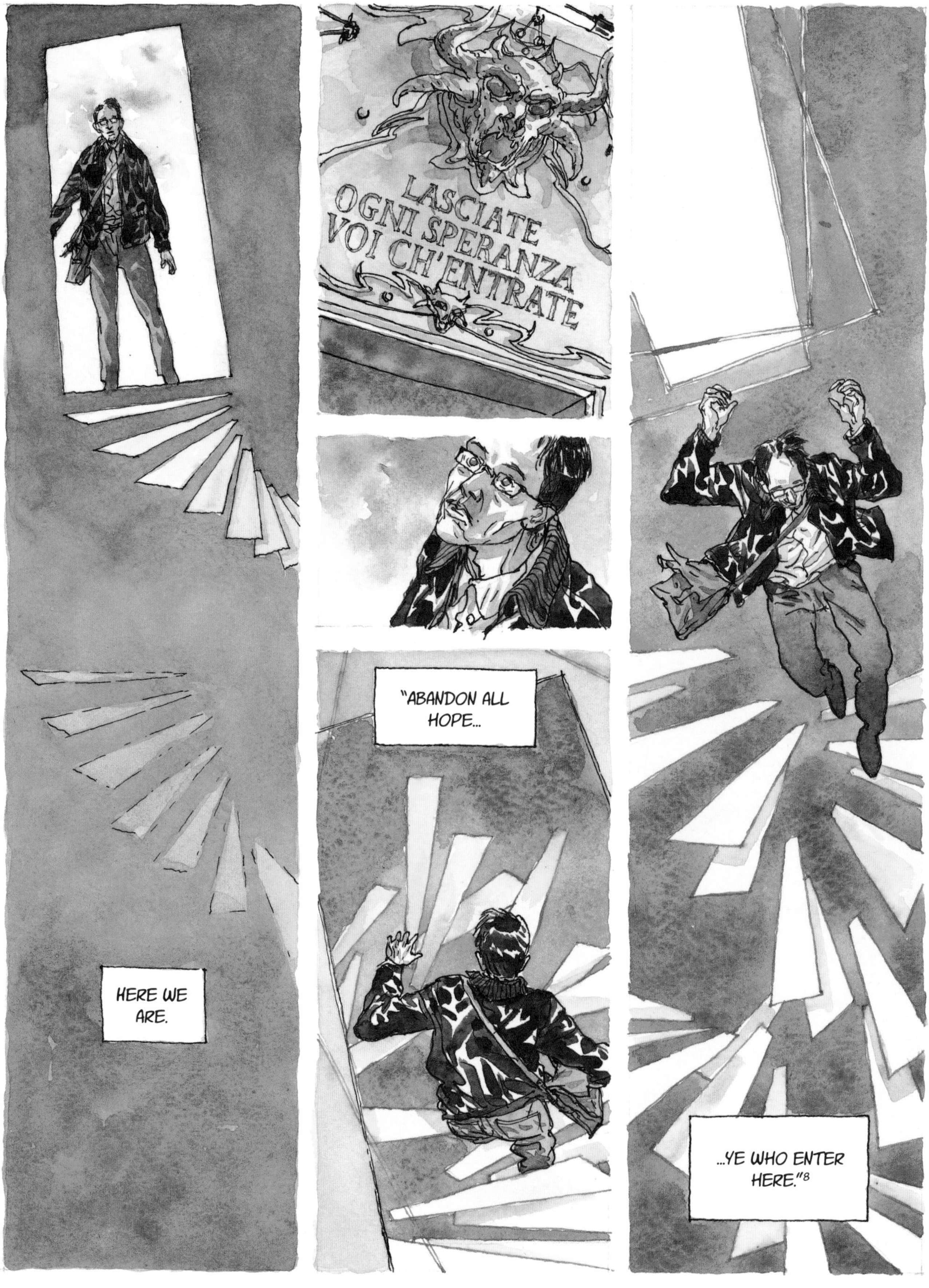
LASCIATE
OGNI SPERANZA
VOI CH'ENTRATE
HERE WE ARE.
"ABANDON ALL HOPE...
...YE WHO ENTER HERE."8

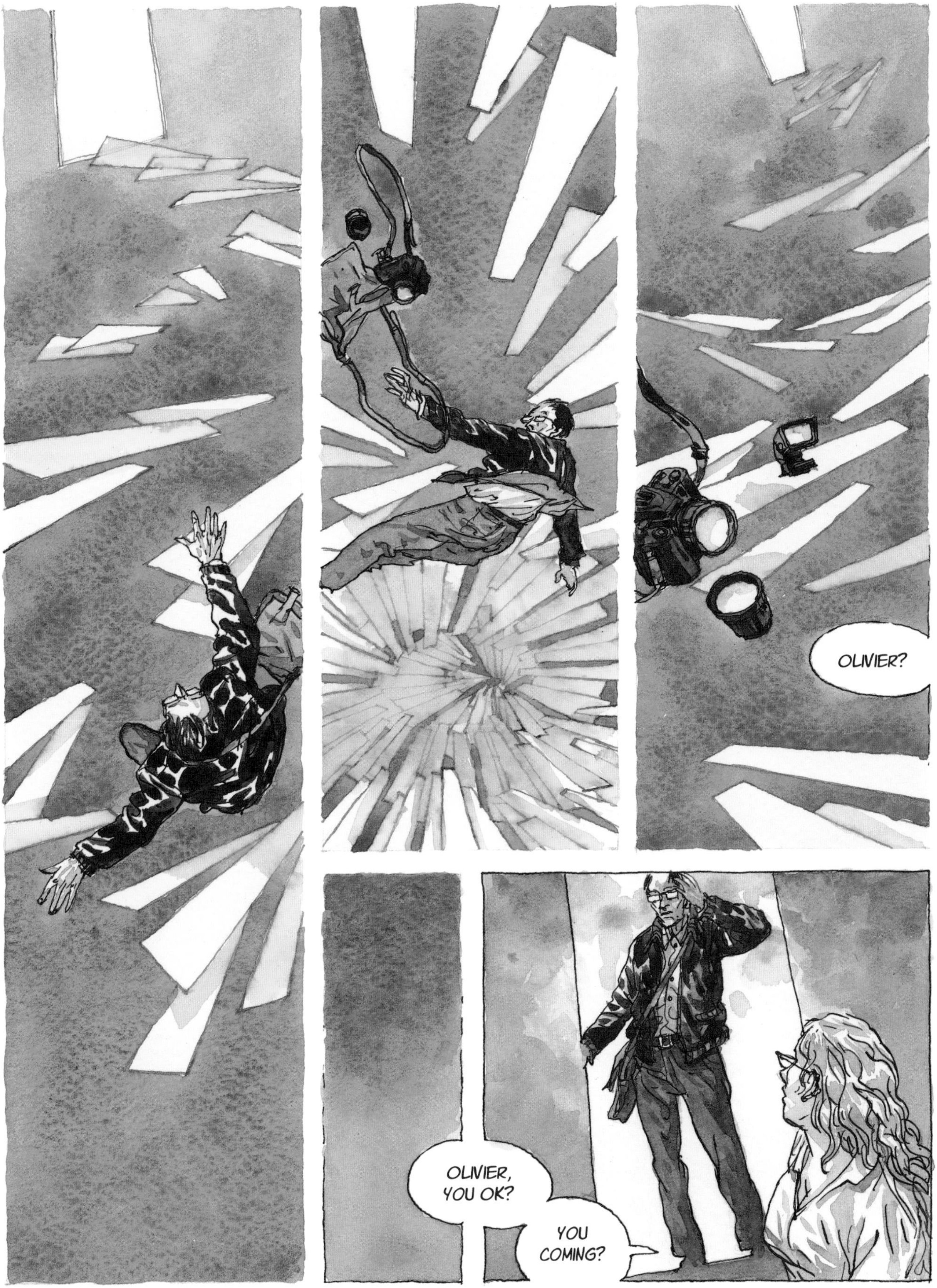
OLIVIER?
OLIVIER, YOU OK?
YOU COMING?

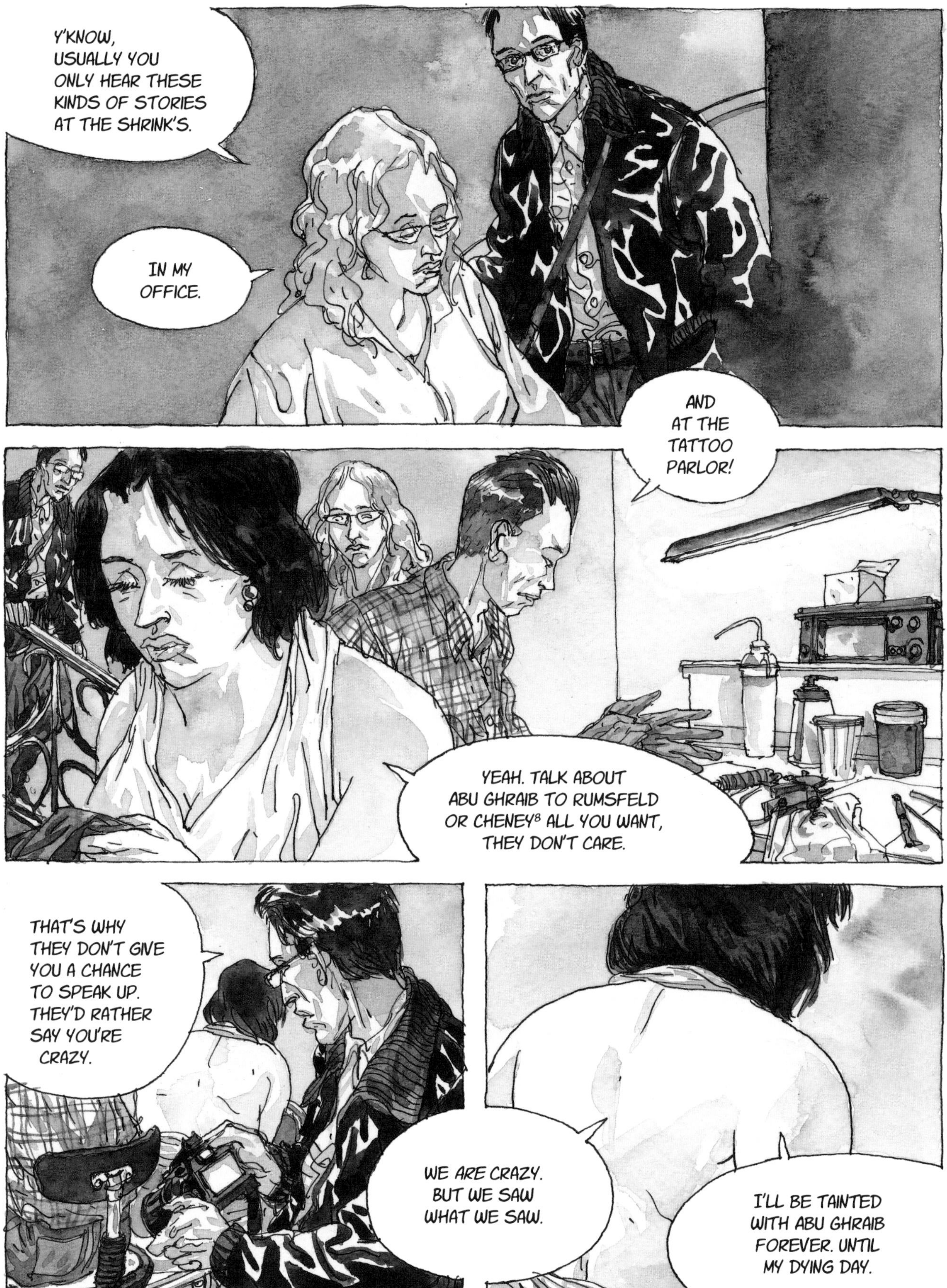
Y'KNOW, USUALLY YOU ONLY HEAR THESE KINDS OF STORIES AT THE SHRINK'S.
IN MY OFFICE.
AND AT THE TATTOO PARLOR!
YEAH. TALK ABOUT ABU GHRAIB TO RUMSFELD OR CHENEY[8] ALL YOU WANT, THEY DON'T CARE.
THAT'S WHY THEY DON'T GIVE YOU A CHANCE TO SPEAK UP. THEY'D RATHER SAY YOU'RE CRAZY.
WE ARE CRAZY. BUT WE SAW WHAT WE SAW.
I'LL BE TAINTED WITH ABU GHRAIB FOREVER. UNTIL MY DYING DAY.

AT ABU GHRAIB, I WAS...

ONE OF MY DUTIES WAS HANDLING THE BLOOD BANK...

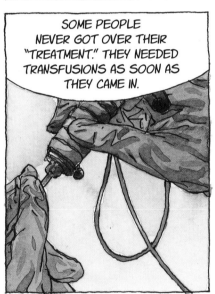

SOME PEOPLE NEVER GOT OVER THEIR "TREATMENT." THEY NEEDED TRANSFUSIONS AS SOON AS THEY CAME IN.

OR THEY'D BRING US PRISONERS WITH SERIOUS INJURIES. I NEVER KNEW WHAT'D HAPPENED TO THEM, BUT I KNOW WE WERE RESPONSIBLE FOR THOSE INJURIES.

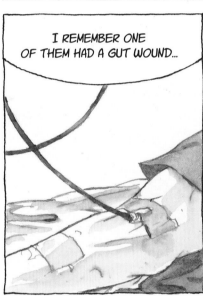

I REMEMBER ONE OF THEM HAD A GUT WOUND...

WE KNEW HE WOULDN'T MAKE IT.

THE LOOK IN HIS EYES, BEGGING US...

I'LL NEVER FORGET IT.

I REALLY LIKED HIM.

IT TIES MY STOMACH UP IN KNOTS. I STRUGGLE WITH THEIR GHOSTS...

OK, I'M READY. YOU GOOD?

I...

I DON'T KNOW IF I WANT—

WANT WHAT?

THIS TATTOO.

IT'S LIKE THE PAIN FROM A PHANTOM LIMB: I WANT TO SEE MY PAIN RIGHT THERE ON THE SURFACE, BUT I ALSO REALIZE IT'LL BE THERE FOREVER.

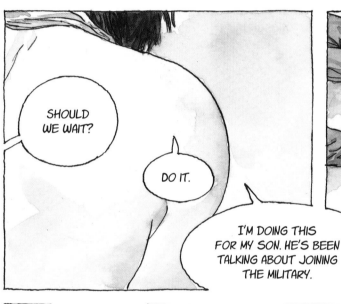

SHOULD WE WAIT?

DO IT.

I'M DOING THIS FOR MY SON. HE'S BEEN TALKING ABOUT JOINING THE MILITARY.

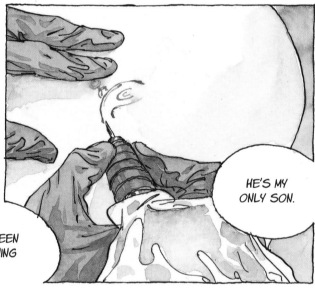

HE'S MY ONLY SON.

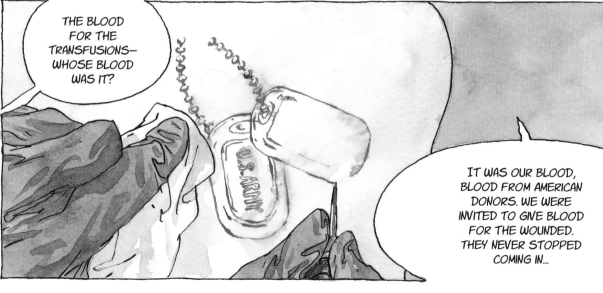

THE BLOOD FOR THE TRANSFUSIONS— WHOSE BLOOD WAS IT?

IT WAS OUR BLOOD, BLOOD FROM AMERICAN DONORS. WE WERE INVITED TO GIVE BLOOD FOR THE WOUNDED. THEY NEVER STOPPED COMING IN...

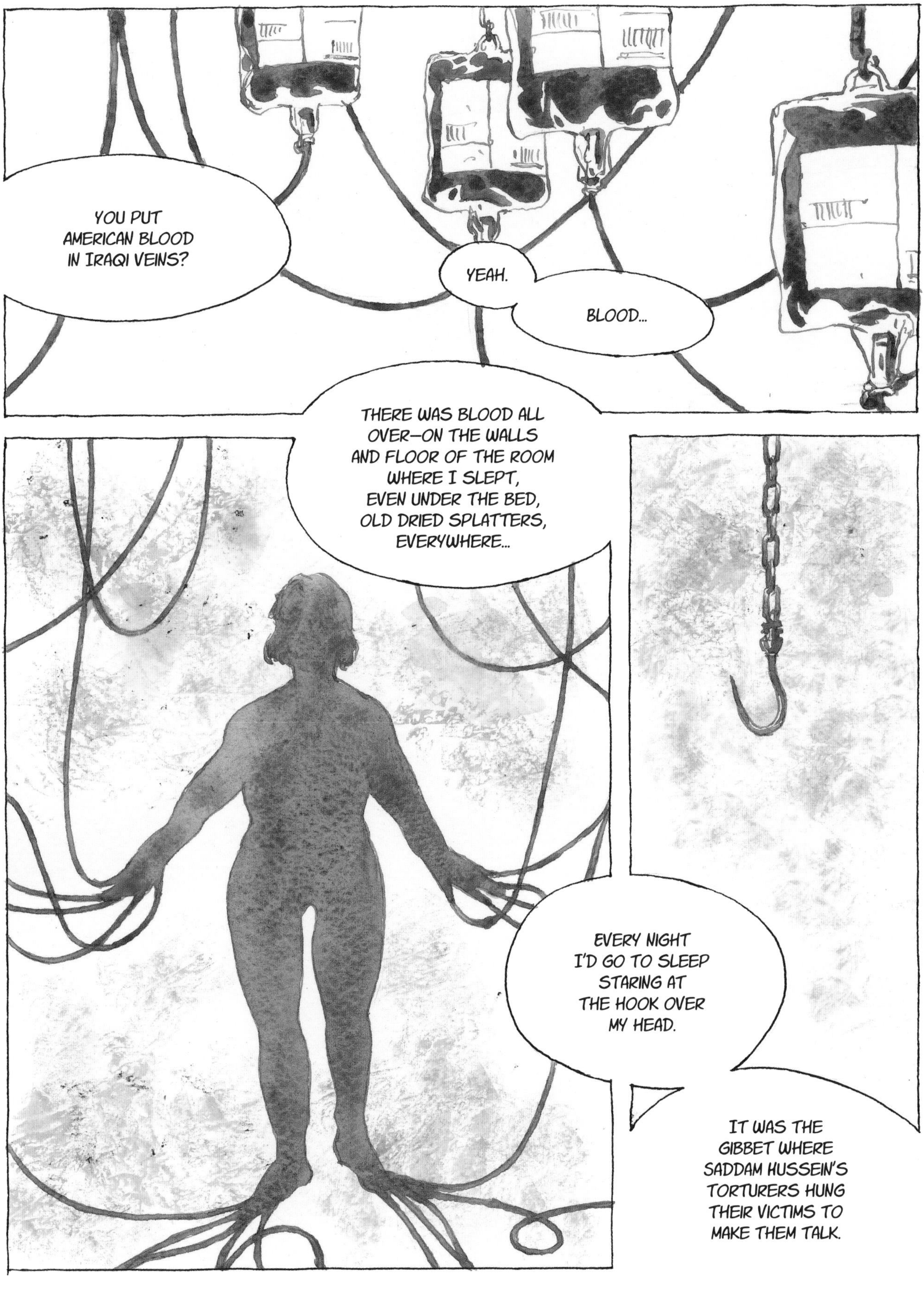
YOU PUT AMERICAN BLOOD IN IRAQI VEINS?
YEAH.
BLOOD...
THERE WAS BLOOD ALL OVER—ON THE WALLS AND FLOOR OF THE ROOM WHERE I SLEPT, EVEN UNDER THE BED, OLD DRIED SPLATTERS, EVERYWHERE...
EVERY NIGHT I'D GO TO SLEEP STARING AT THE HOOK OVER MY HEAD.
IT WAS THE GIBBET WHERE SADDAM HUSSEIN'S TORTURERS HUNG THEIR VICTIMS TO MAKE THEM TALK.

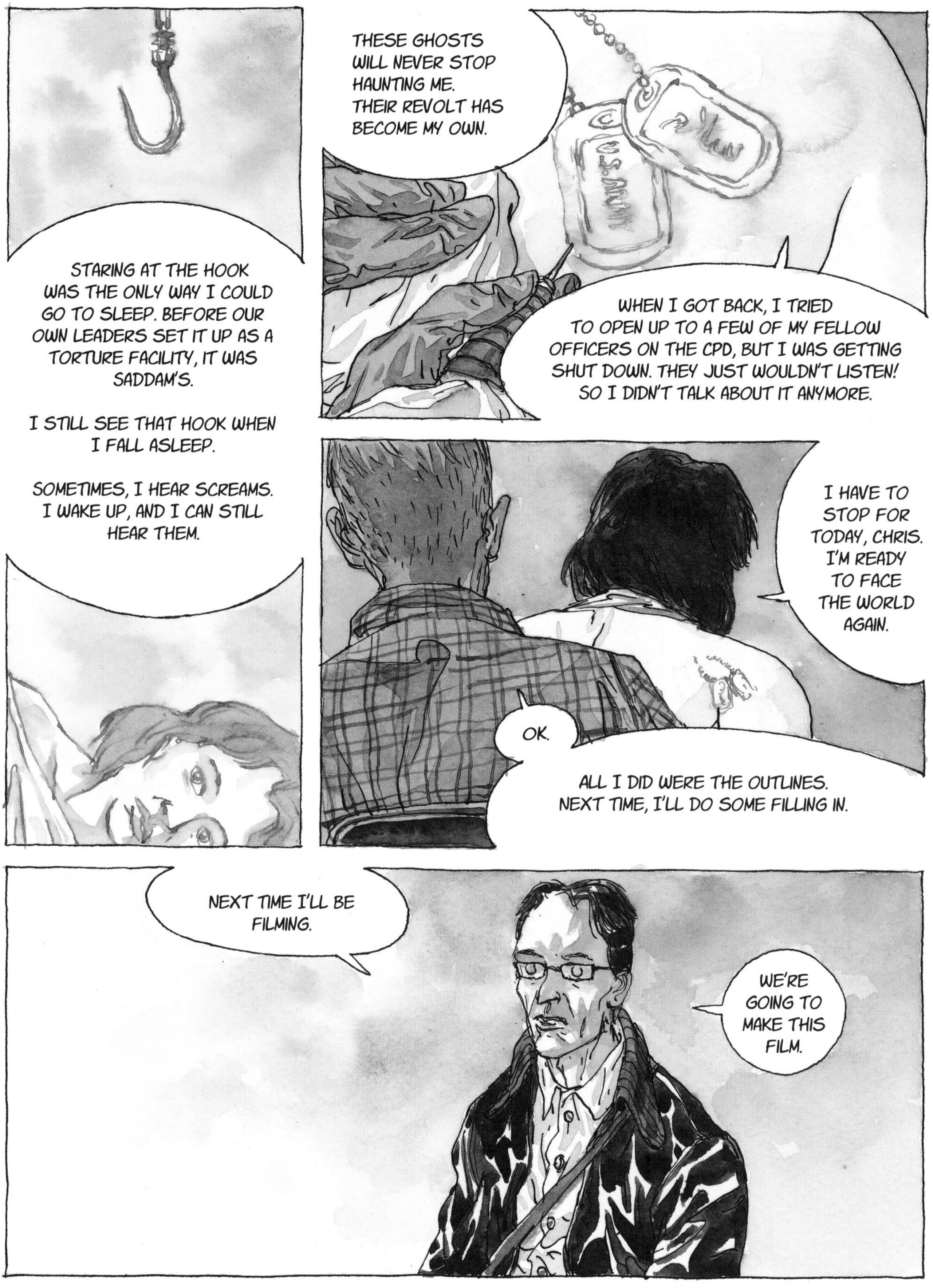
THESE GHOSTS WILL NEVER STOP HAUNTING ME. THEIR REVOLT HAS BECOME MY OWN.
STARING AT THE HOOK WAS THE ONLY WAY I COULD GO TO SLEEP. BEFORE OUR OWN LEADERS SET IT UP AS A TORTURE FACILITY, IT WAS SADDAM'S.
I STILL SEE THAT HOOK WHEN I FALL ASLEEP.
SOMETIMES, I HEAR SCREAMS. I WAKE UP, AND I CAN STILL HEAR THEM.
U.S. ARMY
WHEN I GOT BACK, I TRIED TO OPEN UP TO A FEW OF MY FELLOW OFFICERS ON THE CPD, BUT I WAS GETTING SHUT DOWN. THEY JUST WOULDN'T LISTEN! SO I DIDN'T TALK ABOUT IT ANYMORE.
I HAVE TO STOP FOR TODAY, CHRIS. I'M READY TO FACE THE WORLD AGAIN.
OK.
ALL I DID WERE THE OUTLINES. NEXT TIME, I'LL DO SOME FILLING IN.
NEXT TIME I'LL BE FILMING.
WE'RE GOING TO MAKE THIS FILM.

chapter 2

Ghosts

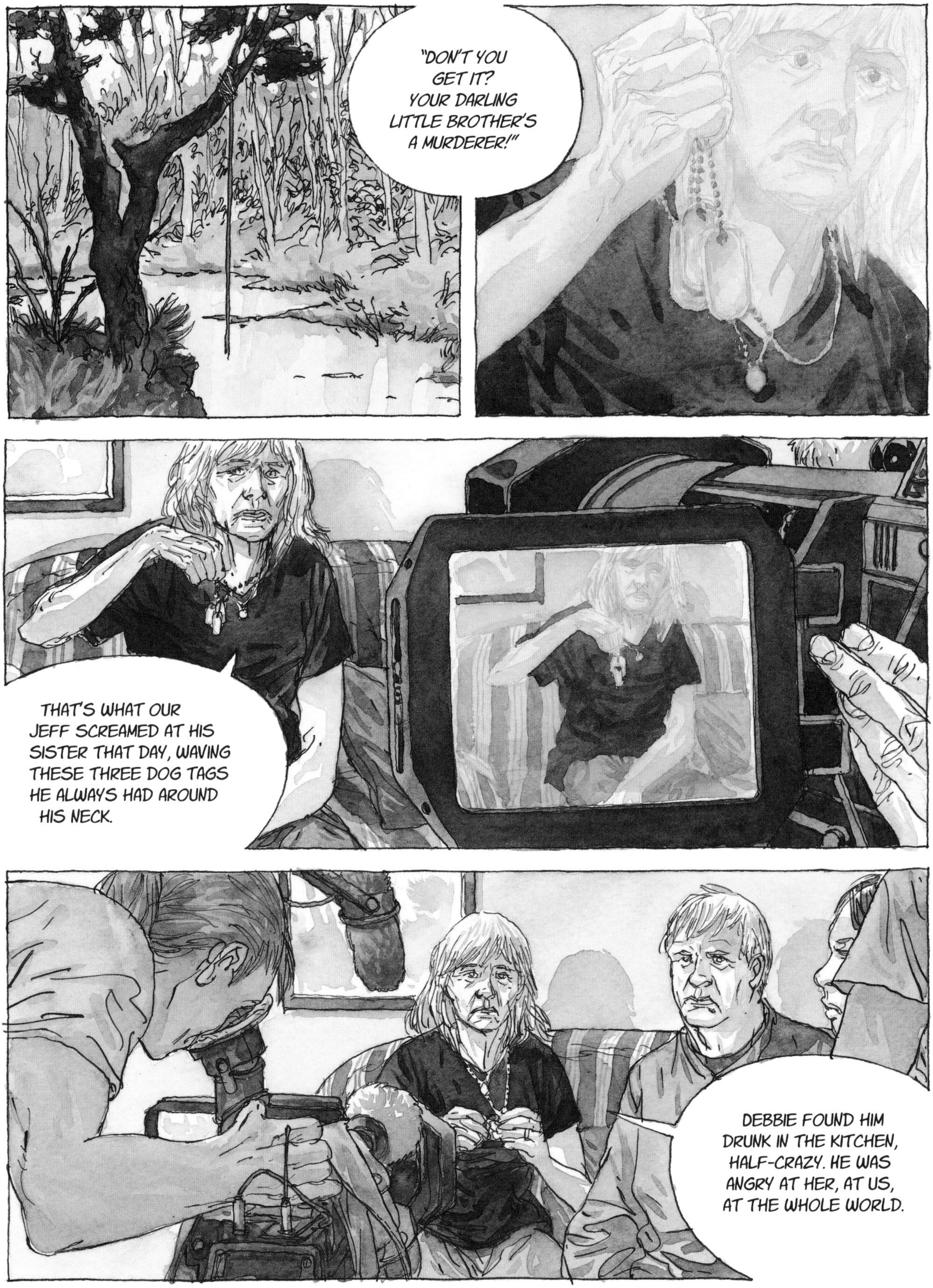
"DON'T YOU GET IT? YOUR DARLING LITTLE BROTHER'S A MURDERER!"
THAT'S WHAT OUR JEFF SCREAMED AT HIS SISTER THAT DAY, WAVING THESE THREE DOG TAGS HE ALWAYS HAD AROUND HIS NECK.
DEBBIE FOUND HIM DRUNK IN THE KITCHEN, HALF-CRAZY. HE WAS ANGRY AT HER, AT US, AT THE WHOLE WORLD.

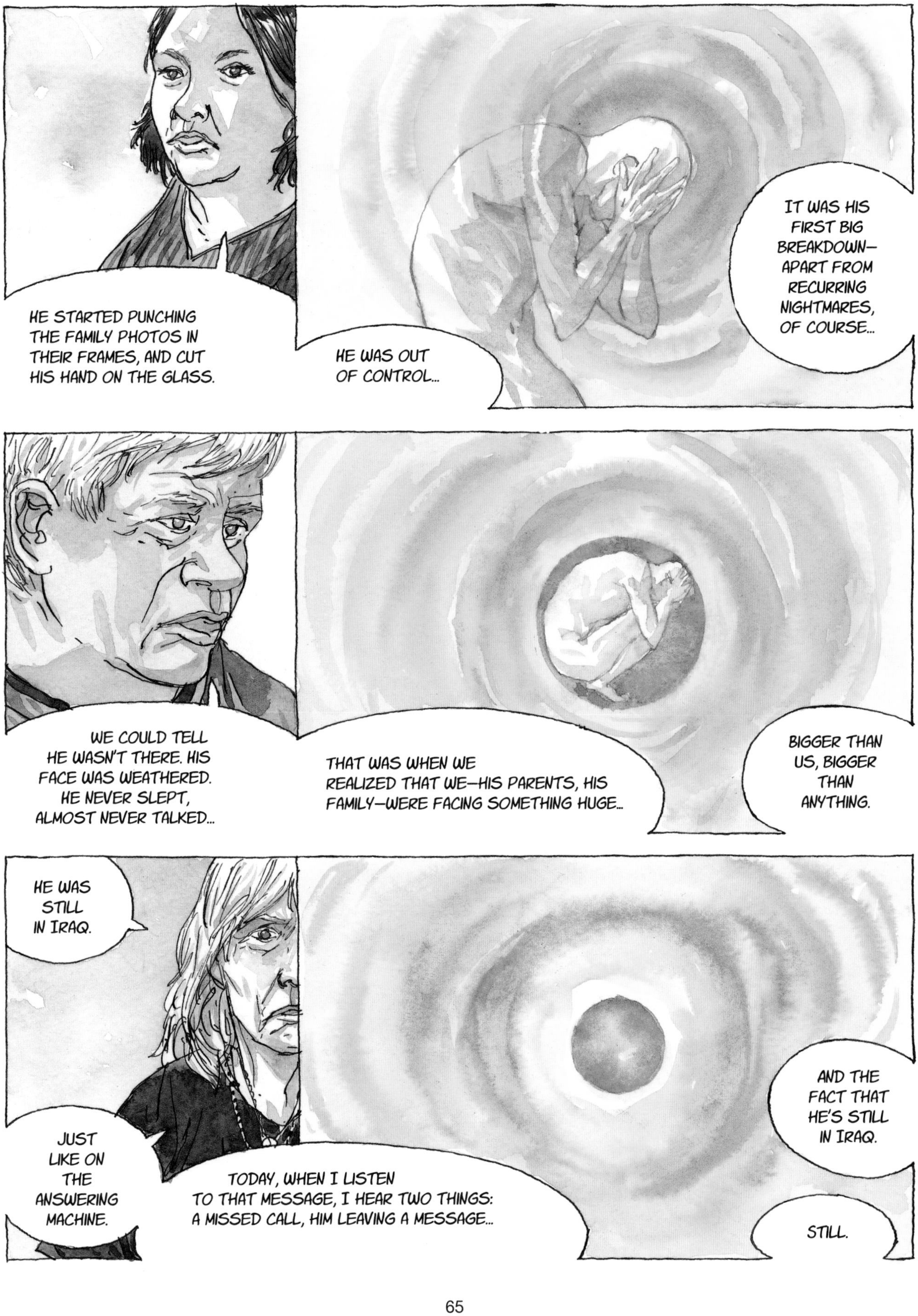
HE STARTED PUNCHING THE FAMILY PHOTOS IN THEIR FRAMES, AND CUT HIS HAND ON THE GLASS.
HE WAS OUT OF CONTROL...
IT WAS HIS FIRST BIG BREAKDOWN—APART FROM RECURRING NIGHTMARES, OF COURSE...
WE COULD TELL HE WASN'T THERE. HIS FACE WAS WEATHERED. HE NEVER SLEPT, ALMOST NEVER TALKED...
THAT WAS WHEN WE REALIZED THAT WE—HIS PARENTS, HIS FAMILY—WERE FACING SOMETHING HUGE...
BIGGER THAN US, BIGGER THAN ANYTHING.
HE WAS STILL IN IRAQ.
JUST LIKE ON THE ANSWERING MACHINE.
TODAY, WHEN I LISTEN TO THAT MESSAGE, I HEAR TWO THINGS: A MISSED CALL, HIM LEAVING A MESSAGE...
AND THE FACT THAT HE'S STILL IN IRAQ.
STILL.

PHYSICALLY, HE CAME BACK. BUT THE IMPORTANT PART GOT LEFT BEHIND.

HE CAME BACK, BUT HE WAS JUST A GHOST OF HIMSELF.

A GHOST HAUNTED BY OTHER GHOSTS.

SO THE DOG TAGS ROUND HIS NECK—

YES, THOSE WERE WHAT HAUNTED JEFF.

HE SAW FACES, THOUGHT HE WAS BEING CHASED...

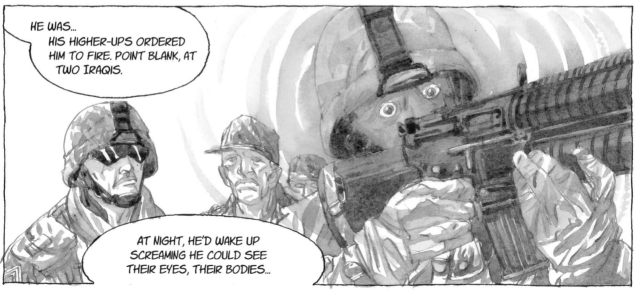

HE WAS... HIS HIGHER-UPS ORDERED HIM TO FIRE. POINT BLANK, AT TWO IRAQIS.

AT NIGHT, HE'D WAKE UP SCREAMING HE COULD SEE THEIR EYES, THEIR BODIES...

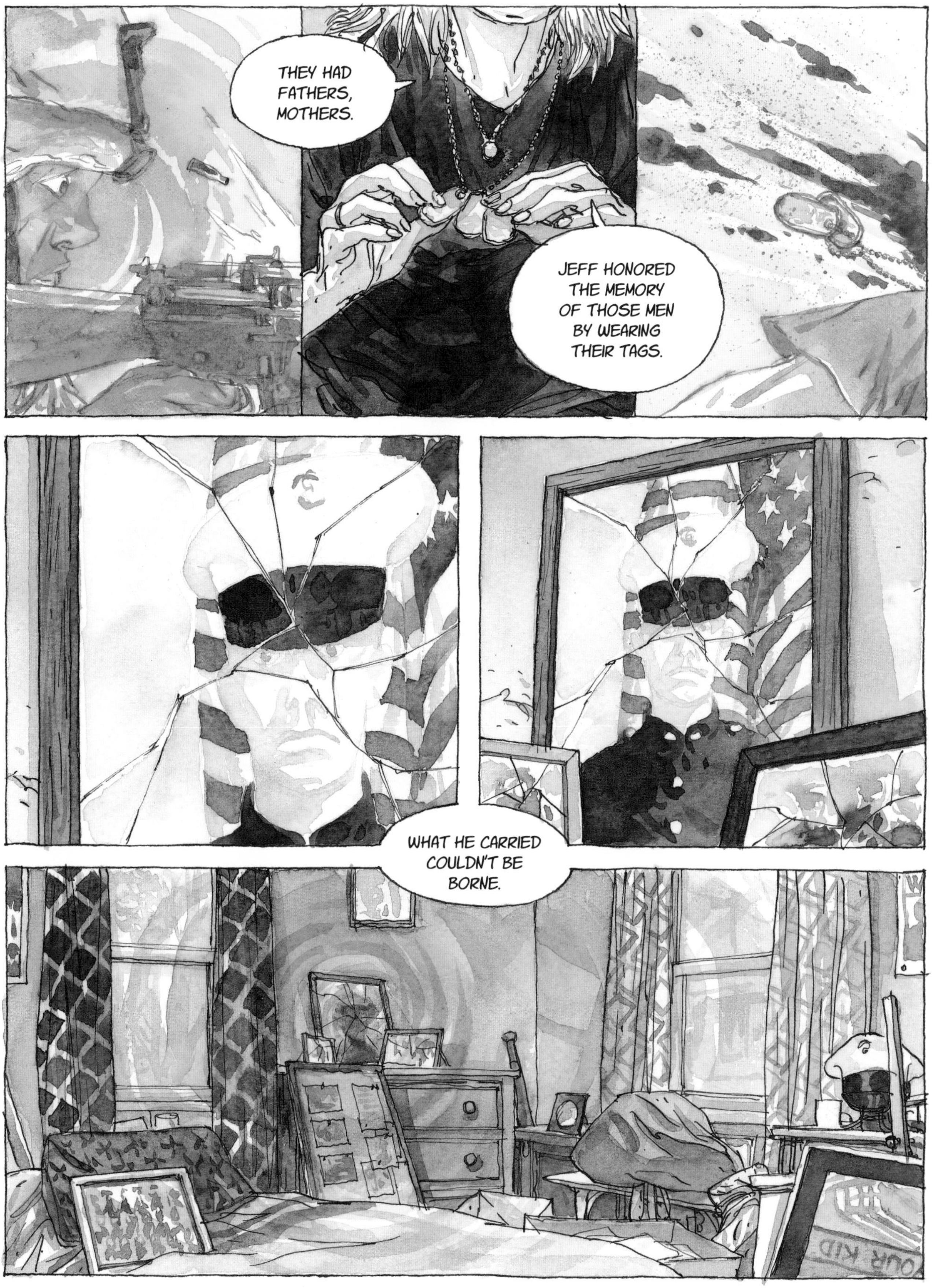
THEY HAD FATHERS, MOTHERS.
JEFF HONORED THE MEMORY OF THOSE MEN BY WEARING THEIR TAGS.
WHAT HE CARRIED COULDN'T BE BORNE.
OUR KID

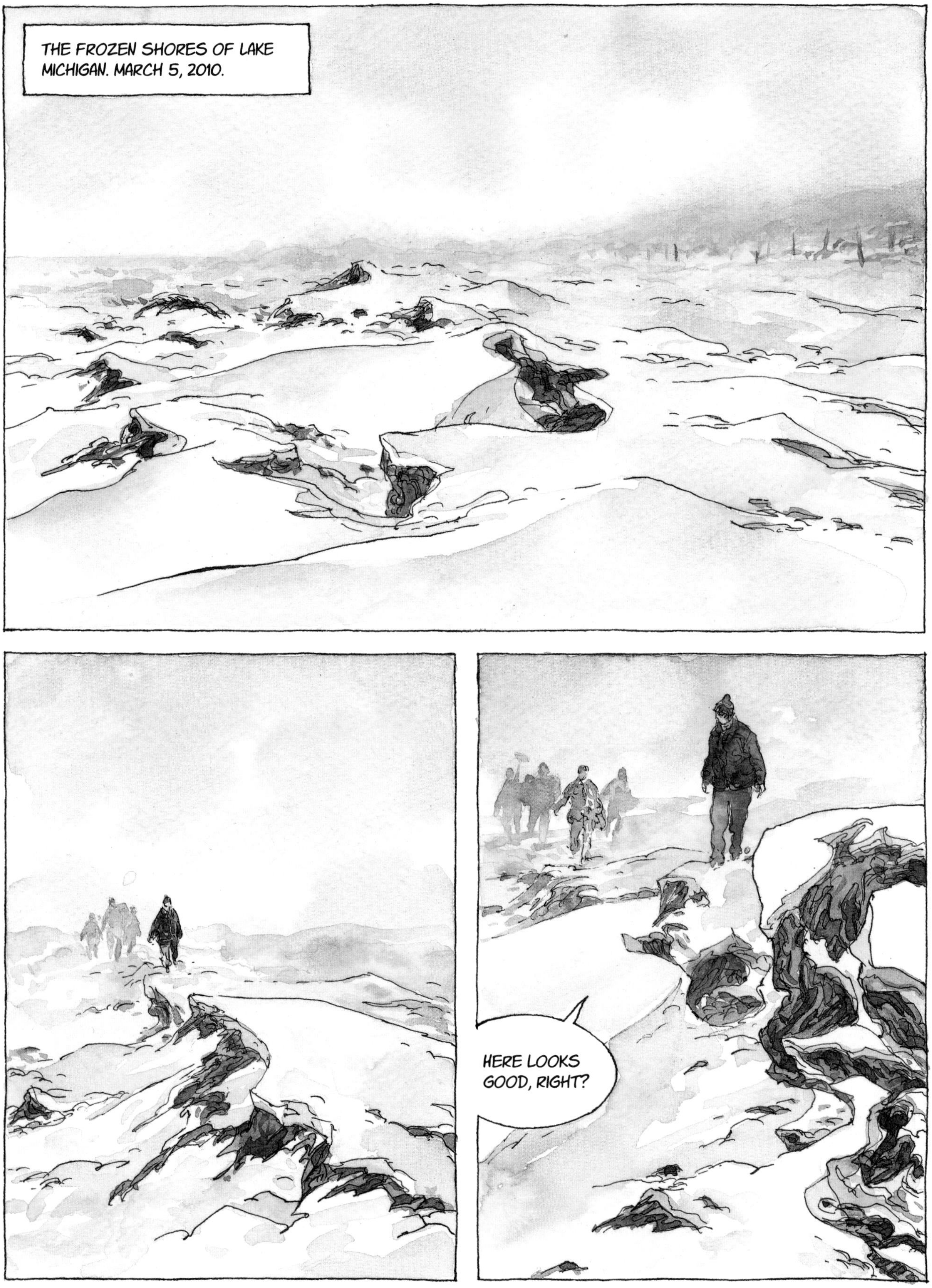
THE FROZEN SHORES OF LAKE MICHIGAN. MARCH 5, 2010.
HERE LOOKS GOOD, RIGHT?

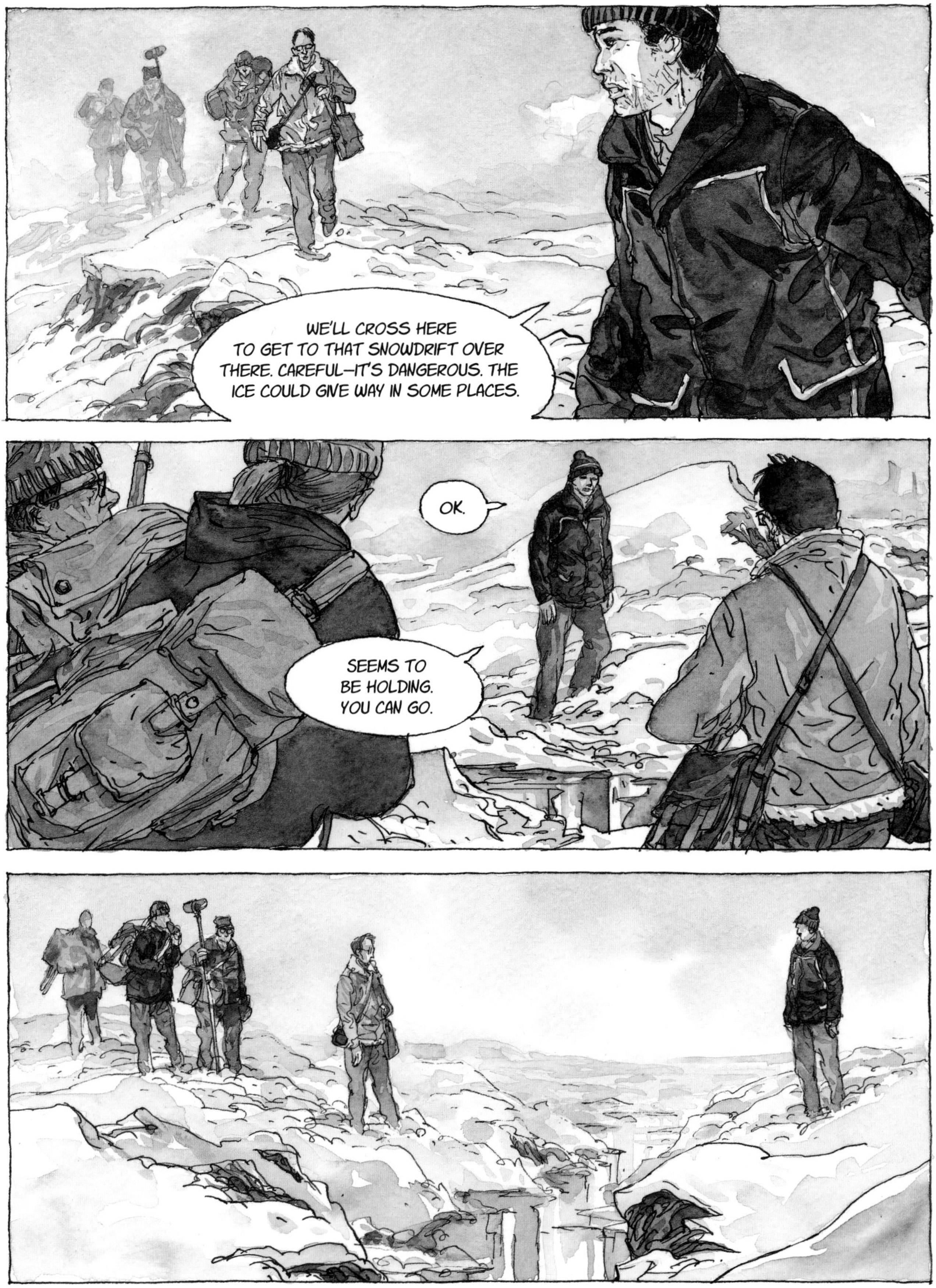
WE'LL CROSS HERE TO GET TO THAT SNOWDRIFT OVER THERE. CAREFUL—IT'S DANGEROUS. THE ICE COULD GIVE WAY IN SOME PLACES.
OK.
SEEMS TO BE HOLDING. YOU CAN GO.

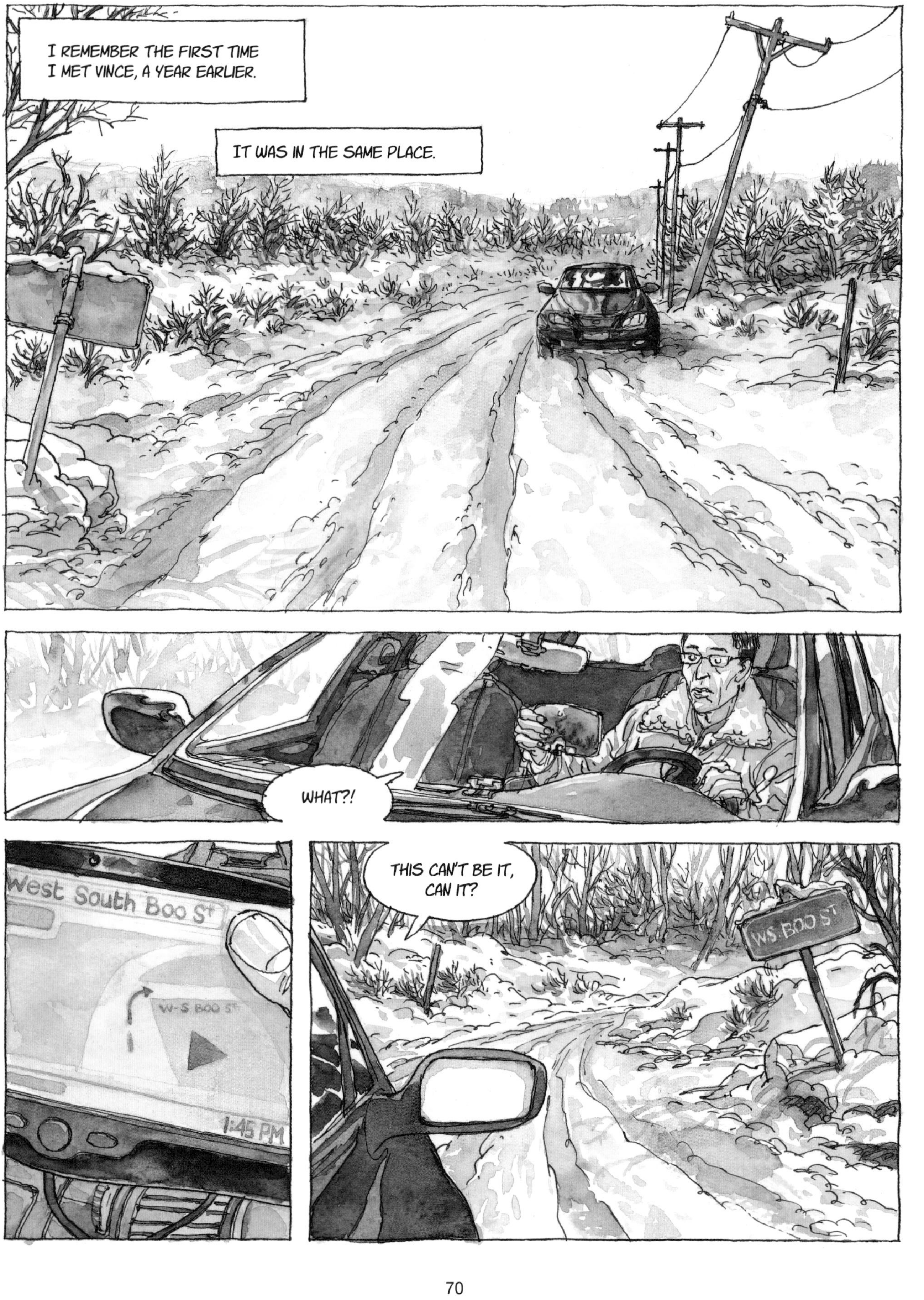
I REMEMBER THE FIRST TIME I MET VINCE, A YEAR EARLIER.
IT WAS IN THE SAME PLACE.
WHAT?!
West South Boo St
W-S BOO ST
1:45 PM
THIS CAN'T BE IT, CAN IT?
W.S. BOO ST

I REMEMBER BEING AFRAID
ALL OF A SUDDEN.

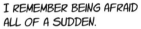

OK.

GOTTA
GO.

I WAS AFRAID... OF WHAT? AFRAID
OF WHAT I'D FIND?

AND I ASKED MYSELF: WHY AM I
DOING THIS? WHY COME ALL THE
WAY OUT HERE TO TORMENT VINCE
EMANUELE'S WOUNDED SOUL?

WHY DO I KEEP OBSESSIVELY
READING HIS CONFESSION,
"DEADLY DAYS"?[10]

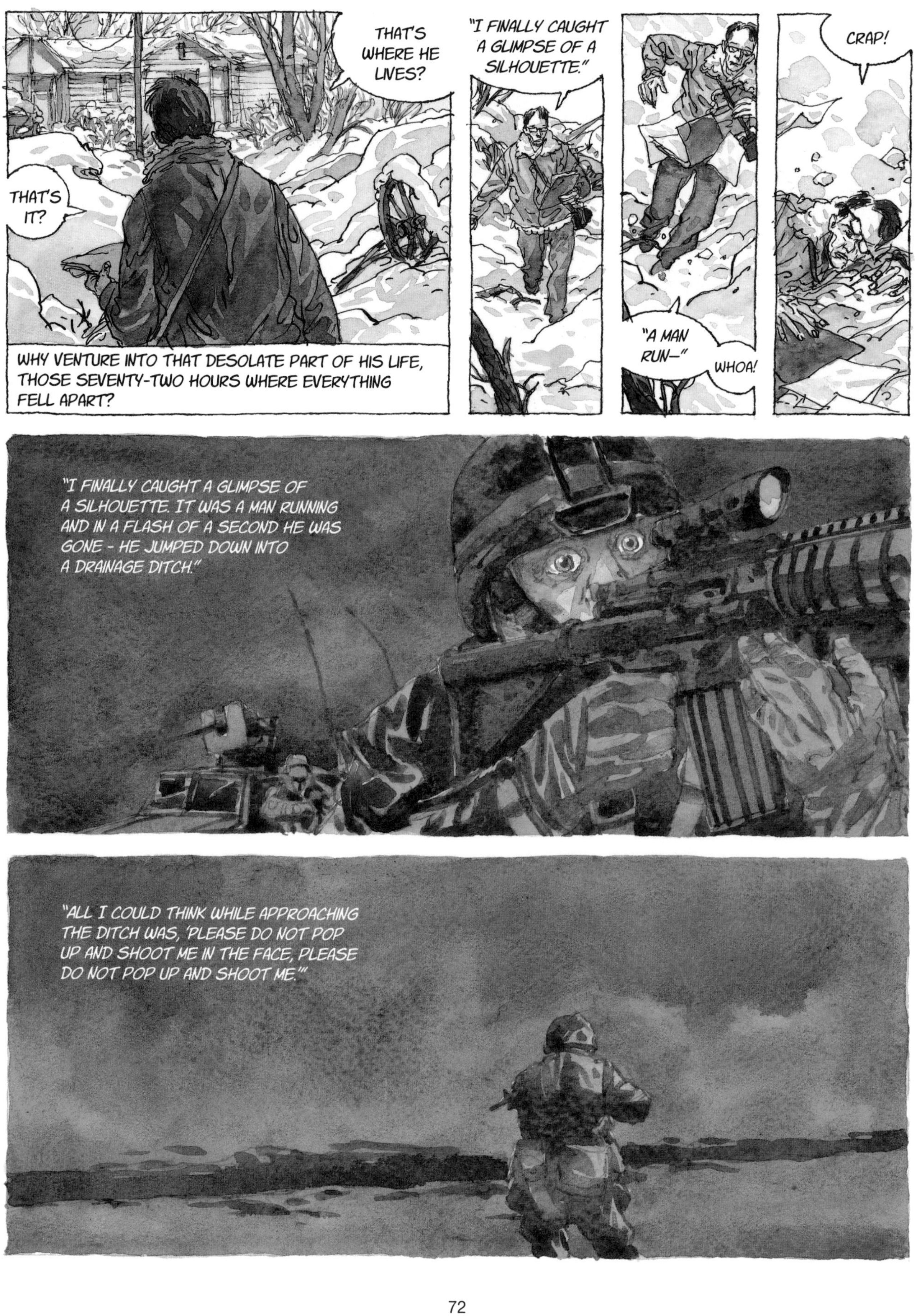
THAT'S IT?
THAT'S WHERE HE LIVES?
WHY VENTURE INTO THAT DESOLATE PART OF HIS LIFE, THOSE SEVENTY-TWO HOURS WHERE EVERYTHING FELL APART?
"I FINALLY CAUGHT A GLIMPSE OF A SILHOUETTE."
"A MAN RUN—"
WHOA!
CRAP!
"I FINALLY CAUGHT A GLIMPSE OF A SILHOUETTE. IT WAS A MAN RUNNING AND IN A FLASH OF A SECOND HE WAS GONE - HE JUMPED DOWN INTO A DRAINAGE DITCH."
"ALL I COULD THINK WHILE APPROACHING THE DITCH WAS, 'PLEASE DO NOT POP UP AND SHOOT ME IN THE FACE, PLEASE DO NOT POP UP AND SHOOT ME.'"

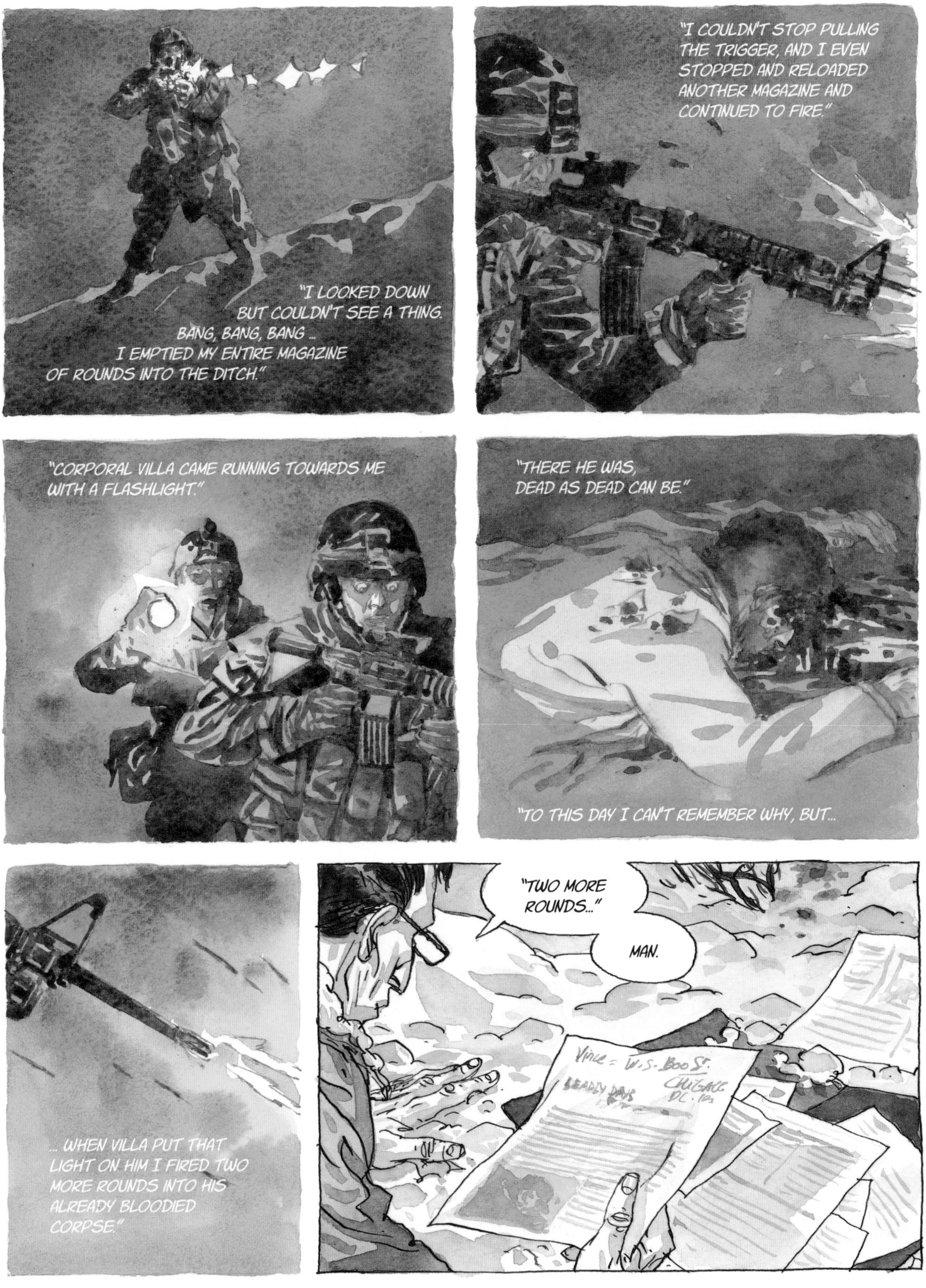
"I LOOKED DOWN BUT COULDN'T SEE A THING. BANG, BANG, BANG ... I EMPTIED MY ENTIRE MAGAZINE OF ROUNDS INTO THE DITCH."
"I COULDN'T STOP PULLING THE TRIGGER, AND I EVEN STOPPED AND RELOADED ANOTHER MAGAZINE AND CONTINUED TO FIRE."
"CORPORAL VILLA CAME RUNNING TOWARDS ME WITH A FLASHLIGHT."
"THERE HE WAS, DEAD AS DEAD CAN BE."
"TO THIS DAY I CAN'T REMEMBER WHY, BUT...
... WHEN VILLA PUT THAT LIGHT ON HIM I FIRED TWO MORE ROUNDS INTO HIS ALREADY BLOODIED CORPSE."
"TWO MORE ROUNDS..."
MAN.

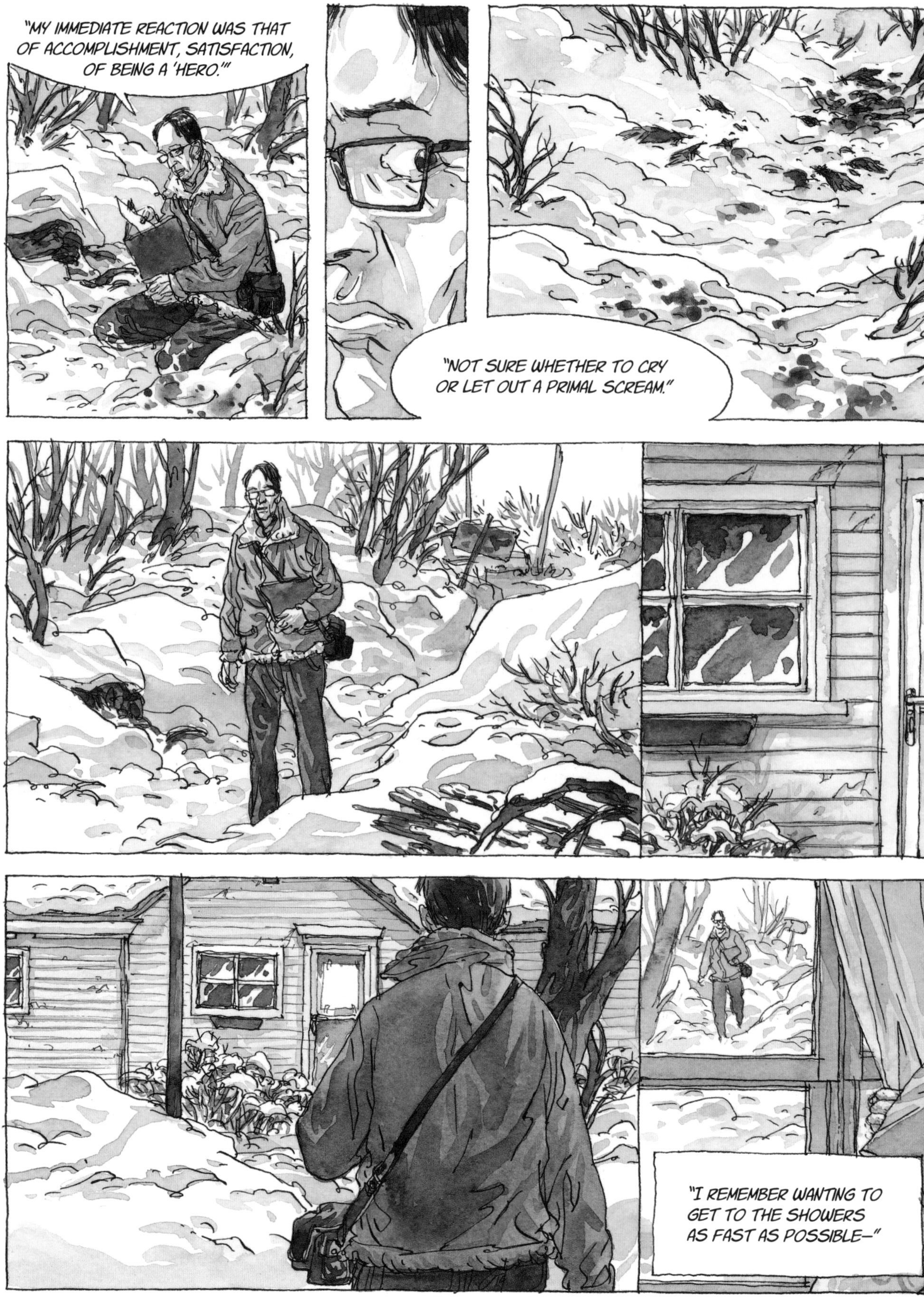
"MY IMMEDIATE REACTION WAS THAT OF ACCOMPLISHMENT, SATISFACTION, OF BEING A 'HERO.'"
"NOT SURE WHETHER TO CRY OR LET OUT A PRIMAL SCREAM."
"I REMEMBER WANTING TO GET TO THE SHOWERS AS FAST AS POSSIBLE–"

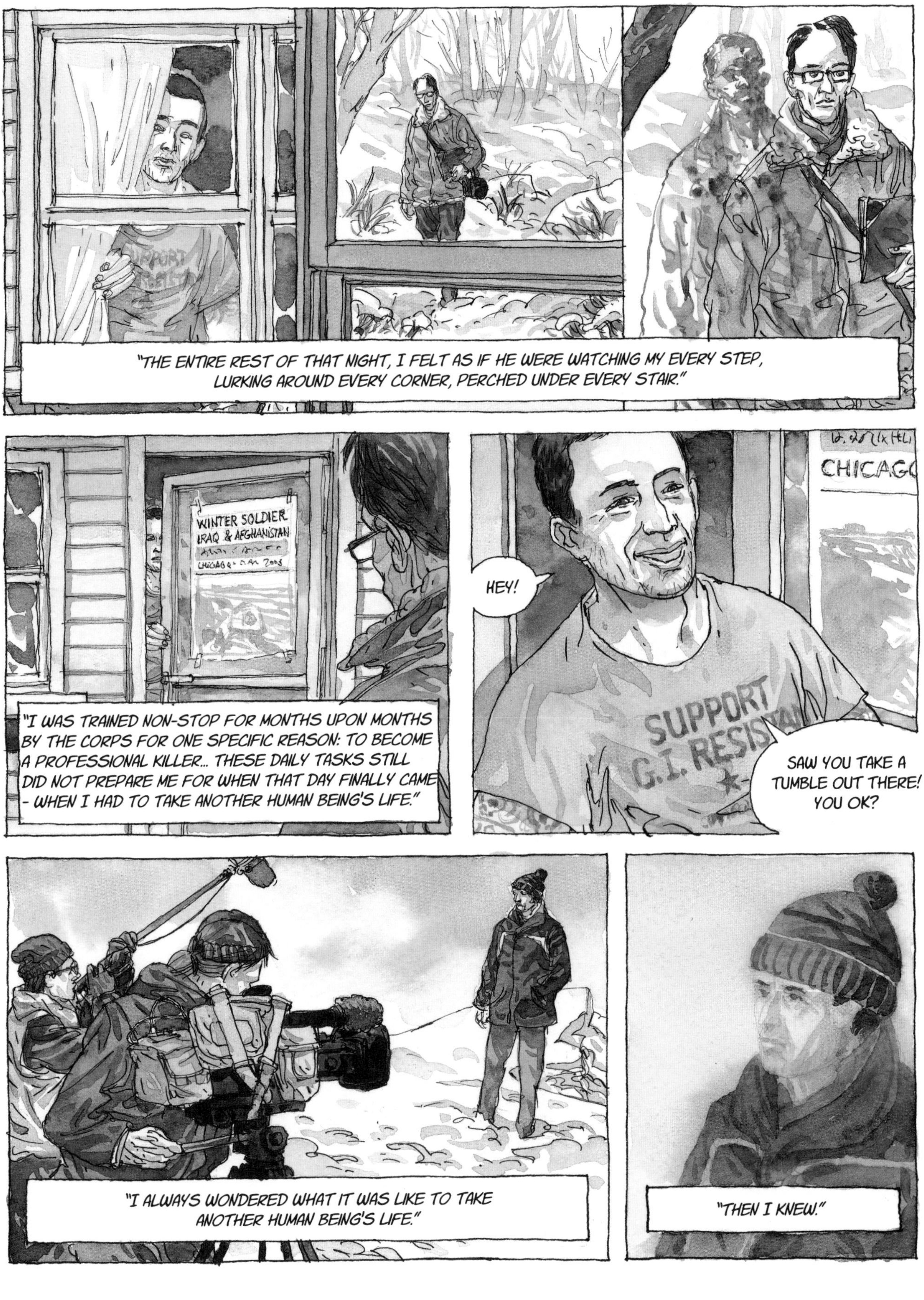
"THE ENTIRE REST OF THAT NIGHT, I FELT AS IF HE WERE WATCHING MY EVERY STEP, LURKING AROUND EVERY CORNER, PERCHED UNDER EVERY STAIR."
WINTER SOLDIER
IRAQ & AFGHANISTAN
"I WAS TRAINED NON-STOP FOR MONTHS UPON MONTHS BY THE CORPS FOR ONE SPECIFIC REASON: TO BECOME A PROFESSIONAL KILLER... THESE DAILY TASKS STILL DID NOT PREPARE ME FOR WHEN THAT DAY FINALLY CAME - WHEN I HAD TO TAKE ANOTHER HUMAN BEING'S LIFE."
CHICAGO
HEY!
SUPPORT
G.I. RESIST
SAW YOU TAKE A TUMBLE OUT THERE! YOU OK?
"I ALWAYS WONDERED WHAT IT WAS LIKE TO TAKE ANOTHER HUMAN BEING'S LIFE."
"THEN I KNEW."

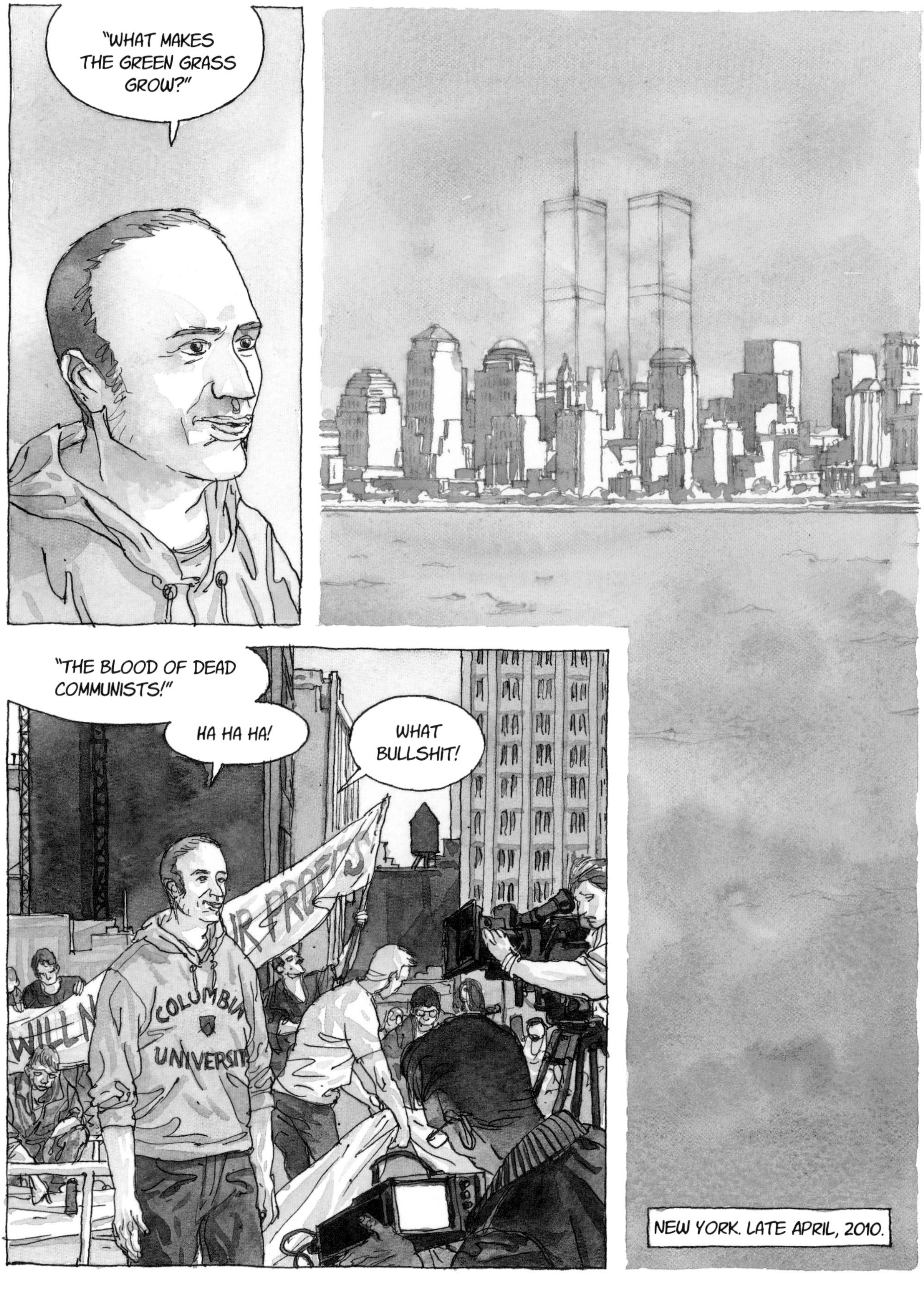

"WHAT MAKES THE GREEN GRASS GROW?"
NEW YORK. LATE APRIL, 2010.
"THE BLOOD OF DEAD COMMUNISTS!"
HA HA HA!
WHAT BULLSHIT!
COLUMBIA UNIVERSITY

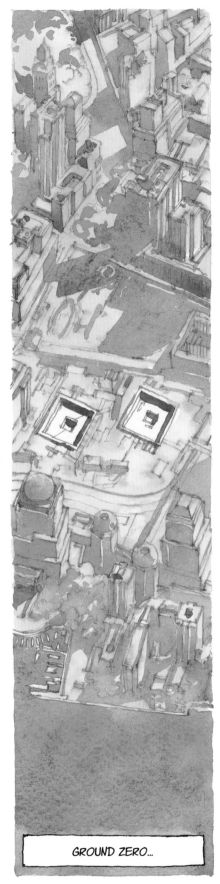

GROUND ZERO...

I WAS IN THE MARINES AROUND THE END OF THE COLD WAR, FROM 1988 TO 1992. THEY STUFFED OUR SKULLS WITH HATE-FILLED JOKES AGAINST THE "COMMIES." I COME FROM A FAMILY OF "MILITARY FETISHISTS," Y'KNOW... PEOPLE WHO LIKE GUNS, UNIFORMS—I GREW UP WITH ALL THAT.

I SAW THE TOWERS FALL ON TV FROM THE DOG GROOMING PARLOR WHERE I WORKED AS A SHAMPOOER.

IT WAS LIKE I'D BEEN AWAKENED FROM A DEEP SLEEP.

WITH KEVIN (AND A FEW OTHERS).

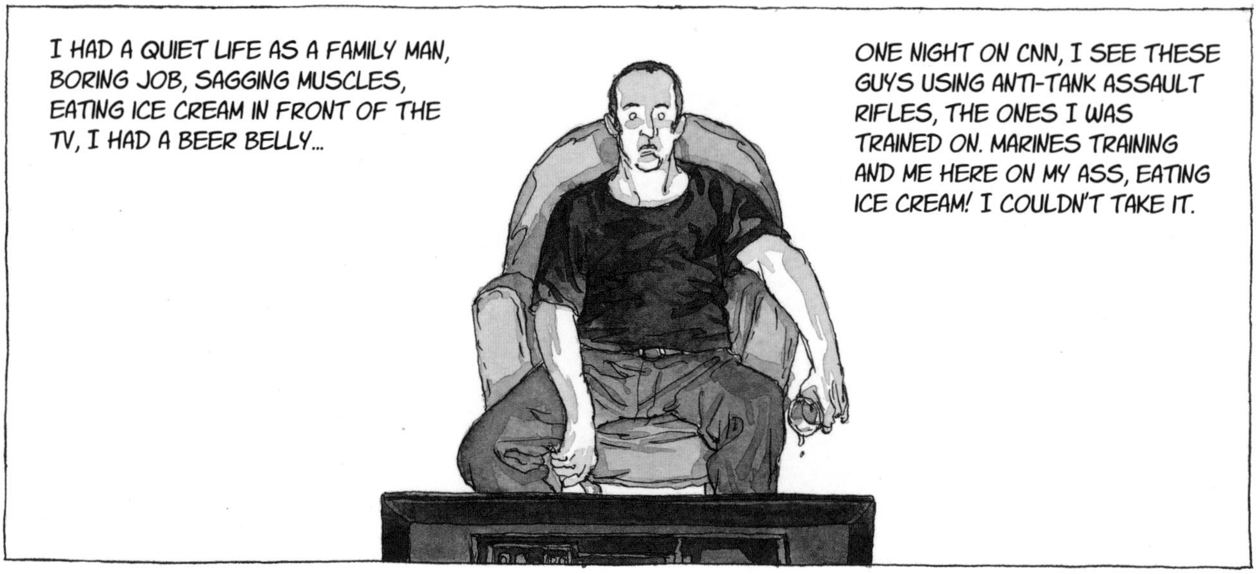
I HAD A QUIET LIFE AS A FAMILY MAN, BORING JOB, SAGGING MUSCLES, EATING ICE CREAM IN FRONT OF THE TV, I HAD A BEER BELLY...
ONE NIGHT ON CNN, I SEE THESE GUYS USING ANTI-TANK ASSAULT RIFLES, THE ONES I WAS TRAINED ON. MARINES TRAINING AND ME HERE ON MY ASS, EATING ICE CREAM! I COULDN'T TAKE IT.

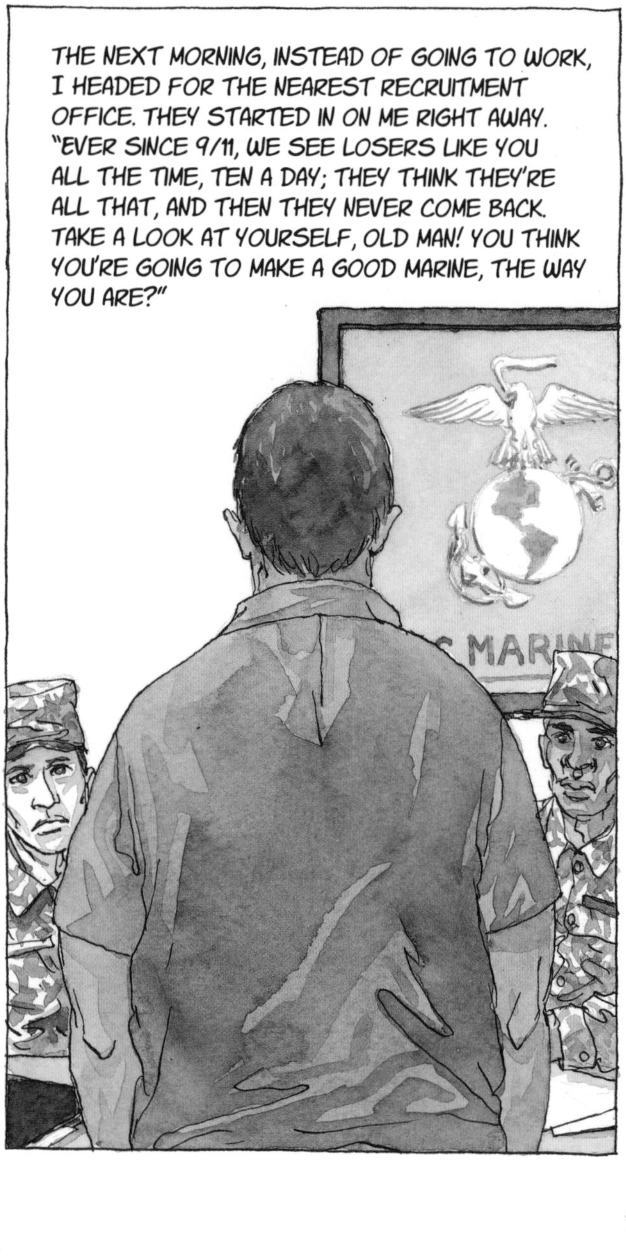
THE NEXT MORNING, INSTEAD OF GOING TO WORK, I HEADED FOR THE NEAREST RECRUITMENT OFFICE. THEY STARTED IN ON ME RIGHT AWAY. "EVER SINCE 9/11, WE SEE LOSERS LIKE YOU ALL THE TIME, TEN A DAY; THEY THINK THEY'RE ALL THAT, AND THEN THEY NEVER COME BACK. TAKE A LOOK AT YOURSELF, OLD MAN! YOU THINK YOU'RE GOING TO MAKE A GOOD MARINE, THE WAY YOU ARE?"

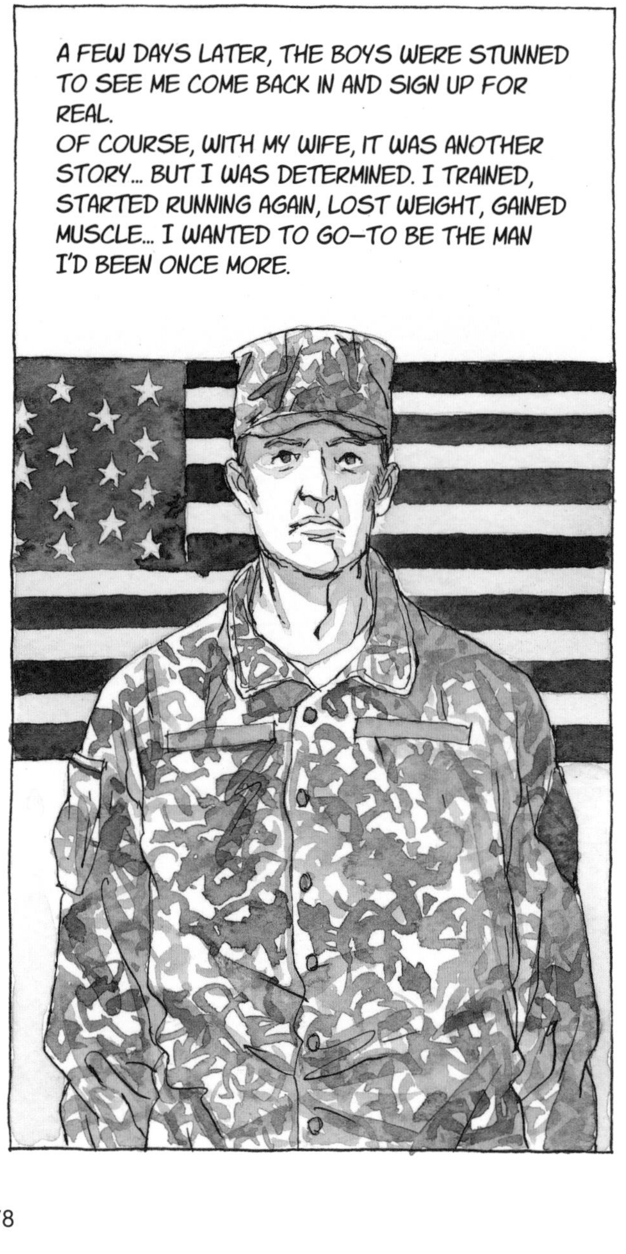
A FEW DAYS LATER, THE BOYS WERE STUNNED TO SEE ME COME BACK IN AND SIGN UP FOR REAL.
OF COURSE, WITH MY WIFE, IT WAS ANOTHER STORY... BUT I WAS DETERMINED. I TRAINED, STARTED RUNNING AGAIN, LOST WEIGHT, GAINED MUSCLE... I WANTED TO GO—TO BE THE MAN I'D BEEN ONCE MORE.

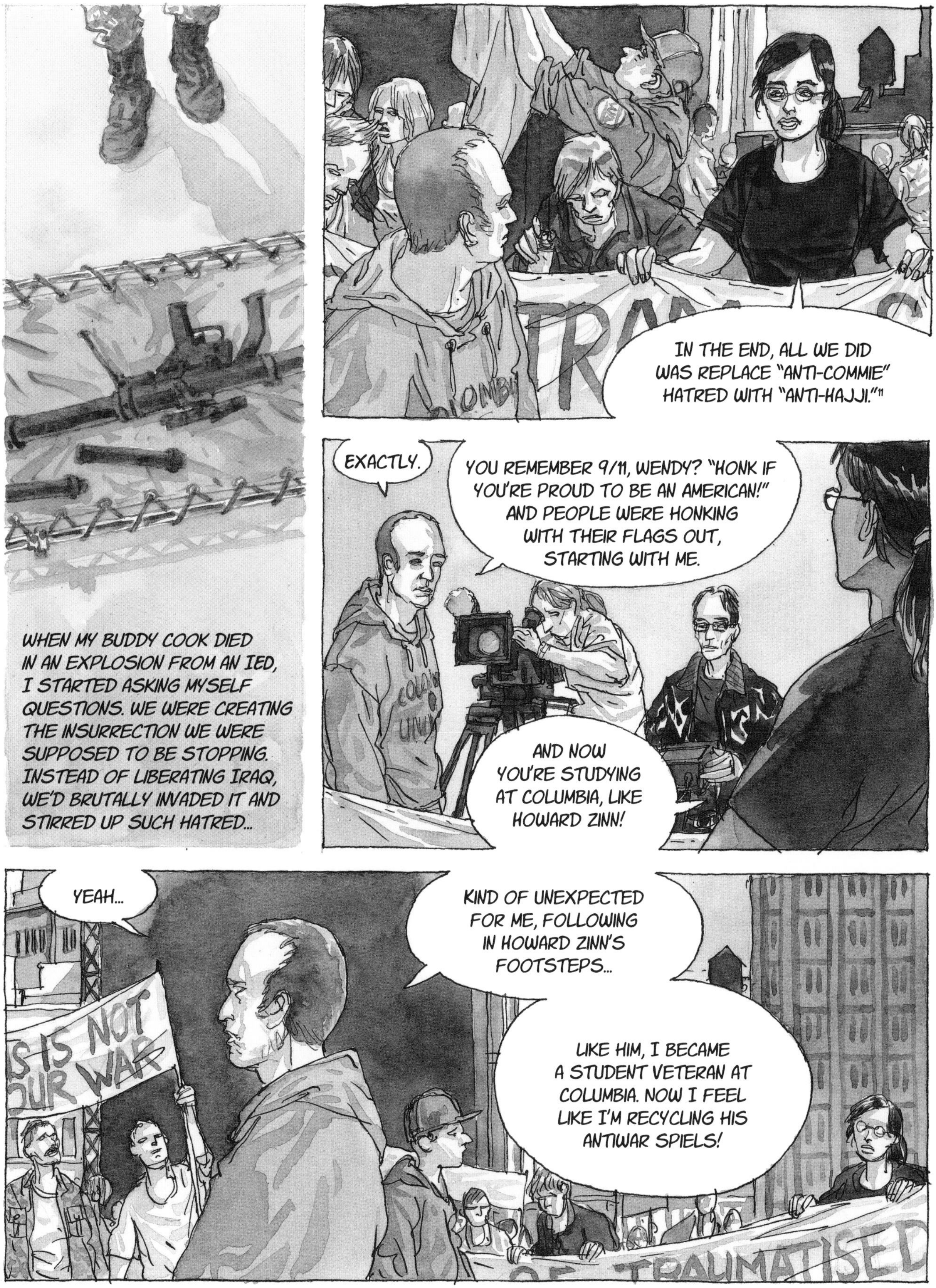
WHEN MY BUDDY COOK DIED IN AN EXPLOSION FROM AN IED, I STARTED ASKING MYSELF QUESTIONS. WE WERE CREATING THE INSURRECTION WE WERE SUPPOSED TO BE STOPPING. INSTEAD OF LIBERATING IRAQ, WE'D BRUTALLY INVADED IT AND STIRRED UP SUCH HATRED...
IN THE END, ALL WE DID WAS REPLACE "ANTI-COMMIE" HATRED WITH "ANTI-HAJJI."[11]
EXACTLY.
YOU REMEMBER 9/11, WENDY? "HONK IF YOU'RE PROUD TO BE AN AMERICAN!" AND PEOPLE WERE HONKING WITH THEIR FLAGS OUT, STARTING WITH ME.
AND NOW YOU'RE STUDYING AT COLUMBIA, LIKE HOWARD ZINN!
YEAH...
KIND OF UNEXPECTED FOR ME, FOLLOWING IN HOWARD ZINN'S FOOTSTEPS...
LIKE HIM, I BECAME A STUDENT VETERAN AT COLUMBIA. NOW I FEEL LIKE I'M RECYCLING HIS ANTIWAR SPIELS!

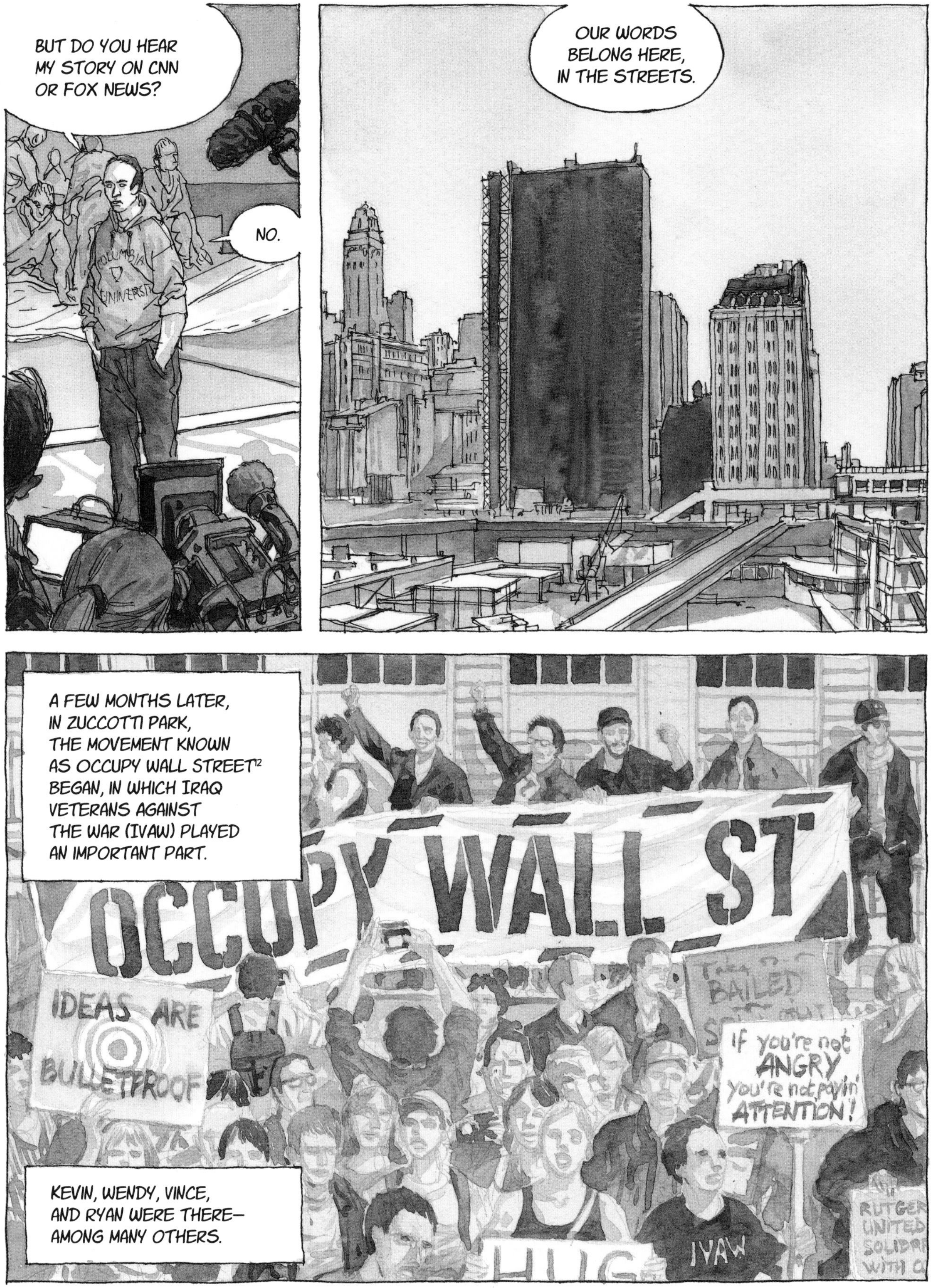
BUT DO YOU HEAR MY STORY ON CNN OR FOX NEWS?
NO.
OUR WORDS BELONG HERE, IN THE STREETS.
A FEW MONTHS LATER, IN ZUCCOTTI PARK, THE MOVEMENT KNOWN AS OCCUPY WALL STREET[12] BEGAN, IN WHICH IRAQ VETERANS AGAINST THE WAR (IVAW) PLAYED AN IMPORTANT PART.
OCCUPY WALL ST
IDEAS ARE BULLETPROOF
If you're not ANGRY you're not payin' ATTENTION!
IVAW
KEVIN, WENDY, VINCE, AND RYAN WERE THERE— AMONG MANY OTHERS.

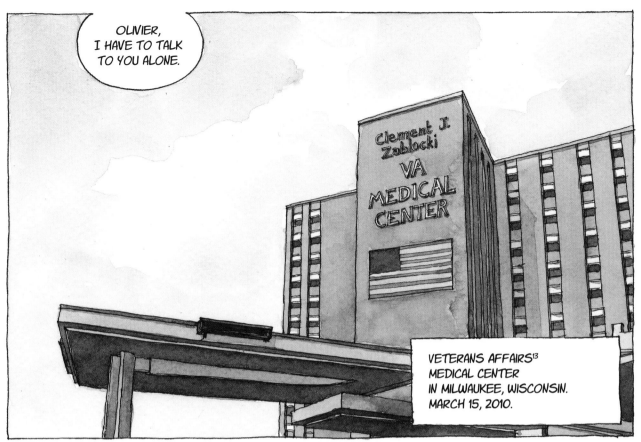

OLIVIER, I HAVE TO TALK TO YOU ALONE.

Clement J. Zablocki VA MEDICAL CENTER

VETERANS AFFAIRS[13] MEDICAL CENTER IN MILWAUKEE, WISCONSIN. MARCH 15, 2010.

I'M WORRIED.

YOU'VE BEEN SHOOTING FOR THREE DAYS. YOU KNOW HOW RISKY THIS IS FOR HIM?

WE'VE BEEN TALKING TO JASON RIGHT FROM THE START, FROM OUR FIRST PHONE CALL IN AUGUST 2008.

RIGHT! AND A FEW WEEKS AFTER HE TRIED TO COMMIT SUICIDE! YOU'VE GOT A LOT OF NERVE!

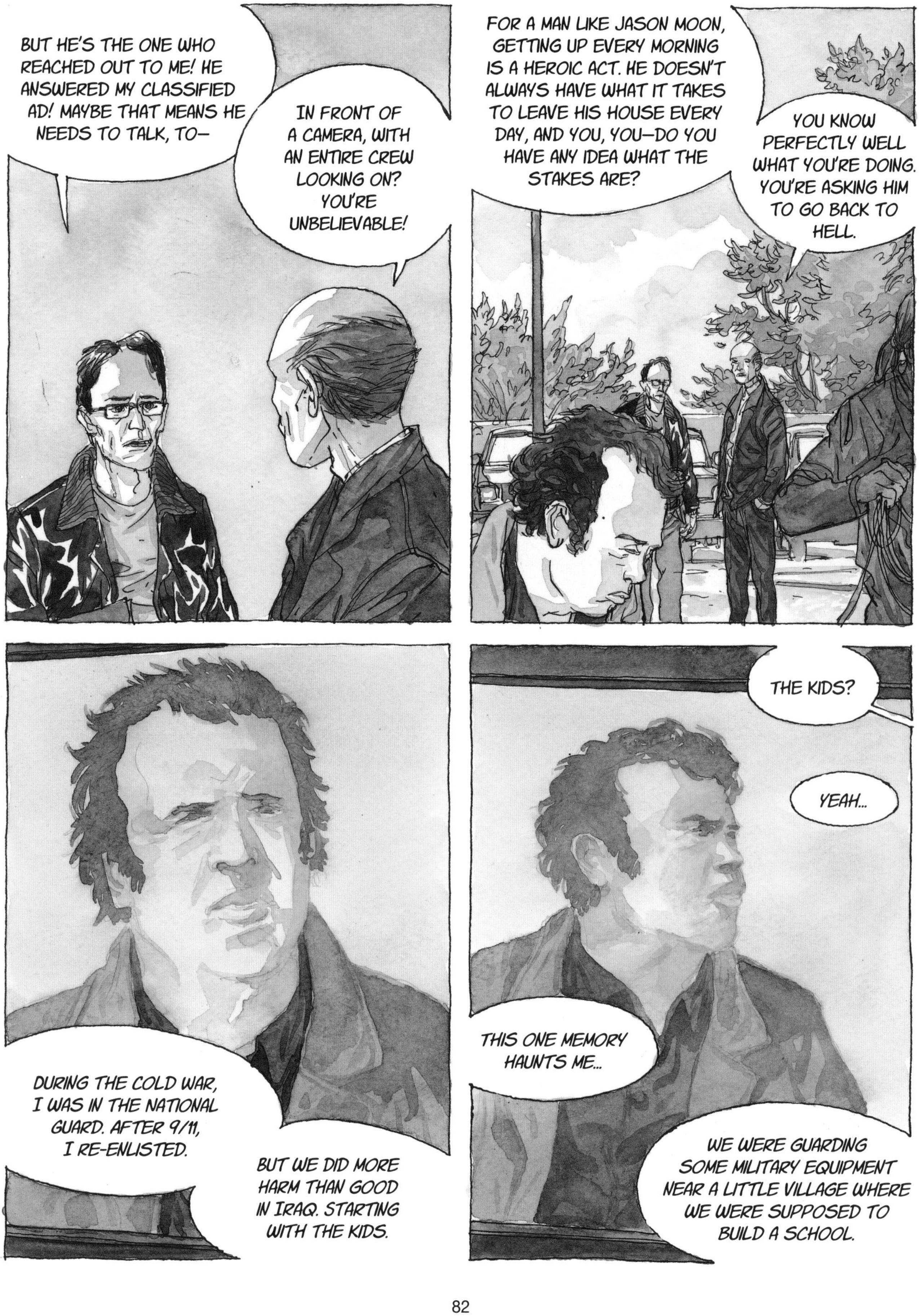
BUT HE'S THE ONE WHO REACHED OUT TO ME! HE ANSWERED MY CLASSIFIED AD! MAYBE THAT MEANS HE NEEDS TO TALK, TO—
IN FRONT OF A CAMERA, WITH AN ENTIRE CREW LOOKING ON? YOU'RE UNBELIEVABLE!
FOR A MAN LIKE JASON MOON, GETTING UP EVERY MORNING IS A HEROIC ACT. HE DOESN'T ALWAYS HAVE WHAT IT TAKES TO LEAVE HIS HOUSE EVERY DAY, AND YOU, YOU—DO YOU HAVE ANY IDEA WHAT THE STAKES ARE?
YOU KNOW PERFECTLY WELL WHAT YOU'RE DOING. YOU'RE ASKING HIM TO GO BACK TO HELL.
DURING THE COLD WAR, I WAS IN THE NATIONAL GUARD. AFTER 9/11, I RE-ENLISTED.
BUT WE DID MORE HARM THAN GOOD IN IRAQ. STARTING WITH THE KIDS.
THE KIDS?
YEAH...
THIS ONE MEMORY HAUNTS ME...
WE WERE GUARDING SOME MILITARY EQUIPMENT NEAR A LITTLE VILLAGE WHERE WE WERE SUPPOSED TO BUILD A SCHOOL.

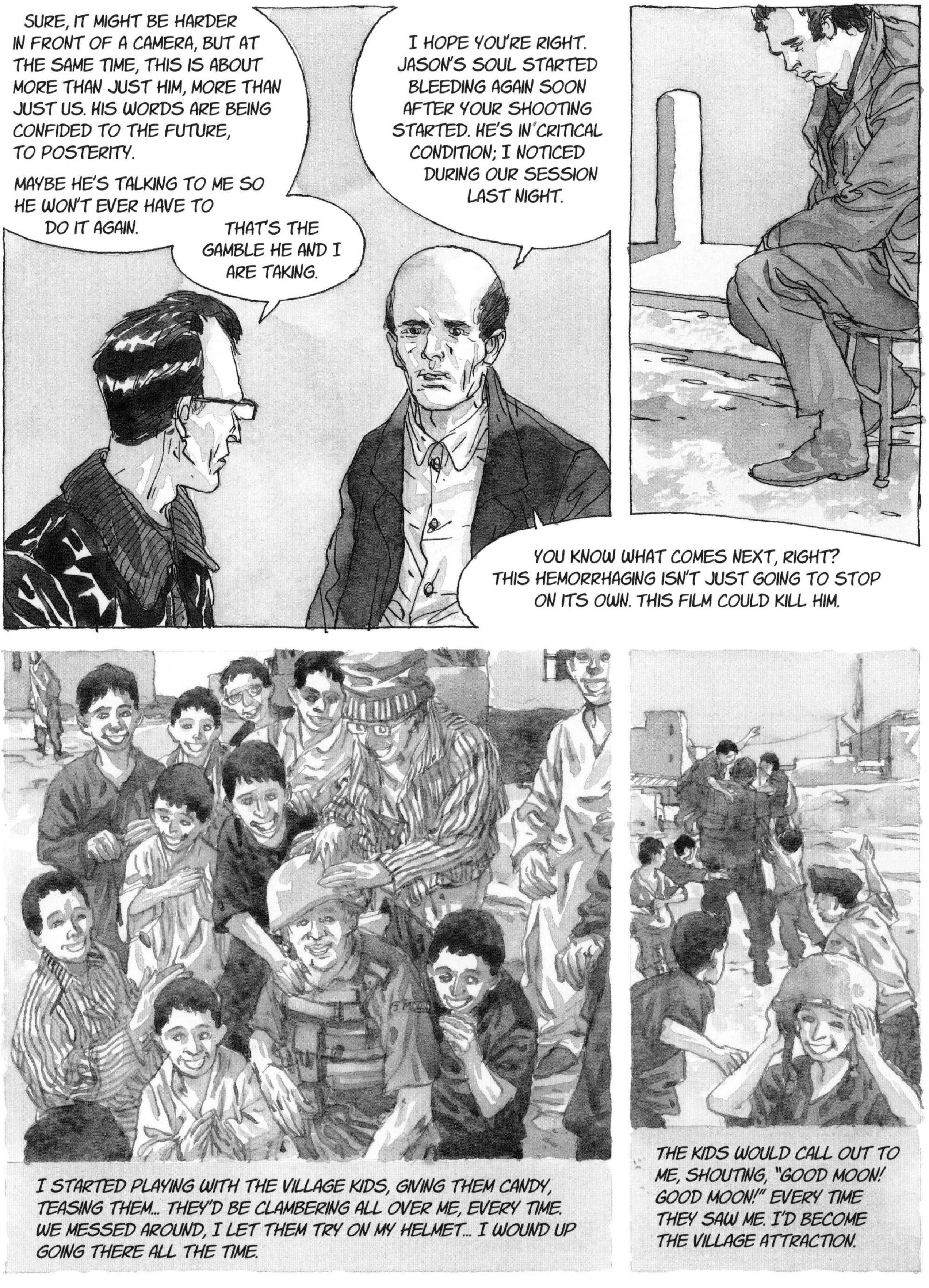
SURE, IT MIGHT BE HARDER IN FRONT OF A CAMERA, BUT AT THE SAME TIME, THIS IS ABOUT MORE THAN JUST HIM, MORE THAN JUST US. HIS WORDS ARE BEING CONFIDED TO THE FUTURE, TO POSTERITY.
MAYBE HE'S TALKING TO ME SO HE WON'T EVER HAVE TO DO IT AGAIN.
THAT'S THE GAMBLE HE AND I ARE TAKING.
I HOPE YOU'RE RIGHT. JASON'S SOUL STARTED BLEEDING AGAIN SOON AFTER YOUR SHOOTING STARTED. HE'S IN CRITICAL CONDITION; I NOTICED DURING OUR SESSION LAST NIGHT.
YOU KNOW WHAT COMES NEXT, RIGHT? THIS HEMORRHAGING ISN'T JUST GOING TO STOP ON ITS OWN. THIS FILM COULD KILL HIM.
I STARTED PLAYING WITH THE VILLAGE KIDS, GIVING THEM CANDY, TEASING THEM... THEY'D BE CLAMBERING ALL OVER ME, EVERY TIME. WE MESSED AROUND, I LET THEM TRY ON MY HELMET... I WOUND UP GOING THERE ALL THE TIME.
THE KIDS WOULD CALL OUT TO ME, SHOUTING, "GOOD MOON! GOOD MOON!" EVERY TIME THEY SAW ME. I'D BECOME THE VILLAGE ATTRACTION.

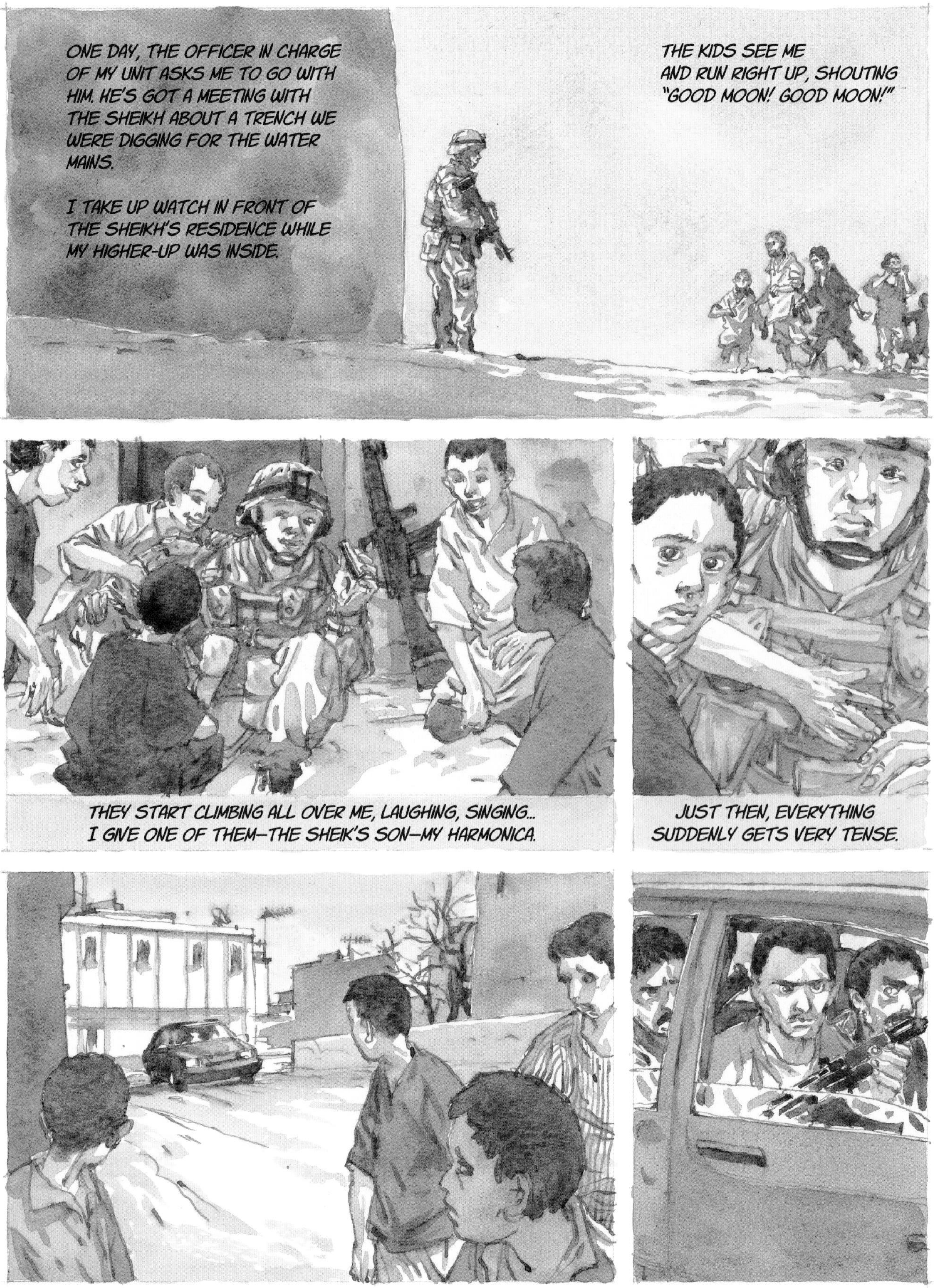
ONE DAY, THE OFFICER IN CHARGE OF MY UNIT ASKS ME TO GO WITH HIM. HE'S GOT A MEETING WITH THE SHEIKH ABOUT A TRENCH WE WERE DIGGING FOR THE WATER MAINS.
I TAKE UP WATCH IN FRONT OF THE SHEIKH'S RESIDENCE WHILE MY HIGHER-UP WAS INSIDE.
THE KIDS SEE ME AND RUN RIGHT UP, SHOUTING "GOOD MOON! GOOD MOON!"
THEY START CLIMBING ALL OVER ME, LAUGHING, SINGING... I GIVE ONE OF THEM—THE SHEIK'S SON—MY HARMONICA.
JUST THEN, EVERYTHING SUDDENLY GETS VERY TENSE.

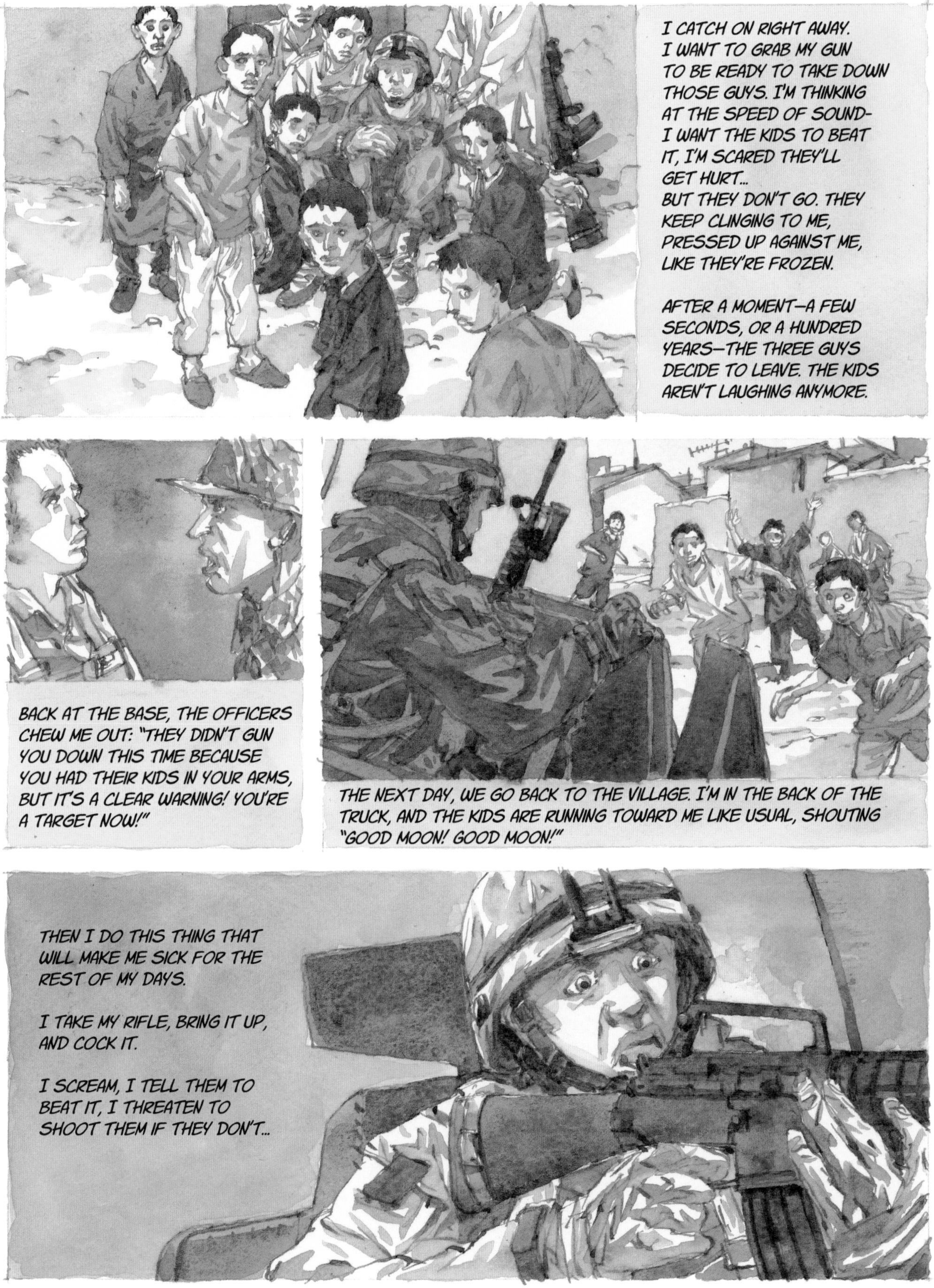
I CATCH ON RIGHT AWAY. I WANT TO GRAB MY GUN TO BE READY TO TAKE DOWN THOSE GUYS. I'M THINKING AT THE SPEED OF SOUND- I WANT THE KIDS TO BEAT IT, I'M SCARED THEY'LL GET HURT... BUT THEY DON'T GO. THEY KEEP CLINGING TO ME, PRESSED UP AGAINST ME, LIKE THEY'RE FROZEN.
AFTER A MOMENT—A FEW SECONDS, OR A HUNDRED YEARS—THE THREE GUYS DECIDE TO LEAVE. THE KIDS AREN'T LAUGHING ANYMORE.
BACK AT THE BASE, THE OFFICERS CHEW ME OUT: "THEY DIDN'T GUN YOU DOWN THIS TIME BECAUSE YOU HAD THEIR KIDS IN YOUR ARMS, BUT IT'S A CLEAR WARNING! YOU'RE A TARGET NOW!"
THE NEXT DAY, WE GO BACK TO THE VILLAGE. I'M IN THE BACK OF THE TRUCK, AND THE KIDS ARE RUNNING TOWARD ME LIKE USUAL, SHOUTING "GOOD MOON! GOOD MOON!"
THEN I DO THIS THING THAT WILL MAKE ME SICK FOR THE REST OF MY DAYS.
I TAKE MY RIFLE, BRING IT UP, AND COCK IT.
I SCREAM, I TELL THEM TO BEAT IT, I THREATEN TO SHOOT THEM IF THEY DON'T...

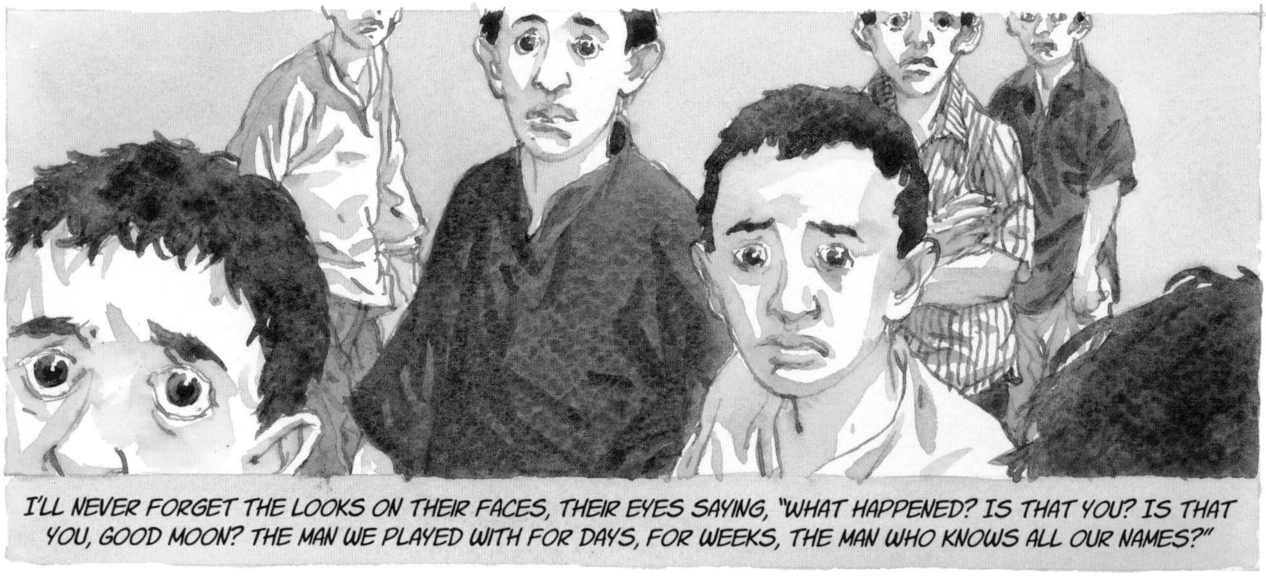
I'LL NEVER FORGET THE LOOKS ON THEIR FACES, THEIR EYES SAYING, "WHAT HAPPENED? IS THAT YOU? IS THAT YOU, GOOD MOON? THE MAN WE PLAYED WITH FOR DAYS, FOR WEEKS, THE MAN WHO KNOWS ALL OUR NAMES?"

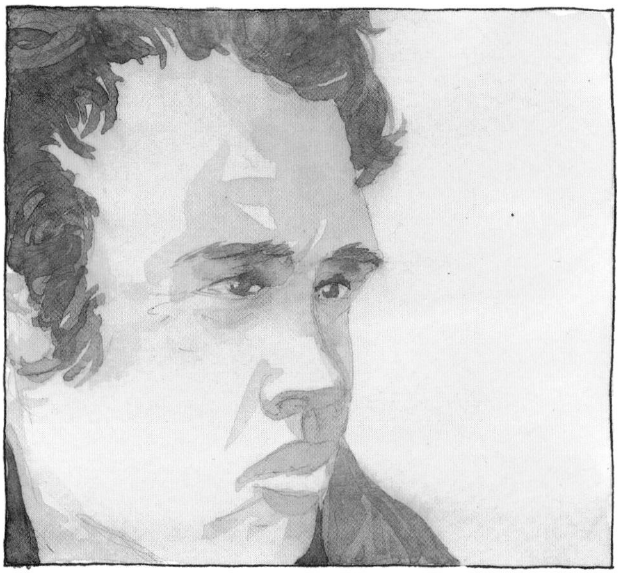

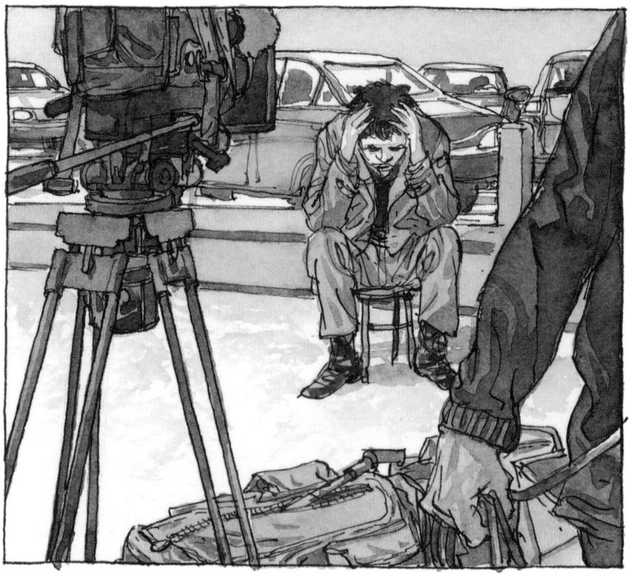

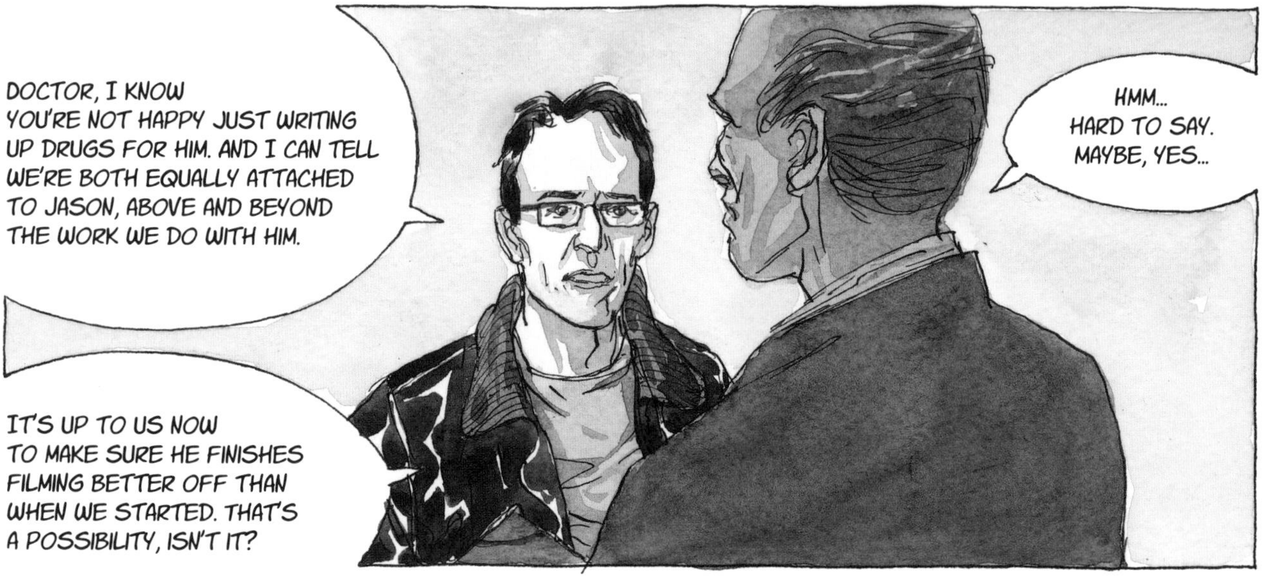
DOCTOR, I KNOW YOU'RE NOT HAPPY JUST WRITING UP DRUGS FOR HIM. AND I CAN TELL WE'RE BOTH EQUALLY ATTACHED TO JASON, ABOVE AND BEYOND THE WORK WE DO WITH HIM.
IT'S UP TO US NOW TO MAKE SURE HE FINISHES FILMING BETTER OFF THAN WHEN WE STARTED. THAT'S A POSSIBILITY, ISN'T IT?
HMM... HARD TO SAY. MAYBE, YES...

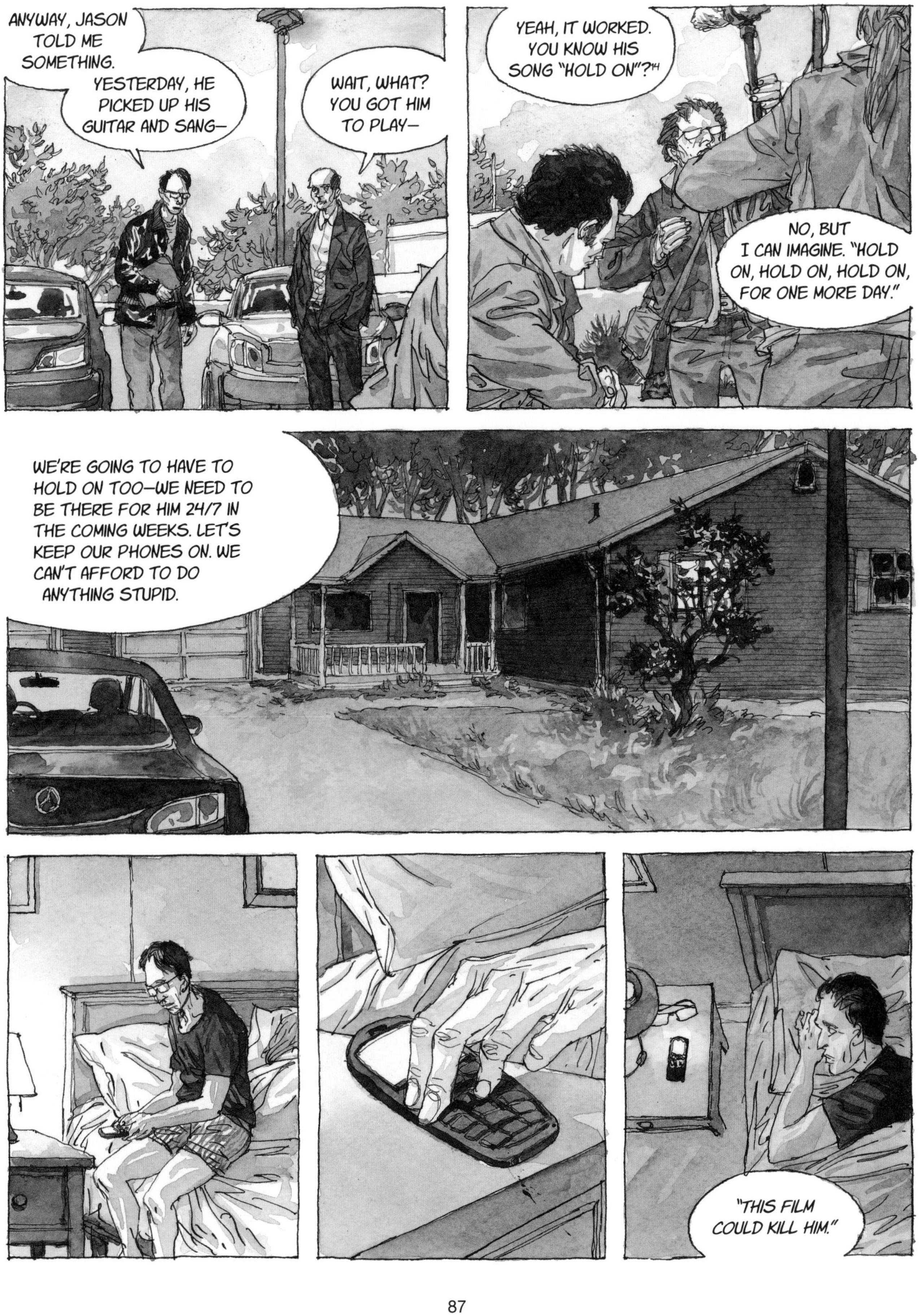
ANYWAY, JASON TOLD ME SOMETHING.
YESTERDAY, HE PICKED UP HIS GUITAR AND SANG—
WAIT, WHAT? YOU GOT HIM TO PLAY—
YEAH, IT WORKED. YOU KNOW HIS SONG "HOLD ON"?[14]
NO, BUT I CAN IMAGINE. "HOLD ON, HOLD ON, HOLD ON, FOR ONE MORE DAY."
WE'RE GOING TO HAVE TO HOLD ON TOO—WE NEED TO BE THERE FOR HIM 24/7 IN THE COMING WEEKS. LET'S KEEP OUR PHONES ON. WE CAN'T AFFORD TO DO ANYTHING STUPID.
"THIS FILM COULD KILL HIM."

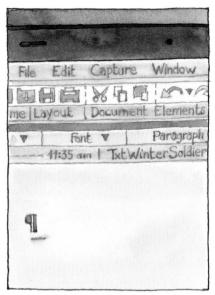

File Edit Capture Window

me | Layout | Document Elements

▽ | Font ▽ | Paragraph

———— 11:35 am | Txt.Winter.Soldier

¶

"BEFORE I START TODAY, I WOULD LIKE TO SAY I'M A PATRIOTIC AMERICAN, AND I LOVE MY COUNTRY. FROM THE MOMENT I LANDED ON DECK IN RAMADI, I WAS SO FILLED WITH HATE..."

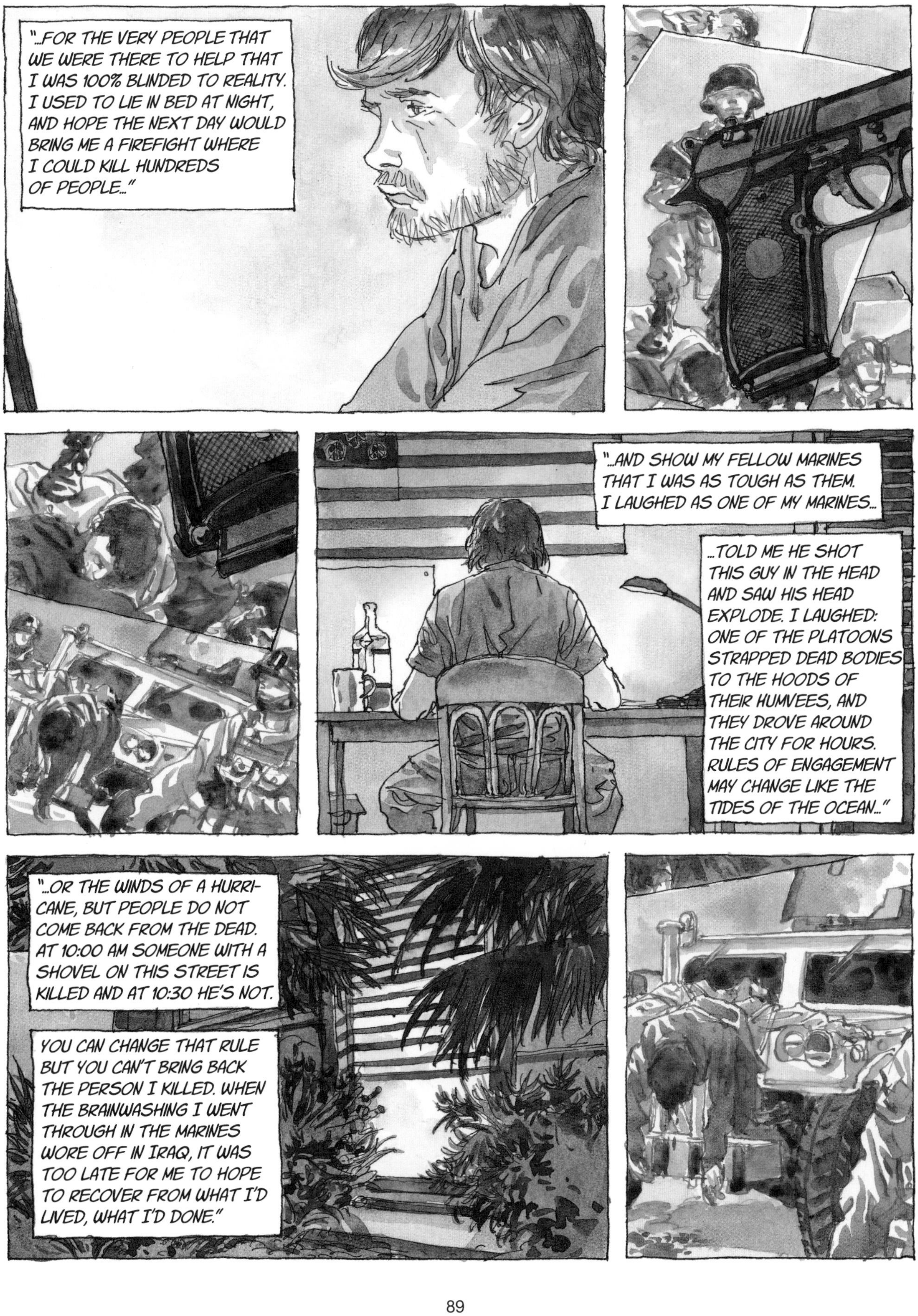
"...FOR THE VERY PEOPLE THAT WE WERE THERE TO HELP THAT I WAS 100% BLINDED TO REALITY. I USED TO LIE IN BED AT NIGHT, AND HOPE THE NEXT DAY WOULD BRING ME A FIREFIGHT WHERE I COULD KILL HUNDREDS OF PEOPLE..."
"...AND SHOW MY FELLOW MARINES THAT I WAS AS TOUGH AS THEM. I LAUGHED AS ONE OF MY MARINES...
...TOLD ME HE SHOT THIS GUY IN THE HEAD AND SAW HIS HEAD EXPLODE. I LAUGHED: ONE OF THE PLATOONS STRAPPED DEAD BODIES TO THE HOODS OF THEIR HUMVEES, AND THEY DROVE AROUND THE CITY FOR HOURS. RULES OF ENGAGEMENT MAY CHANGE LIKE THE TIDES OF THE OCEAN..."
"...OR THE WINDS OF A HURRI-CANE, BUT PEOPLE DO NOT COME BACK FROM THE DEAD. AT 10:00 AM SOMEONE WITH A SHOVEL ON THIS STREET IS KILLED AND AT 10:30 HE'S NOT.
YOU CAN CHANGE THAT RULE BUT YOU CAN'T BRING BACK THE PERSON I KILLED. WHEN THE BRAINWASHING I WENT THROUGH IN THE MARINES WORE OFF IN IRAQ, IT WAS TOO LATE FOR ME TO HOPE TO RECOVER FROM WHAT I'D LIVED, WHAT I'D DONE."

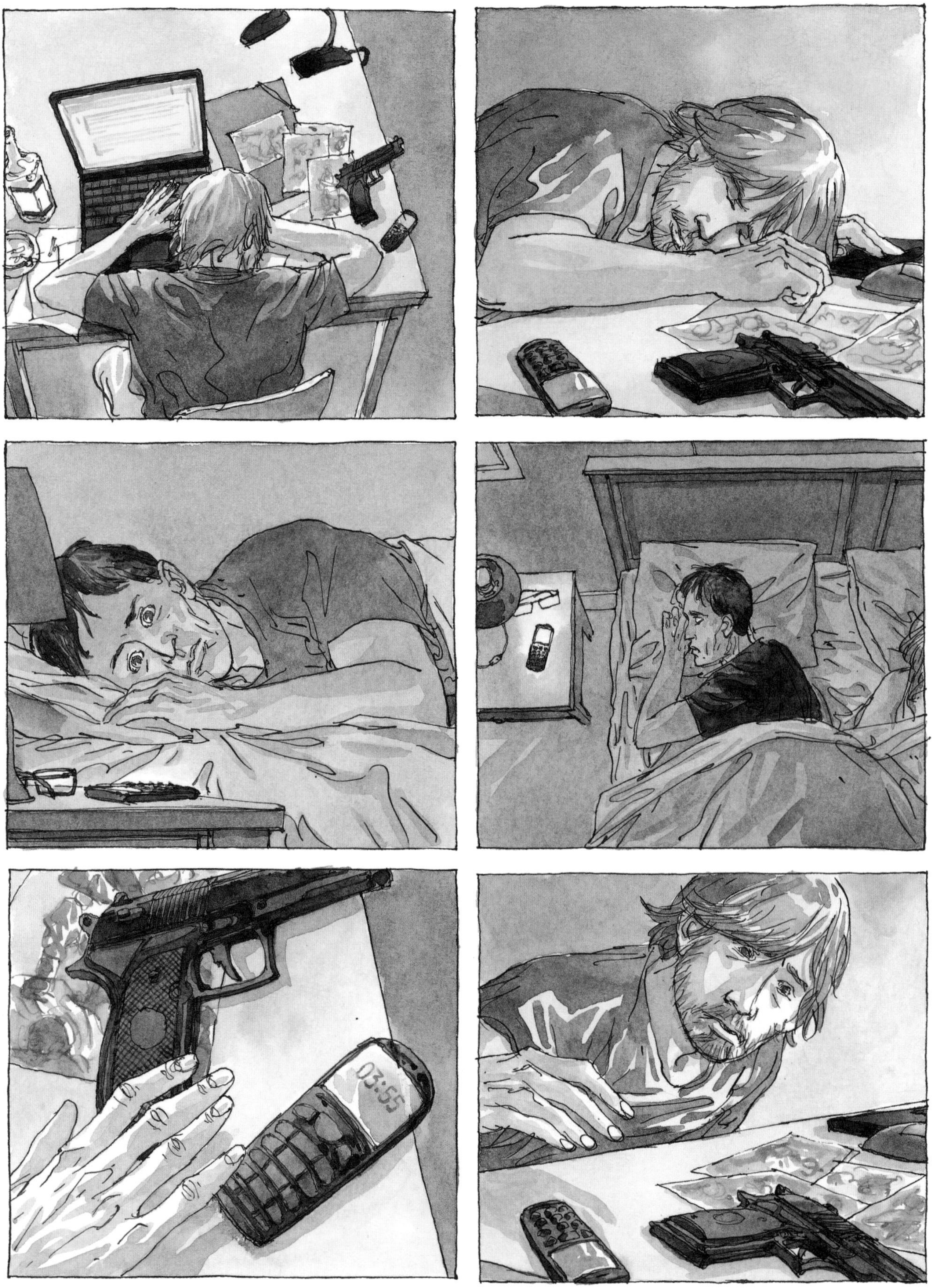
03:55

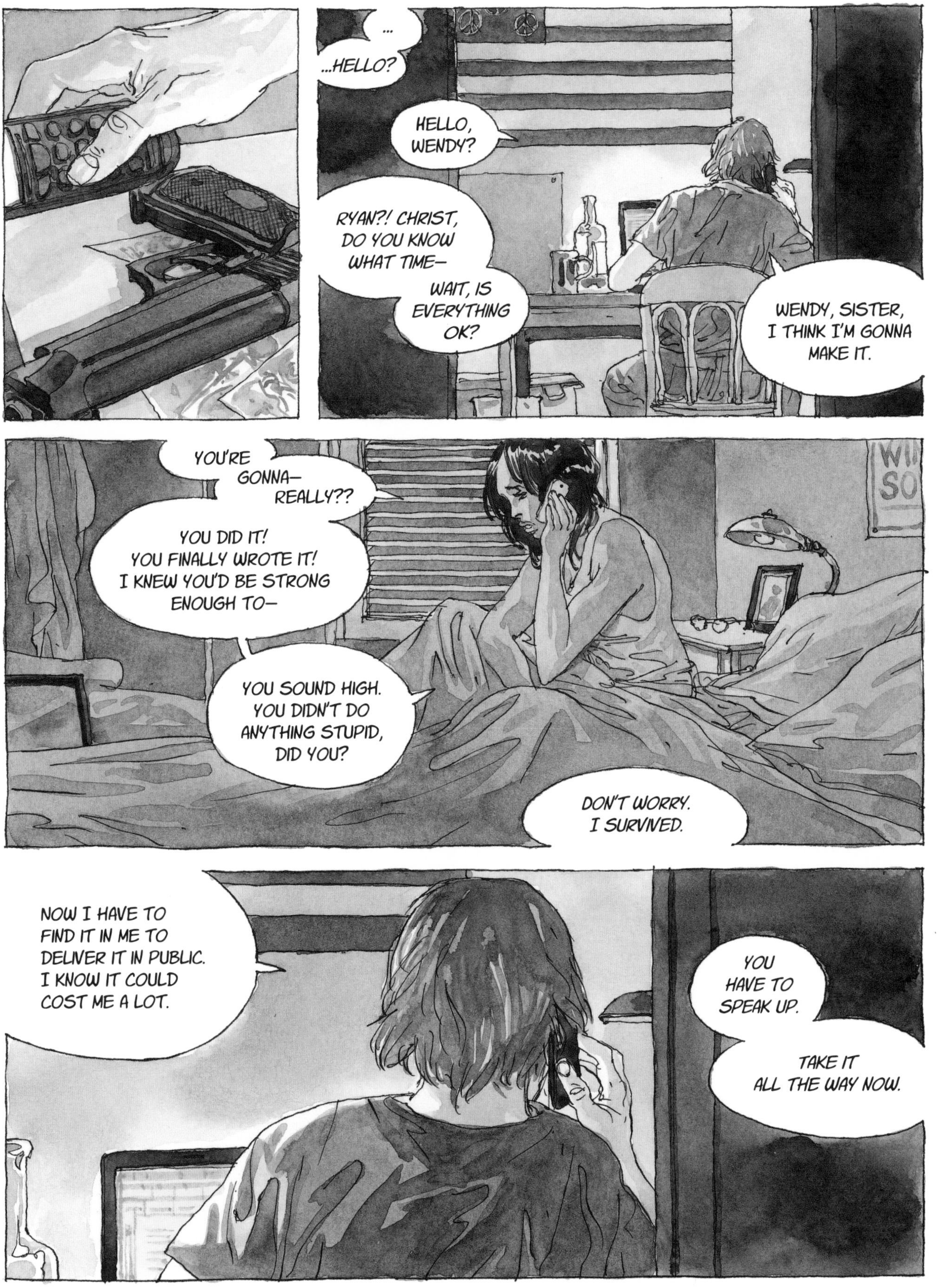
...
...HELLO?
HELLO, WENDY?
RYAN?! CHRIST, DO YOU KNOW WHAT TIME—
WAIT, IS EVERYTHING OK?
WENDY, SISTER, I THINK I'M GONNA MAKE IT.
YOU'RE GONNA—
REALLY??
YOU DID IT! YOU FINALLY WROTE IT! I KNEW YOU'D BE STRONG ENOUGH TO—
YOU SOUND HIGH. YOU DIDN'T DO ANYTHING STUPID, DID YOU?
DON'T WORRY. I SURVIVED.
NOW I HAVE TO FIND IT IN ME TO DELIVER IT IN PUBLIC. I KNOW IT COULD COST ME A LOT.
YOU HAVE TO SPEAK UP.
TAKE IT ALL THE WAY NOW.

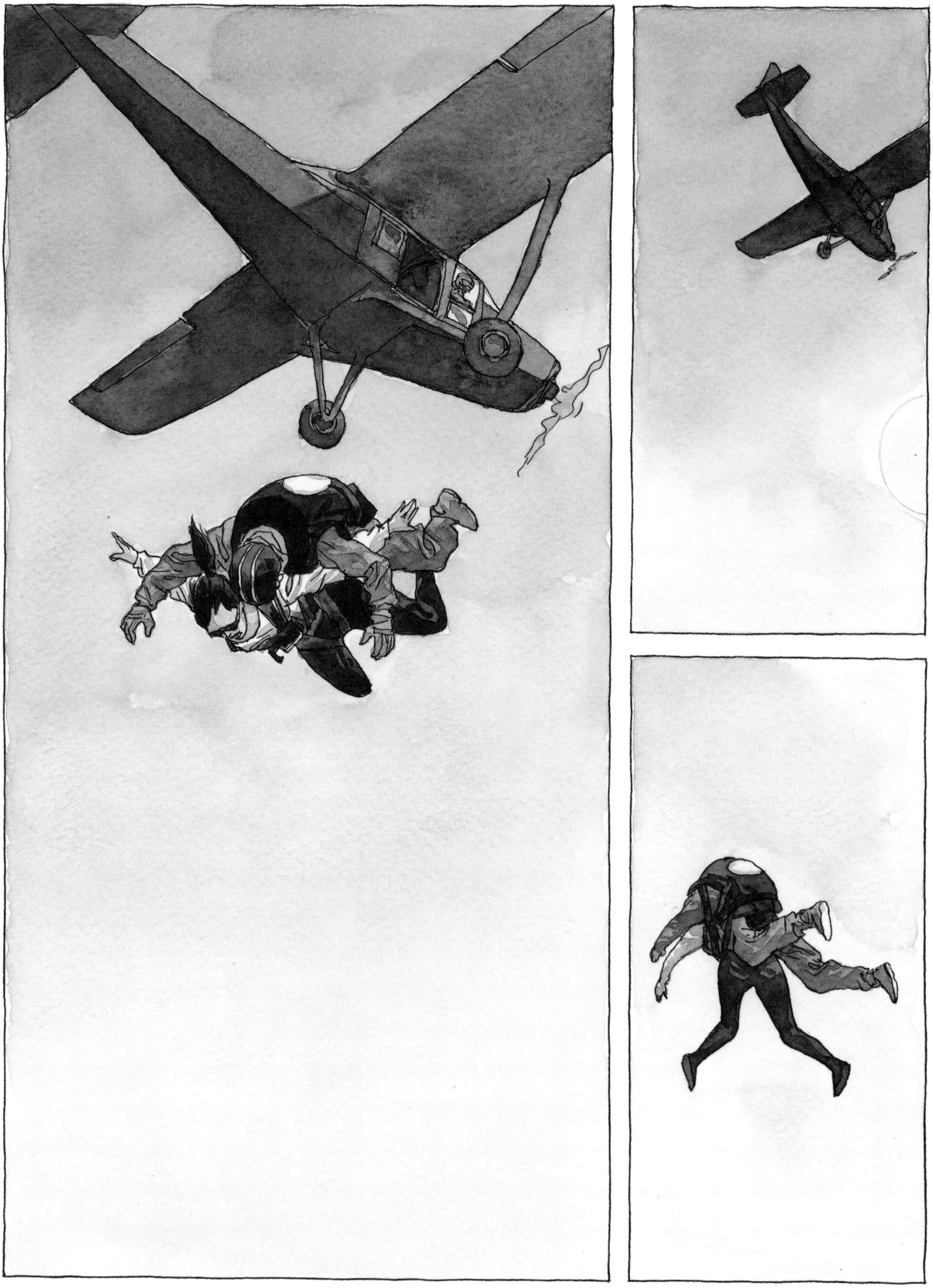

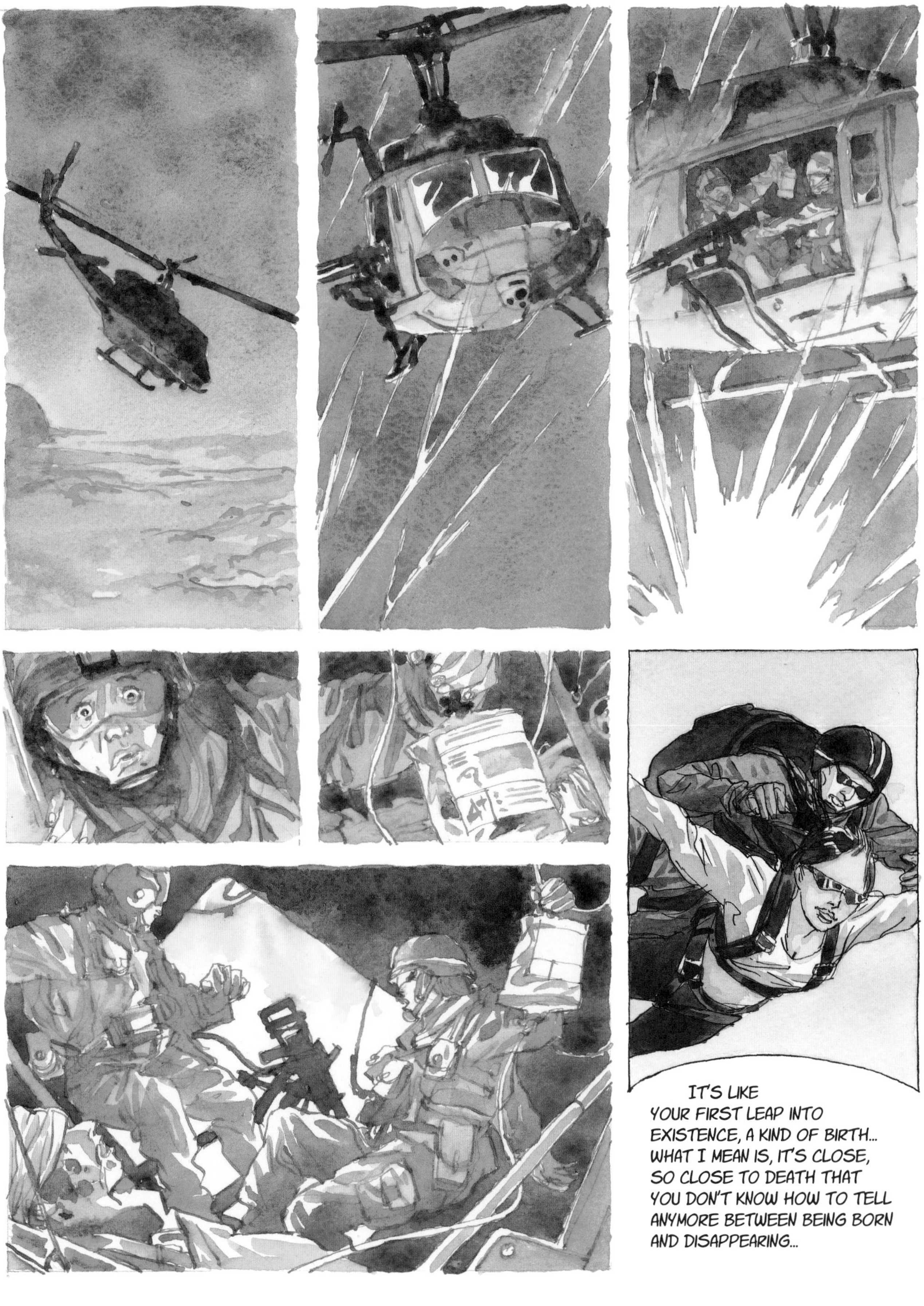
IT'S LIKE
YOUR FIRST LEAP INTO
EXISTENCE, A KIND OF BIRTH...
WHAT I MEAN IS, IT'S CLOSE,
SO CLOSE TO DEATH THAT
YOU DON'T KNOW HOW TO TELL
ANYMORE BETWEEN BEING BORN
AND DISAPPEARING...

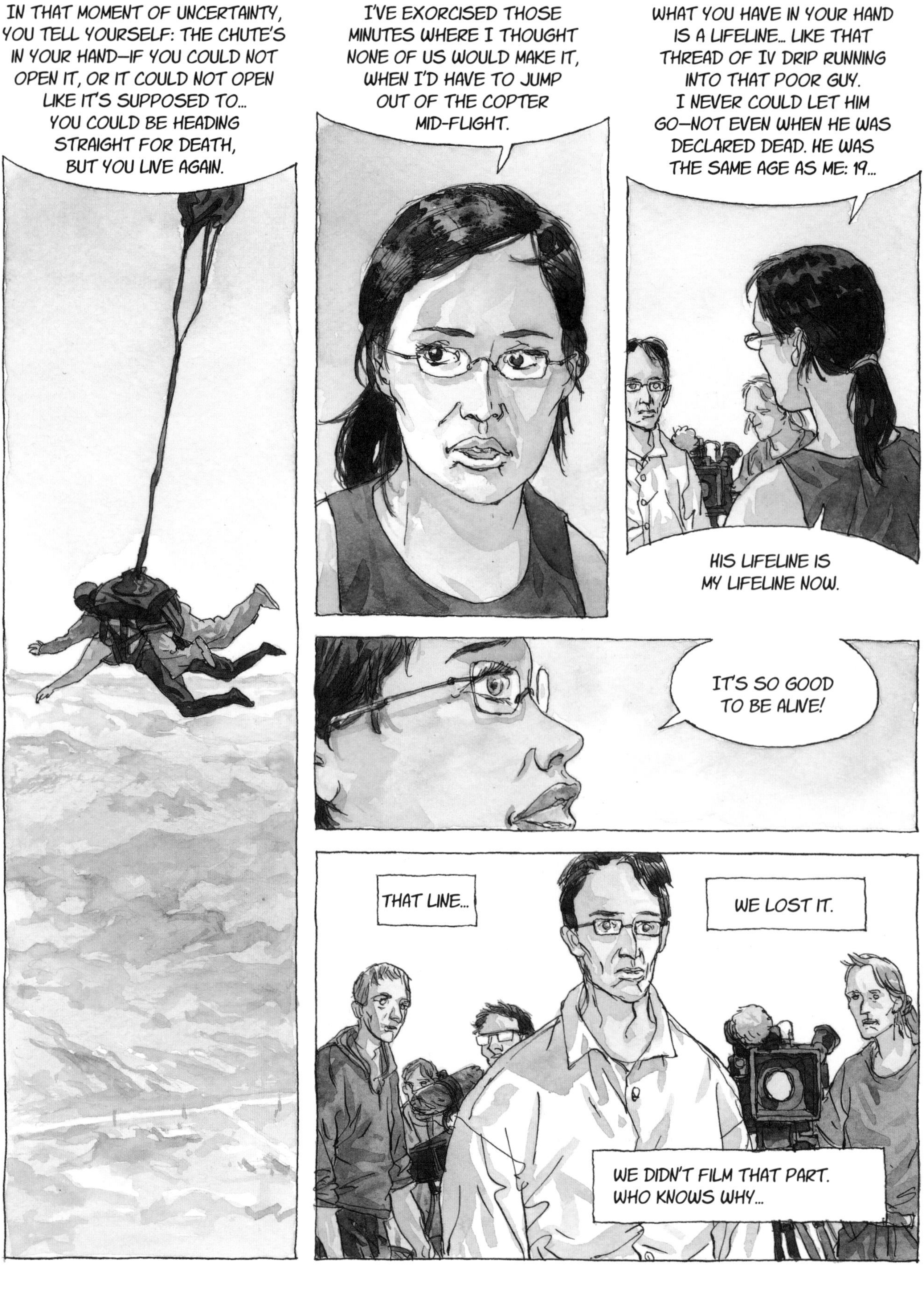
IN THAT MOMENT OF UNCERTAINTY, YOU TELL YOURSELF: THE CHUTE'S IN YOUR HAND—IF YOU COULD NOT OPEN IT, OR IT COULD NOT OPEN LIKE IT'S SUPPOSED TO... YOU COULD BE HEADING STRAIGHT FOR DEATH, BUT YOU LIVE AGAIN.
I'VE EXORCISED THOSE MINUTES WHERE I THOUGHT NONE OF US WOULD MAKE IT, WHEN I'D HAVE TO JUMP OUT OF THE COPTER MID-FLIGHT.
WHAT YOU HAVE IN YOUR HAND IS A LIFELINE... LIKE THAT THREAD OF IV DRIP RUNNING INTO THAT POOR GUY. I NEVER COULD LET HIM GO—NOT EVEN WHEN HE WAS DECLARED DEAD. HE WAS THE SAME AGE AS ME: 19...
HIS LIFELINE IS MY LIFELINE NOW.
IT'S SO GOOD TO BE ALIVE!
THAT LINE...
WE LOST IT.
WE DIDN'T FILM THAT PART. WHO KNOWS WHY...

chapter 3

Midnight

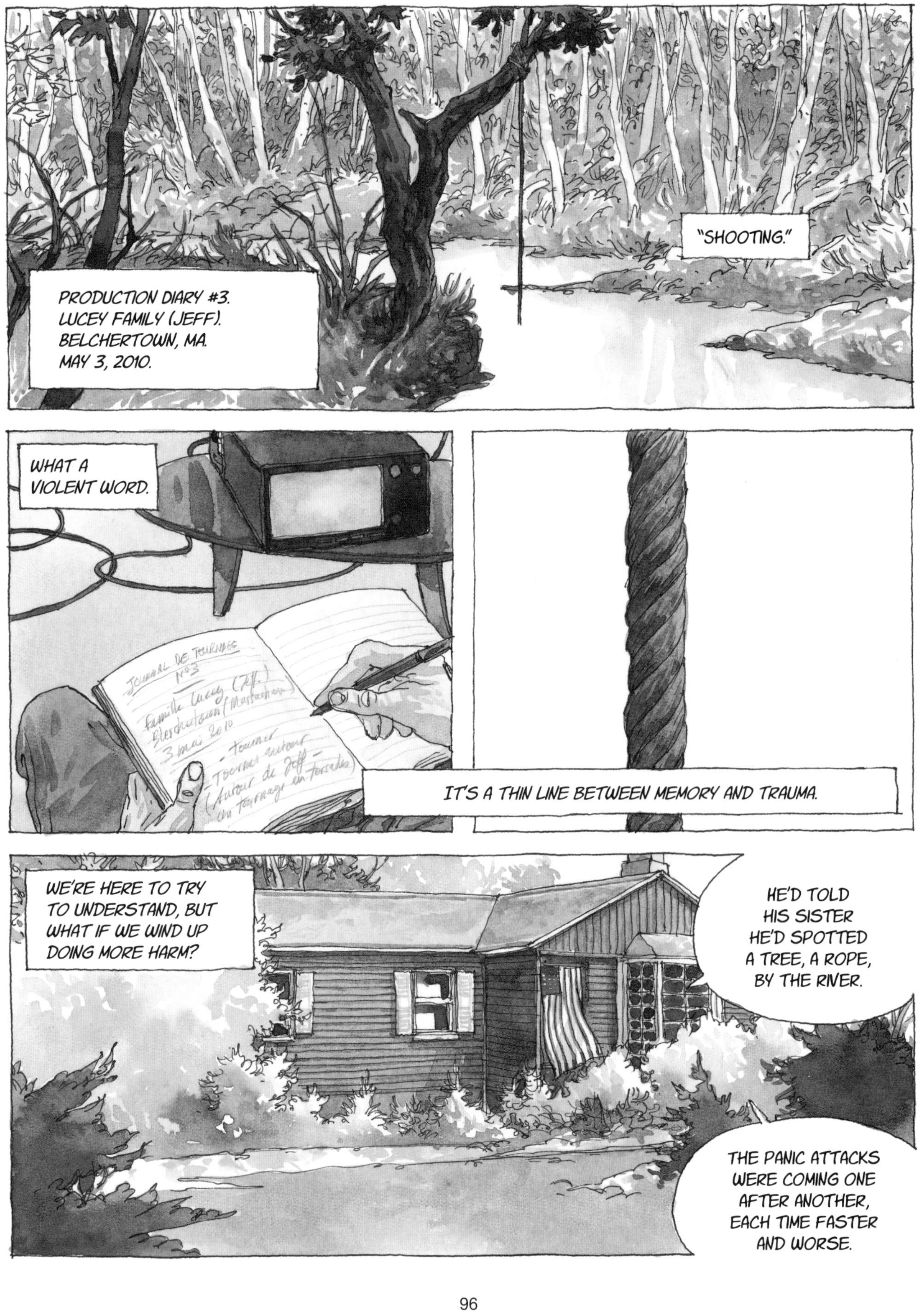

PRODUCTION DIARY #3.
LUCEY FAMILY (JEFF).
BELCHERTOWN, MA.
MAY 3, 2010.
"SHOOTING."
WHAT A VIOLENT WORD.
IT'S A THIN LINE BETWEEN MEMORY AND TRAUMA.
WE'RE HERE TO TRY TO UNDERSTAND, BUT WHAT IF WE WIND UP DOING MORE HARM?
HE'D TOLD HIS SISTER HE'D SPOTTED A TREE, A ROPE, BY THE RIVER.
THE PANIC ATTACKS WERE COMING ONE AFTER ANOTHER, EACH TIME FASTER AND WORSE.

THE NIGHT OF JUNE 21, 2004, WHEN I CAME HOME FROM WORK, HE WAS HAVING A FIT OF RAGE.

A VIOLENT ATTACK.

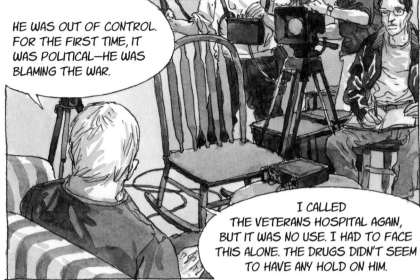

HE WAS OUT OF CONTROL. FOR THE FIRST TIME, IT WAS POLITICAL—HE WAS BLAMING THE WAR.

I CALLED THE VETERANS HOSPITAL AGAIN, BUT IT WAS NO USE. I HAD TO FACE THIS ALONE. THE DRUGS DIDN'T SEEM TO HAVE ANY HOLD ON HIM.

FINALLY, AROUND MIDNIGHT, JEFF ASKED ME TO TAKE HIM IN MY ARMS AND HOLD HIM LIKE A BABY IN THE ROCKING CHAIR.

I HELD HIM THAT WAY FOR 45 MINUTES IN TOTAL SILENCE.

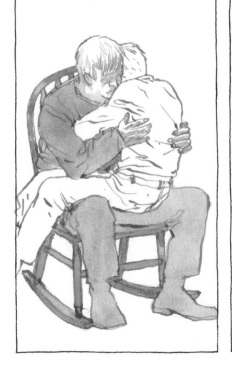

AND HE FELL ASLEEP.

THE NEXT DAY, JUNE 22, IT WAS LATE AFTERNOON WHEN I HELD HIM IN MY ARMS AGAIN—TO TAKE HIM DOWN FROM THE BEAM IN THE BASEMENT.

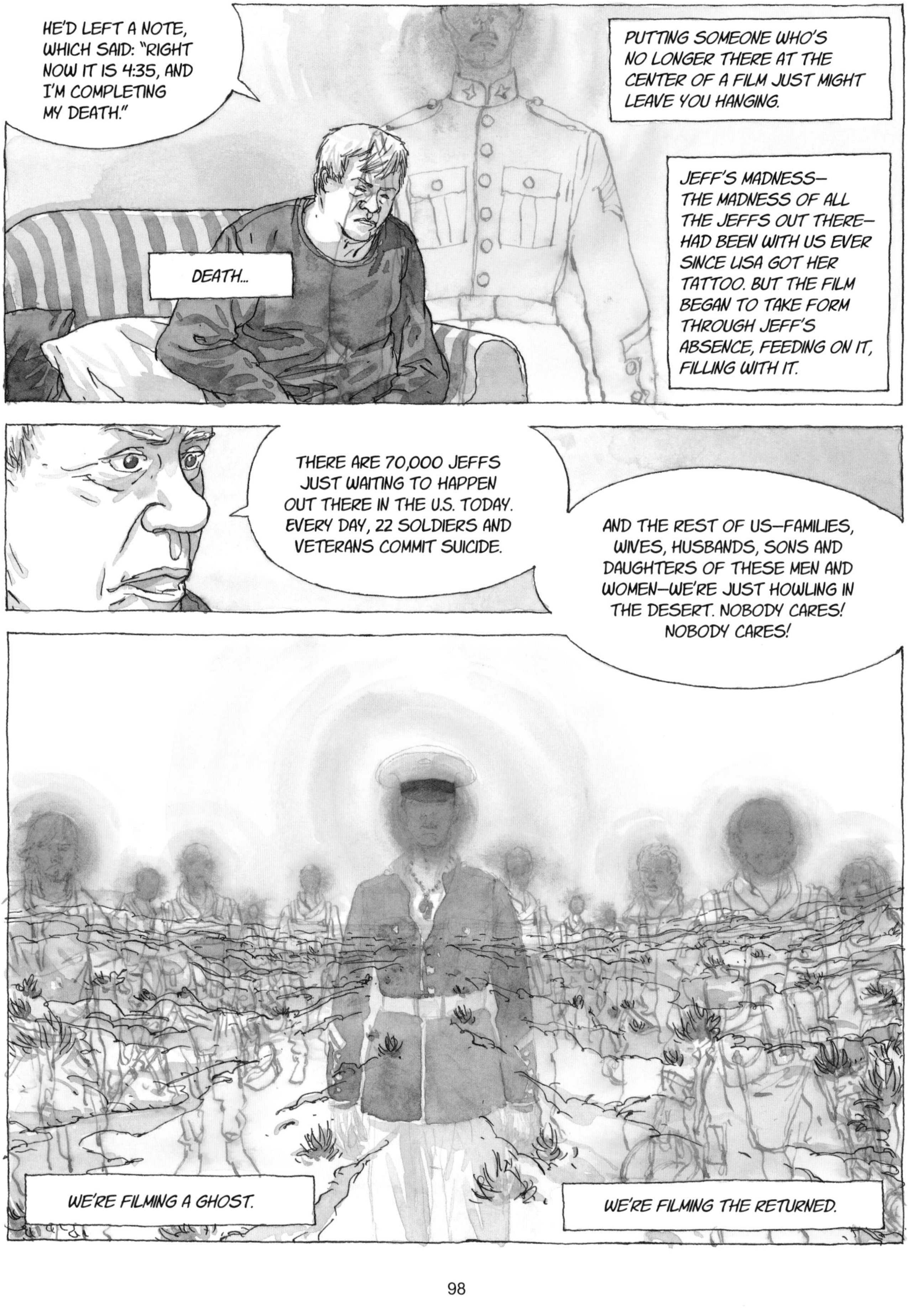
HE'D LEFT A NOTE, WHICH SAID: "RIGHT NOW IT IS 4:35, AND I'M COMPLETING MY DEATH."
PUTTING SOMEONE WHO'S NO LONGER THERE AT THE CENTER OF A FILM JUST MIGHT LEAVE YOU HANGING.
DEATH...
JEFF'S MADNESS—THE MADNESS OF ALL THE JEFFS OUT THERE—HAD BEEN WITH US EVER SINCE LISA GOT HER TATTOO. BUT THE FILM BEGAN TO TAKE FORM THROUGH JEFF'S ABSENCE, FEEDING ON IT, FILLING WITH IT.
THERE ARE 70,000 JEFFS JUST WAITING TO HAPPEN OUT THERE IN THE U.S. TODAY. EVERY DAY, 22 SOLDIERS AND VETERANS COMMIT SUICIDE.
AND THE REST OF US—FAMILIES, WIVES, HUSBANDS, SONS AND DAUGHTERS OF THESE MEN AND WOMEN—WE'RE JUST HOWLING IN THE DESERT. NOBODY CARES! NOBODY CARES!
WE'RE FILMING A GHOST.
WE'RE FILMING THE RETURNED.

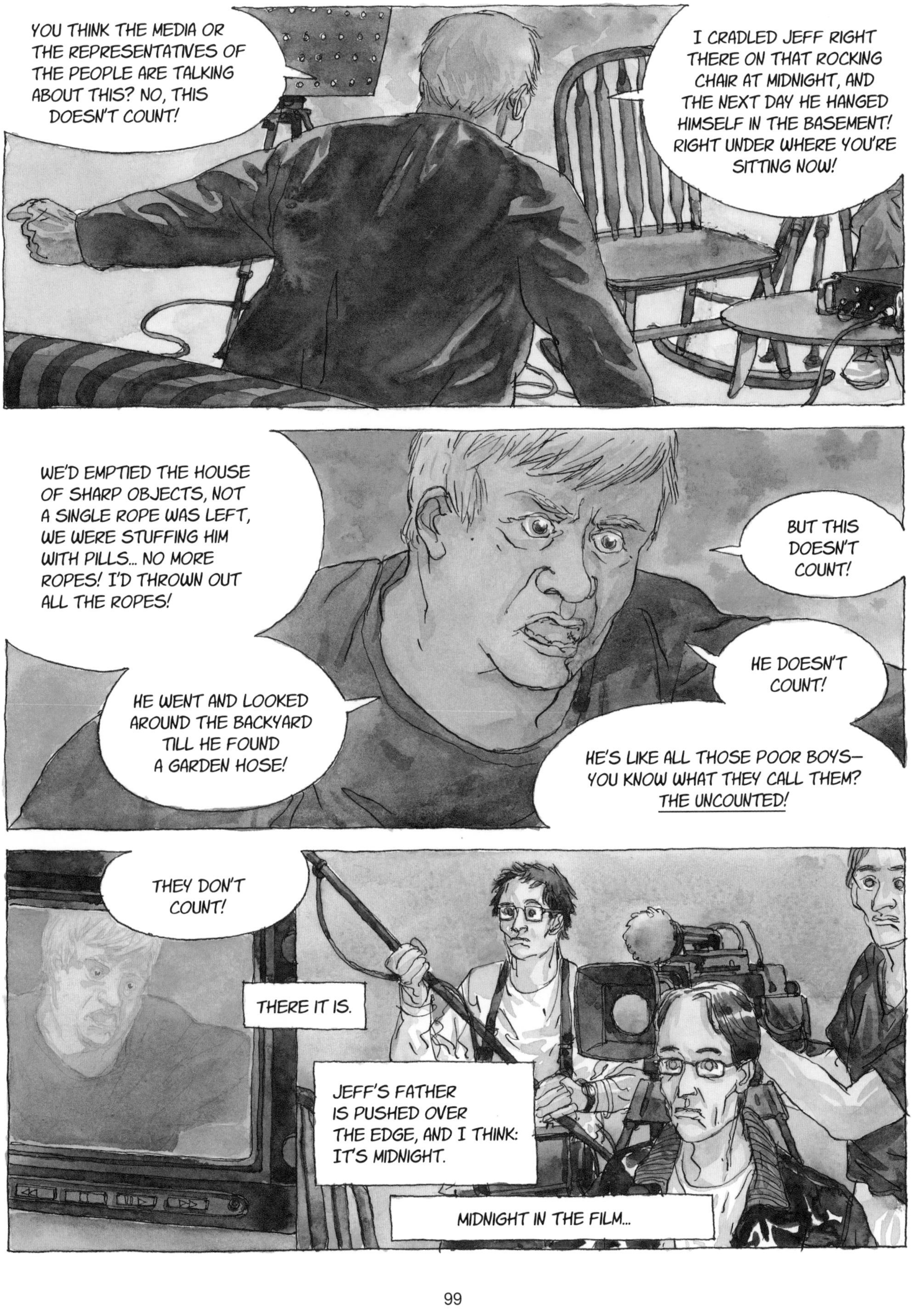
YOU THINK THE MEDIA OR THE REPRESENTATIVES OF THE PEOPLE ARE TALKING ABOUT THIS? NO, THIS DOESN'T COUNT!
I CRADLED JEFF RIGHT THERE ON THAT ROCKING CHAIR AT MIDNIGHT, AND THE NEXT DAY HE HANGED HIMSELF IN THE BASEMENT! RIGHT UNDER WHERE YOU'RE SITTING NOW!
WE'D EMPTIED THE HOUSE OF SHARP OBJECTS, NOT A SINGLE ROPE WAS LEFT, WE WERE STUFFING HIM WITH PILLS... NO MORE ROPES! I'D THROWN OUT ALL THE ROPES!
BUT THIS DOESN'T COUNT!
HE WENT AND LOOKED AROUND THE BACKYARD TILL HE FOUND A GARDEN HOSE!
HE DOESN'T COUNT!
HE'S LIKE ALL THOSE POOR BOYS— YOU KNOW WHAT THEY CALL THEM? THE UNCOUNTED!
THEY DON'T COUNT!
THERE IT IS.
JEFF'S FATHER IS PUSHED OVER THE EDGE, AND I THINK: IT'S MIDNIGHT.
MIDNIGHT IN THE FILM...

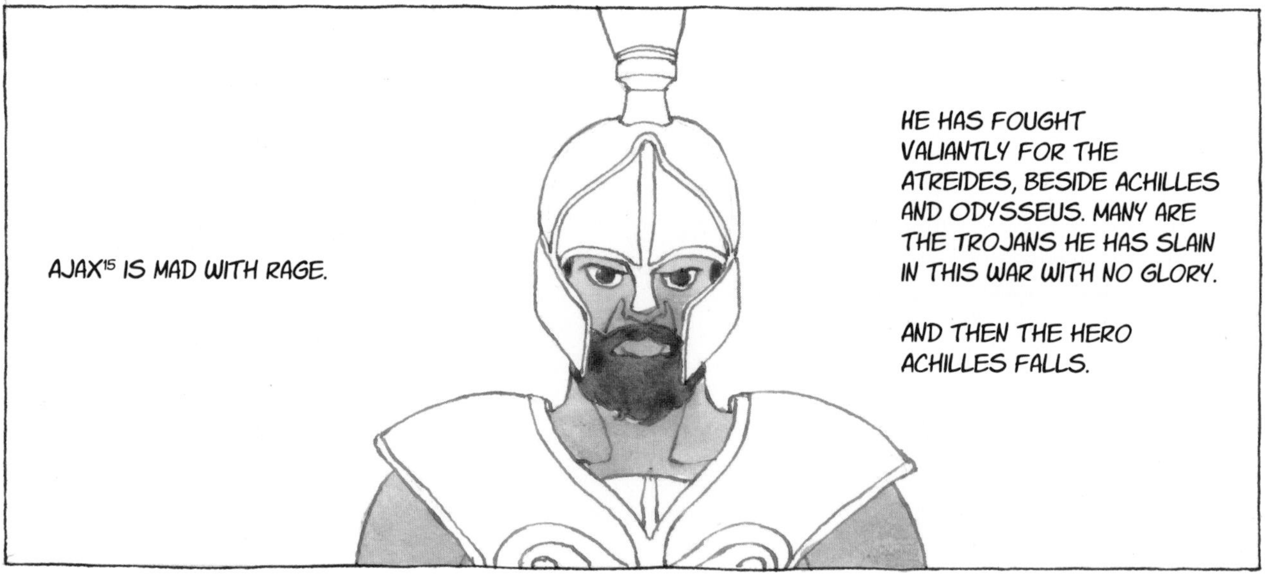
AJAX[15] IS MAD WITH RAGE.
HE HAS FOUGHT VALIANTLY FOR THE ATREIDES, BESIDE ACHILLES AND ODYSSEUS. MANY ARE THE TROJANS HE HAS SLAIN IN THIS WAR WITH NO GLORY.
AND THEN THE HERO ACHILLES FALLS.

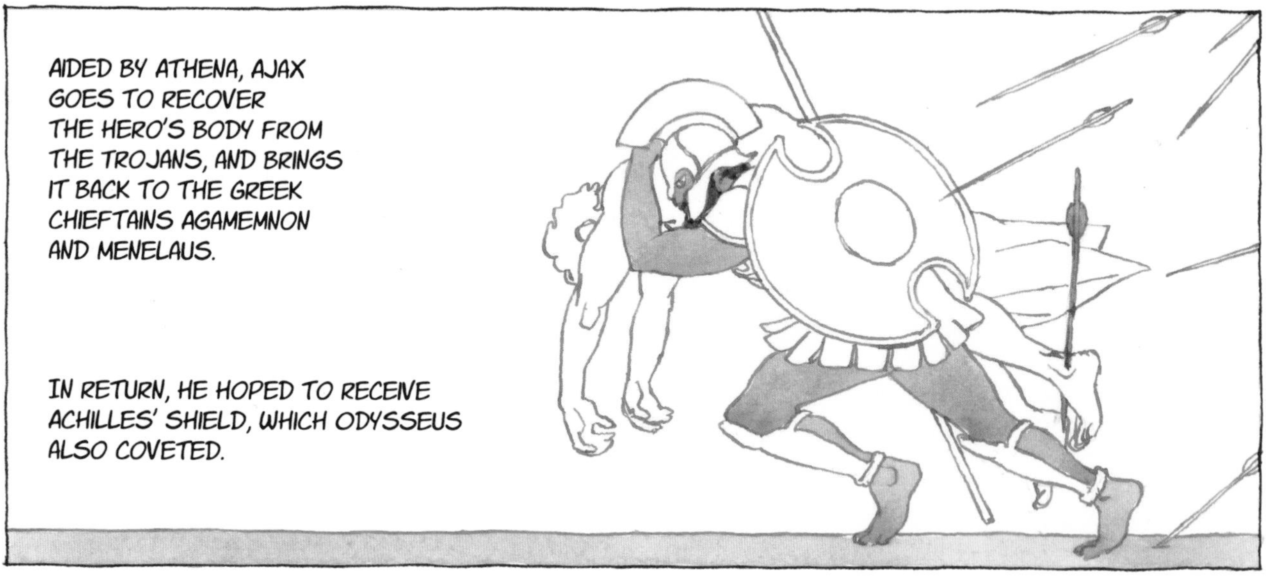
AIDED BY ATHENA, AJAX GOES TO RECOVER THE HERO'S BODY FROM THE TROJANS, AND BRINGS IT BACK TO THE GREEK CHIEFTAINS AGAMEMNON AND MENELAUS.
IN RETURN, HE HOPED TO RECEIVE ACHILLES' SHIELD, WHICH ODYSSEUS ALSO COVETED.

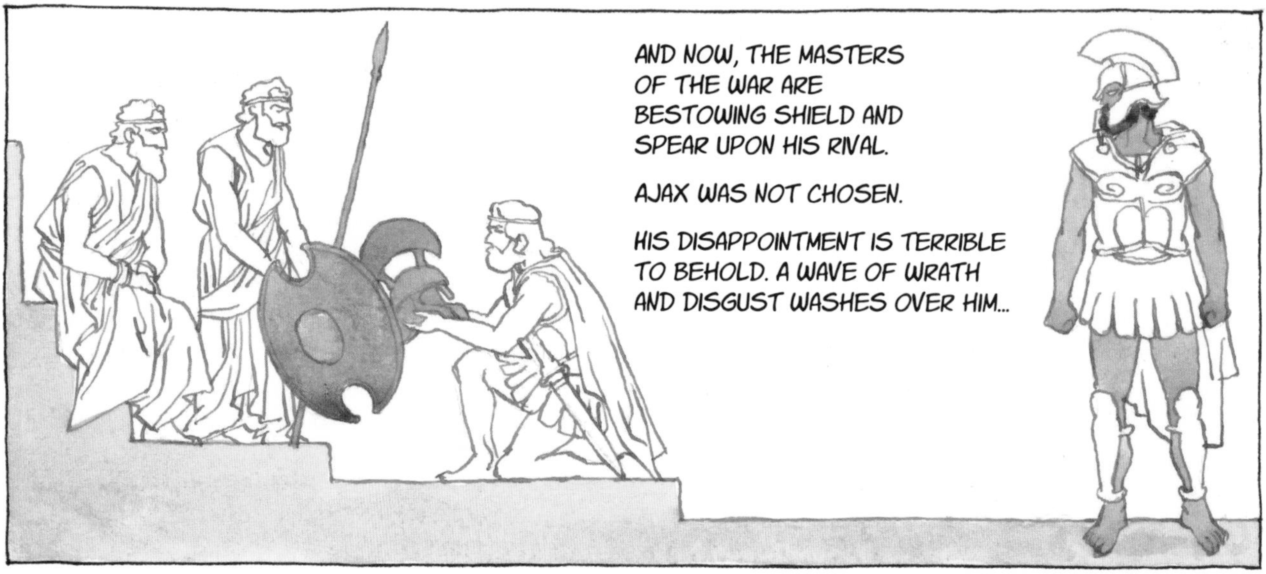
AND NOW, THE MASTERS OF THE WAR ARE BESTOWING SHIELD AND SPEAR UPON HIS RIVAL.
AJAX WAS NOT CHOSEN.
HIS DISAPPOINTMENT IS TERRIBLE TO BEHOLD. A WAVE OF WRATH AND DISGUST WASHES OVER HIM...

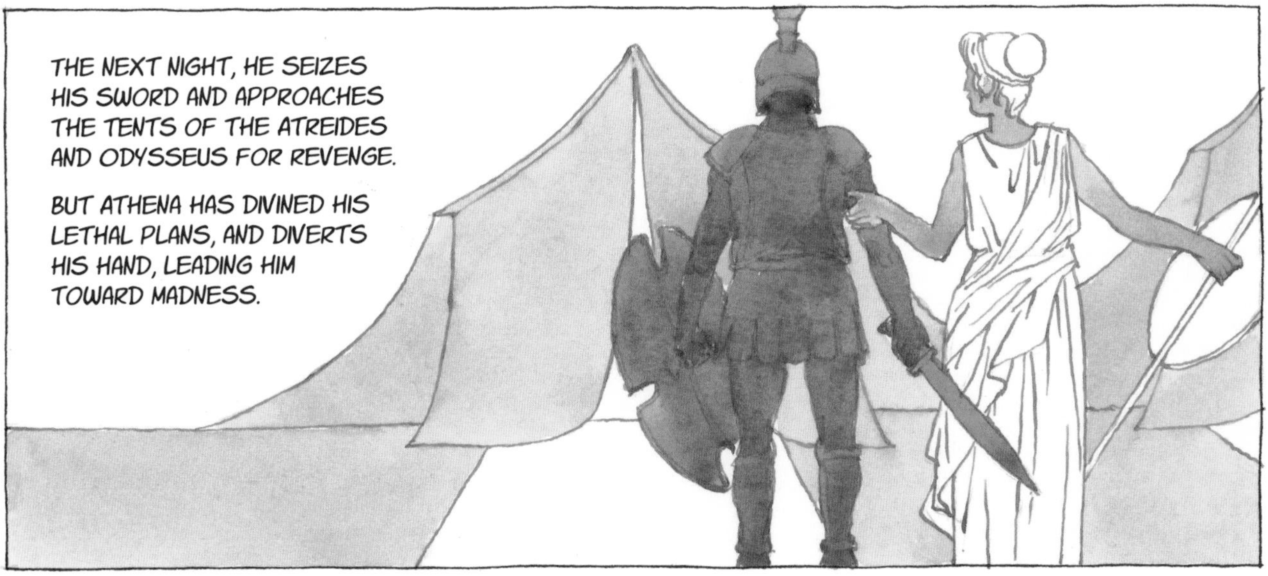
THE NEXT NIGHT, HE SEIZES HIS SWORD AND APPROACHES THE TENTS OF THE ATREIDES AND ODYSSEUS FOR REVENGE.
BUT ATHENA HAS DIVINED HIS LETHAL PLANS, AND DIVERTS HIS HAND, LEADING HIM TOWARD MADNESS.

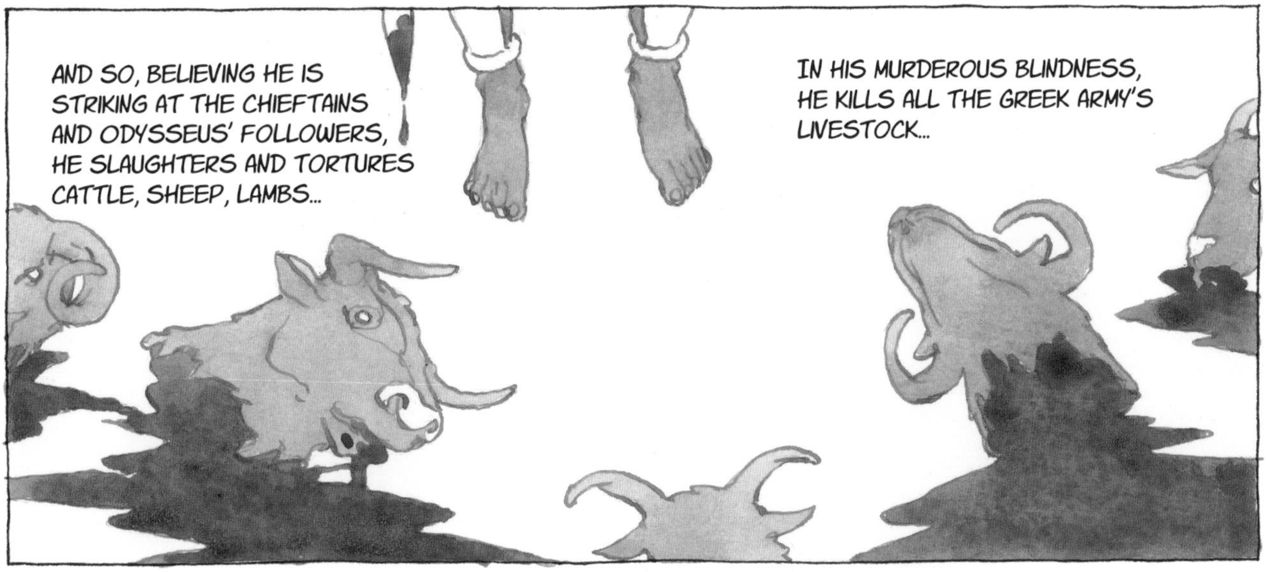
AND SO, BELIEVING HE IS STRIKING AT THE CHIEFTAINS AND ODYSSEUS' FOLLOWERS, HE SLAUGHTERS AND TORTURES CATTLE, SHEEP, LAMBS...
IN HIS MURDEROUS BLINDNESS, HE KILLS ALL THE GREEK ARMY'S LIVESTOCK...

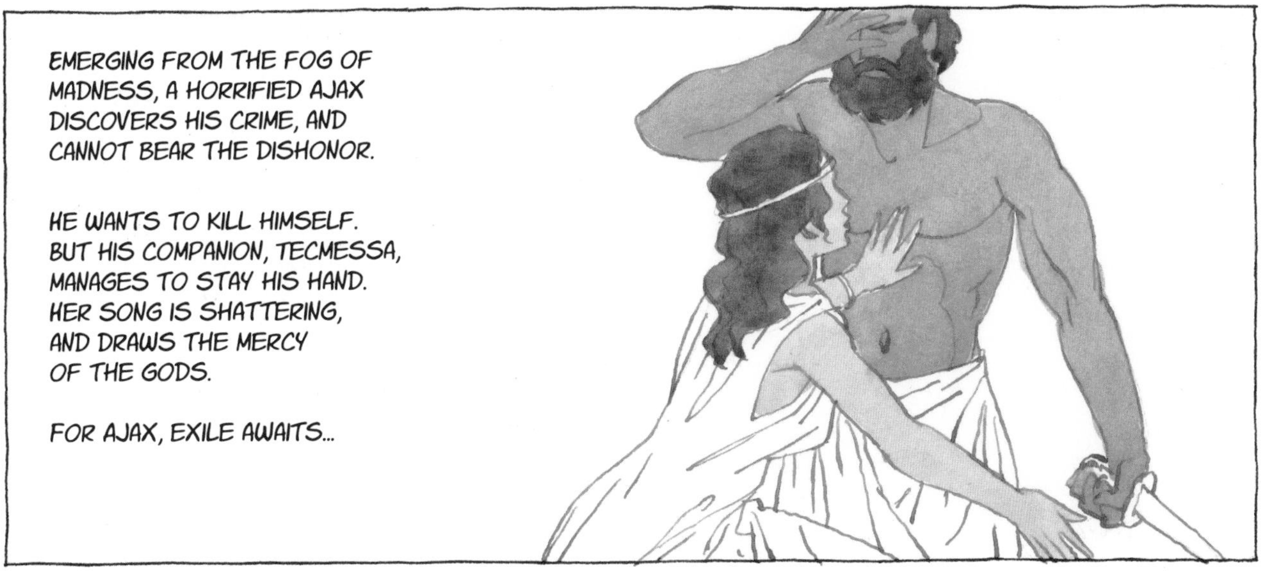
EMERGING FROM THE FOG OF MADNESS, A HORRIFIED AJAX DISCOVERS HIS CRIME, AND CANNOT BEAR THE DISHONOR.
HE WANTS TO KILL HIMSELF. BUT HIS COMPANION, TECMESSA, MANAGES TO STAY HIS HAND. HER SONG IS SHATTERING, AND DRAWS THE MERCY OF THE GODS.
FOR AJAX, EXILE AWAITS...

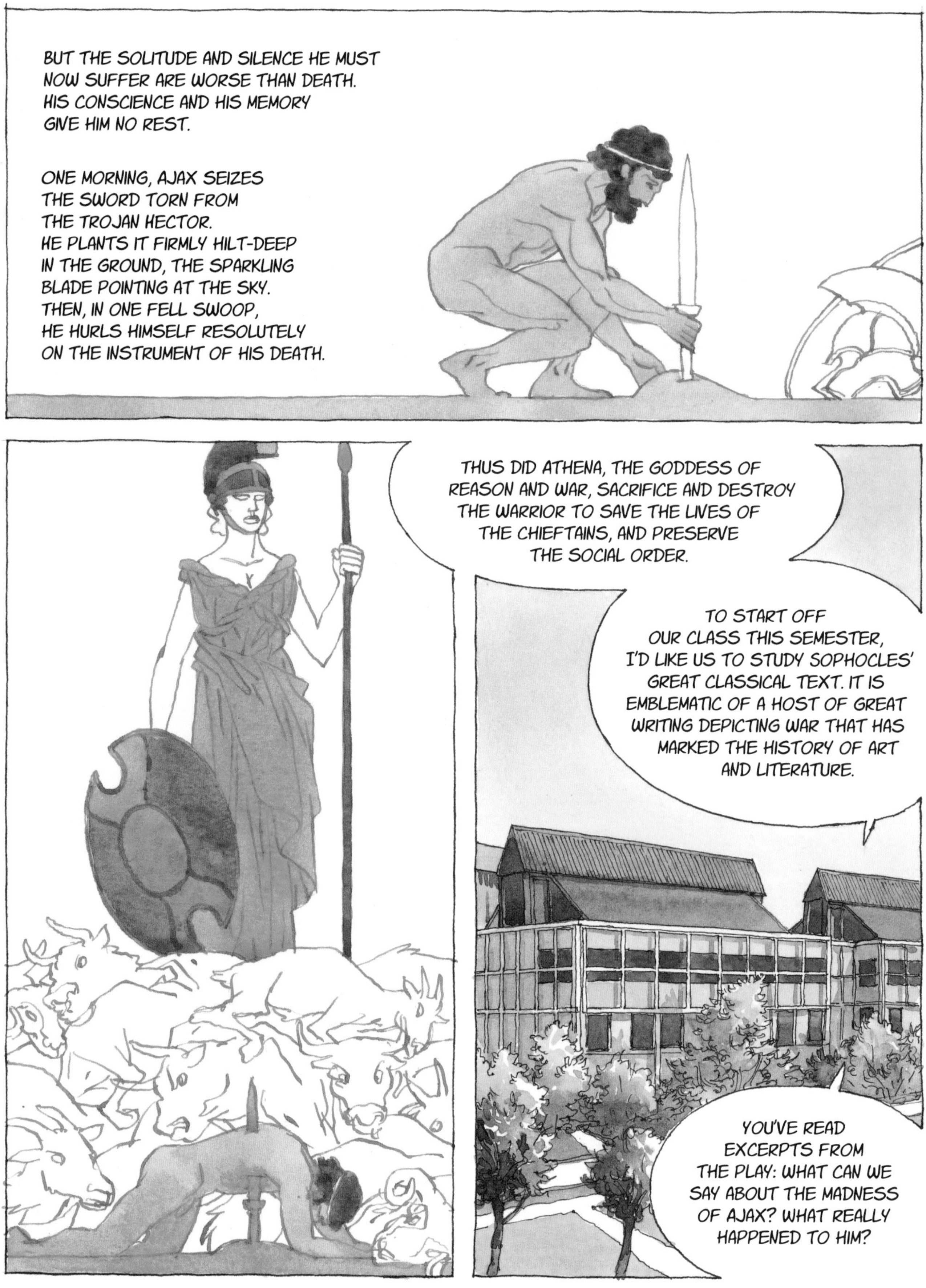
BUT THE SOLITUDE AND SILENCE HE MUST NOW SUFFER ARE WORSE THAN DEATH. HIS CONSCIENCE AND HIS MEMORY GIVE HIM NO REST.
ONE MORNING, AJAX SEIZES THE SWORD TORN FROM THE TROJAN HECTOR. HE PLANTS IT FIRMLY HILT-DEEP IN THE GROUND, THE SPARKLING BLADE POINTING AT THE SKY. THEN, IN ONE FELL SWOOP, HE HURLS HIMSELF RESOLUTELY ON THE INSTRUMENT OF HIS DEATH.
THUS DID ATHENA, THE GODDESS OF REASON AND WAR, SACRIFICE AND DESTROY THE WARRIOR TO SAVE THE LIVES OF THE CHIEFTAINS, AND PRESERVE THE SOCIAL ORDER.
TO START OFF OUR CLASS THIS SEMESTER, I'D LIKE US TO STUDY SOPHOCLES' GREAT CLASSICAL TEXT. IT IS EMBLEMATIC OF A HOST OF GREAT WRITING DEPICTING WAR THAT HAS MARKED THE HISTORY OF ART AND LITERATURE.
YOU'VE READ EXCERPTS FROM THE PLAY: WHAT CAN WE SAY ABOUT THE MADNESS OF AJAX? WHAT REALLY HAPPENED TO HIM?

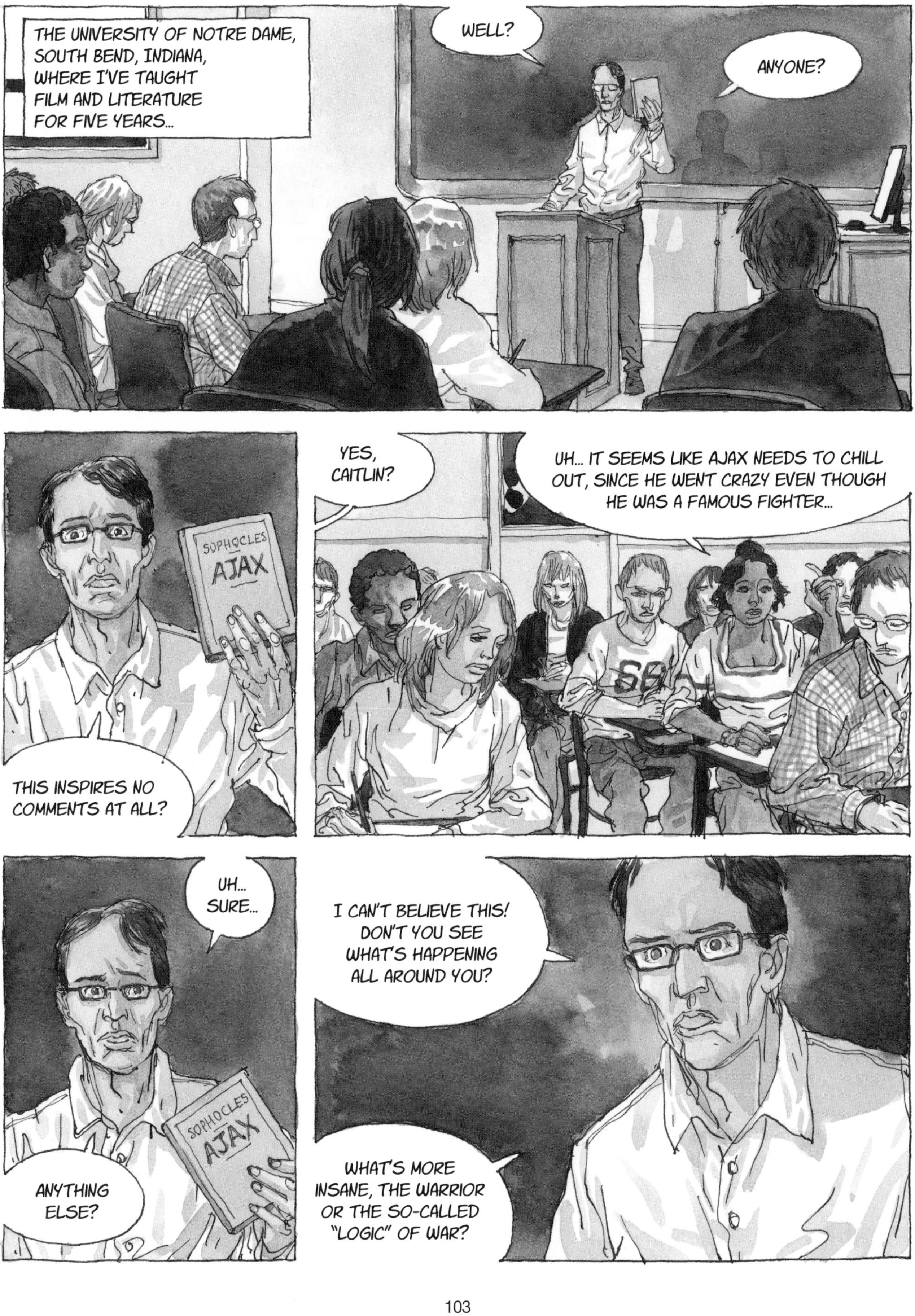
THE UNIVERSITY OF NOTRE DAME, SOUTH BEND, INDIANA, WHERE I'VE TAUGHT FILM AND LITERATURE FOR FIVE YEARS...
WELL?
ANYONE?
SOPHOCLES AJAX
THIS INSPIRES NO COMMENTS AT ALL?
YES, CAITLIN?
UH... IT SEEMS LIKE AJAX NEEDS TO CHILL OUT, SINCE HE WENT CRAZY EVEN THOUGH HE WAS A FAMOUS FIGHTER...
UH... SURE...
SOPHOCLES AJAX
ANYTHING ELSE?
I CAN'T BELIEVE THIS! DON'T YOU SEE WHAT'S HAPPENING ALL AROUND YOU?
WHAT'S MORE INSANE, THE WARRIOR OR THE SO-CALLED "LOGIC" OF WAR?

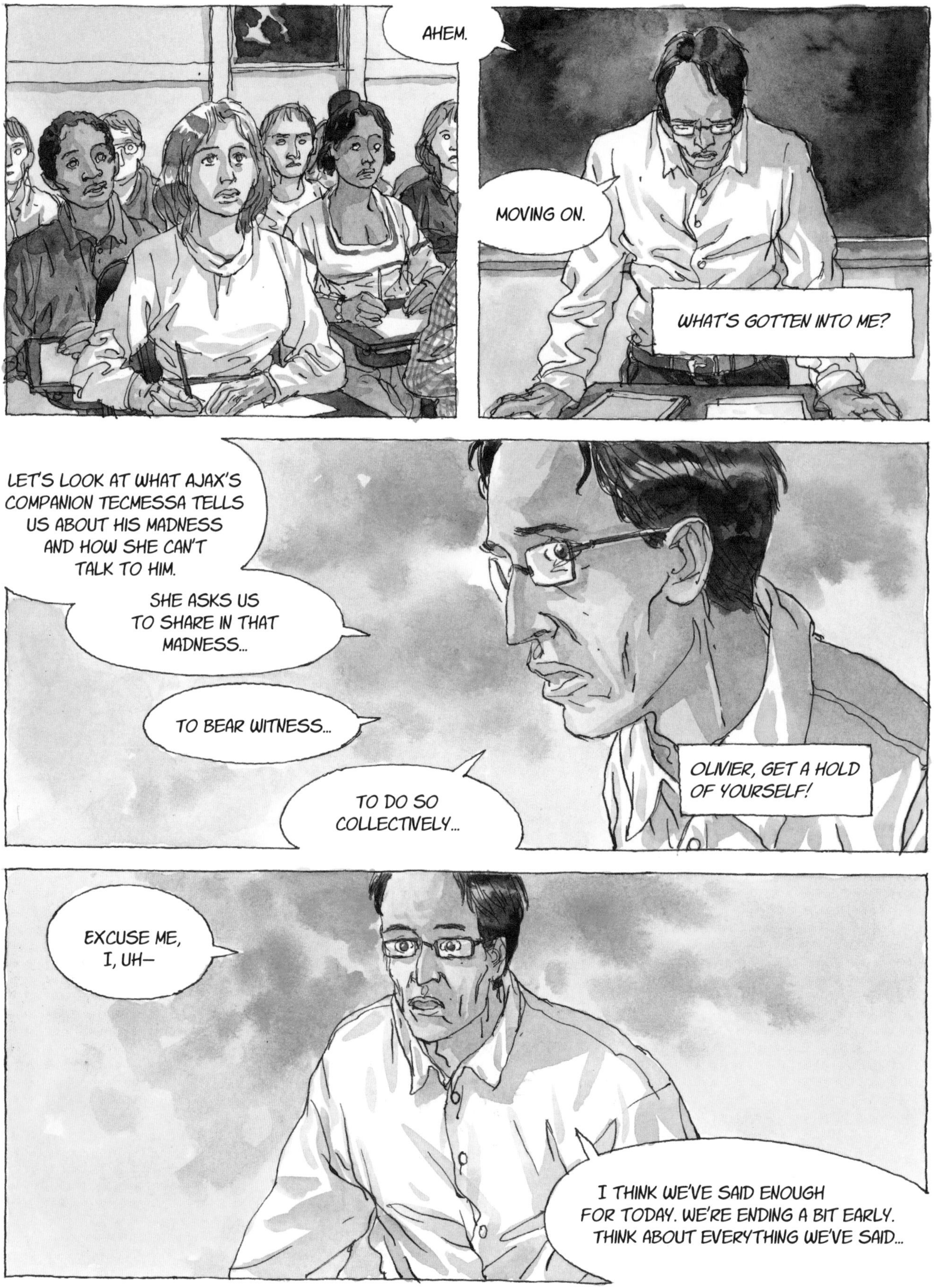
AHEM.
MOVING ON.
WHAT'S GOTTEN INTO ME?
LET'S LOOK AT WHAT AJAX'S COMPANION TECMESSA TELLS US ABOUT HIS MADNESS AND HOW SHE CAN'T TALK TO HIM.
SHE ASKS US TO SHARE IN THAT MADNESS...
TO BEAR WITNESS...
TO DO SO COLLECTIVELY...
OLIVIER, GET A HOLD OF YOURSELF!
EXCUSE ME, I, UH–
I THINK WE'VE SAID ENOUGH FOR TODAY. WE'RE ENDING A BIT EARLY. THINK ABOUT EVERYTHING WE'VE SAID...

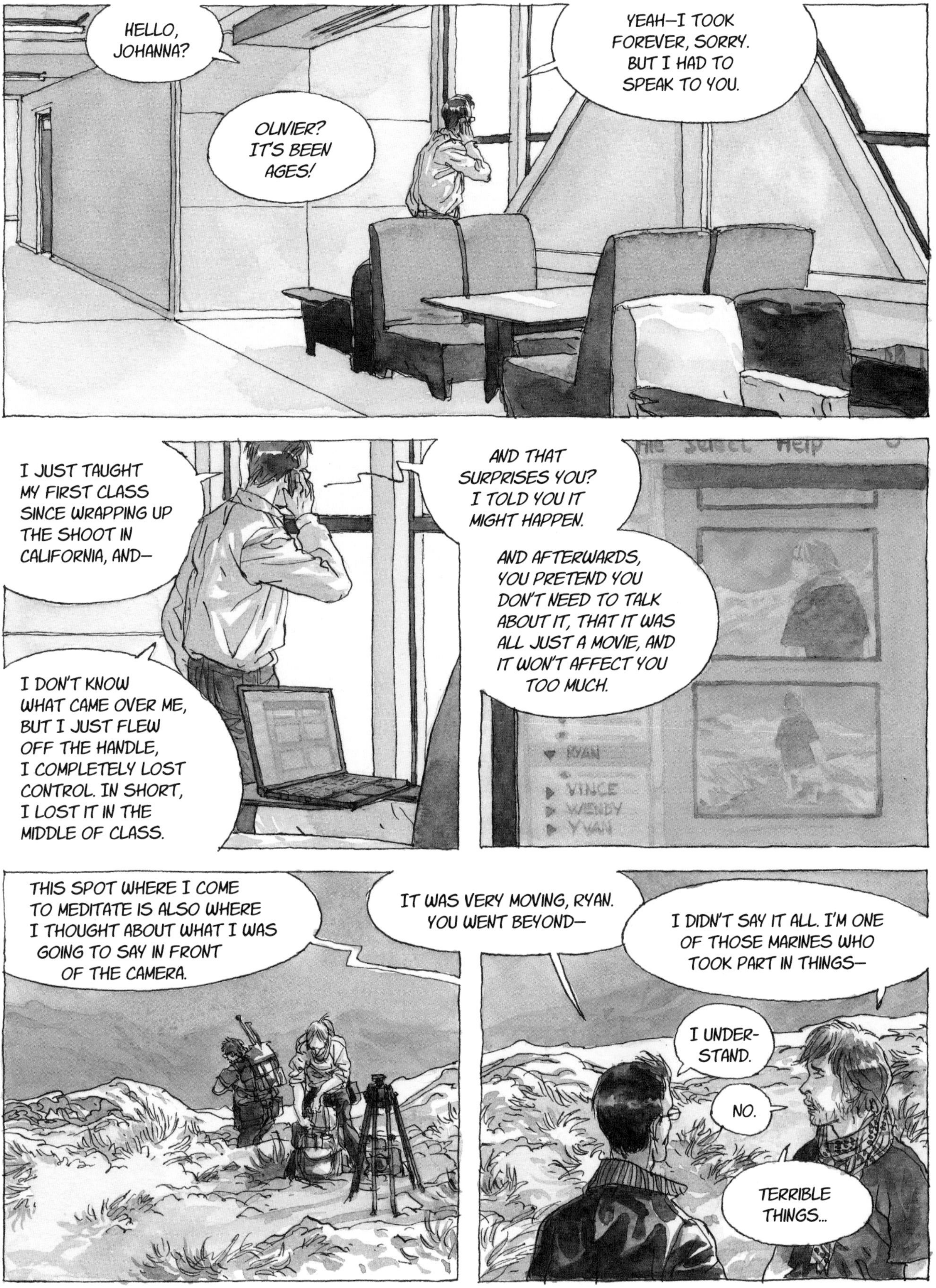
HELLO, JOHANNA?
OLIVIER? IT'S BEEN AGES!
YEAH—I TOOK FOREVER, SORRY. BUT I HAD TO SPEAK TO YOU.
I JUST TAUGHT MY FIRST CLASS SINCE WRAPPING UP THE SHOOT IN CALIFORNIA, AND—
I DON'T KNOW WHAT CAME OVER ME, BUT I JUST FLEW OFF THE HANDLE, I COMPLETELY LOST CONTROL. IN SHORT, I LOST IT IN THE MIDDLE OF CLASS.
AND THAT SURPRISES YOU? I TOLD YOU IT MIGHT HAPPEN.
AND AFTERWARDS, YOU PRETEND YOU DON'T NEED TO TALK ABOUT IT, THAT IT WAS ALL JUST A MOVIE, AND IT WON'T AFFECT YOU TOO MUCH.
RYAN
VINCE
WENDY
YVAN
THIS SPOT WHERE I COME TO MEDITATE IS ALSO WHERE I THOUGHT ABOUT WHAT I WAS GOING TO SAY IN FRONT OF THE CAMERA.
IT WAS VERY MOVING, RYAN. YOU WENT BEYOND—
I DIDN'T SAY IT ALL. I'M ONE OF THOSE MARINES WHO TOOK PART IN THINGS—
I UNDER-STAND.
NO.
TERRIBLE THINGS...

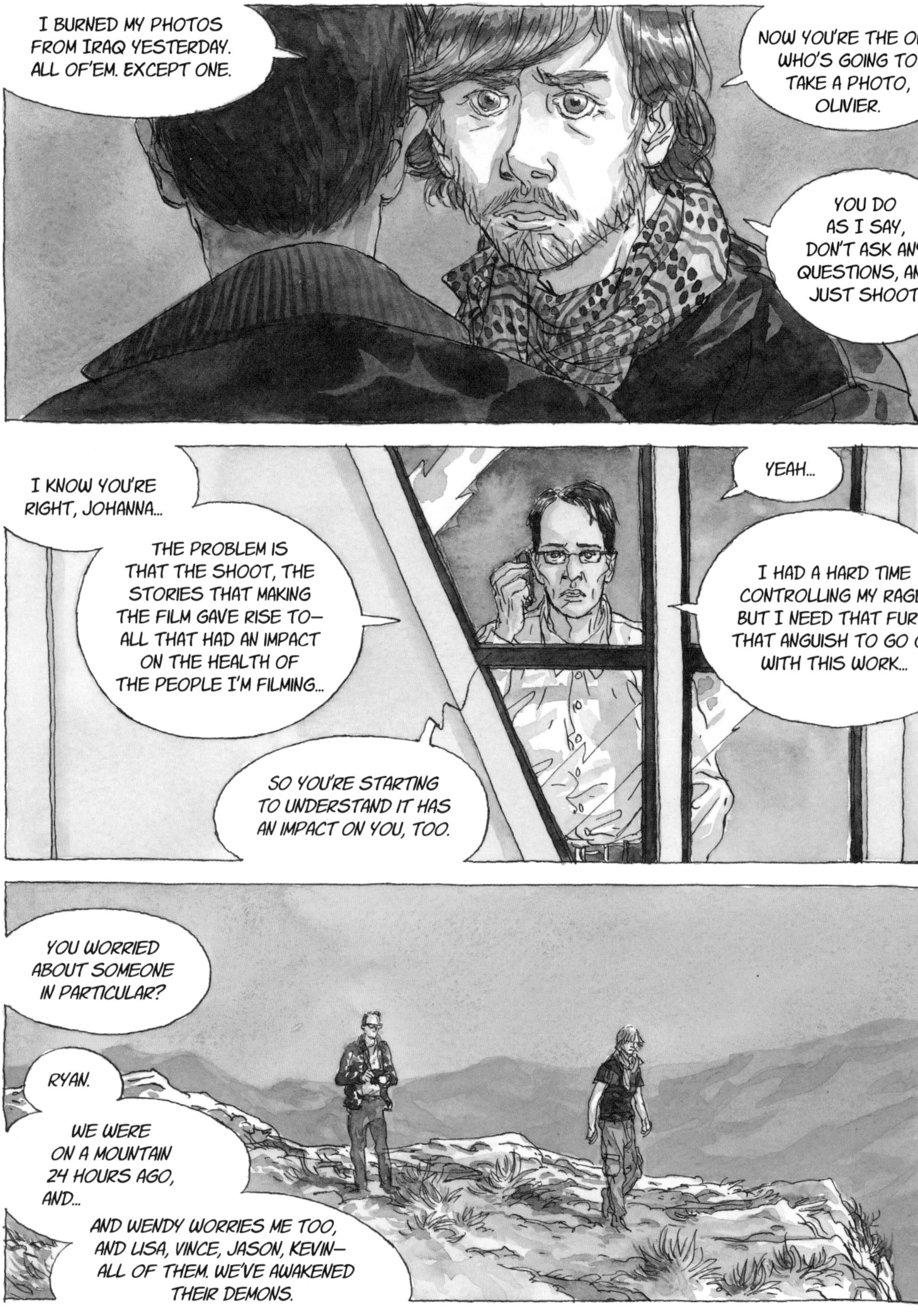
I BURNED MY PHOTOS FROM IRAQ YESTERDAY. ALL OF'EM. EXCEPT ONE.
NOW YOU'RE THE ONE WHO'S GOING TO TAKE A PHOTO, OLIVIER.
YOU DO AS I SAY, DON'T ASK ANY QUESTIONS, AND JUST SHOOT.
I KNOW YOU'RE RIGHT, JOHANNA...
THE PROBLEM IS THAT THE SHOOT, THE STORIES THAT MAKING THE FILM GAVE RISE TO— ALL THAT HAD AN IMPACT ON THE HEALTH OF THE PEOPLE I'M FILMING...
YEAH...
I HAD A HARD TIME CONTROLLING MY RAGE. BUT I NEED THAT FURY, THAT ANGUISH TO GO ON WITH THIS WORK...
SO YOU'RE STARTING TO UNDERSTAND IT HAS AN IMPACT ON YOU, TOO.
YOU WORRIED ABOUT SOMEONE IN PARTICULAR?
RYAN.
WE WERE ON A MOUNTAIN 24 HOURS AGO, AND...
AND WENDY WORRIES ME TOO, AND LISA, VINCE, JASON, KEVIN— ALL OF THEM. WE'VE AWAKENED THEIR DEMONS.

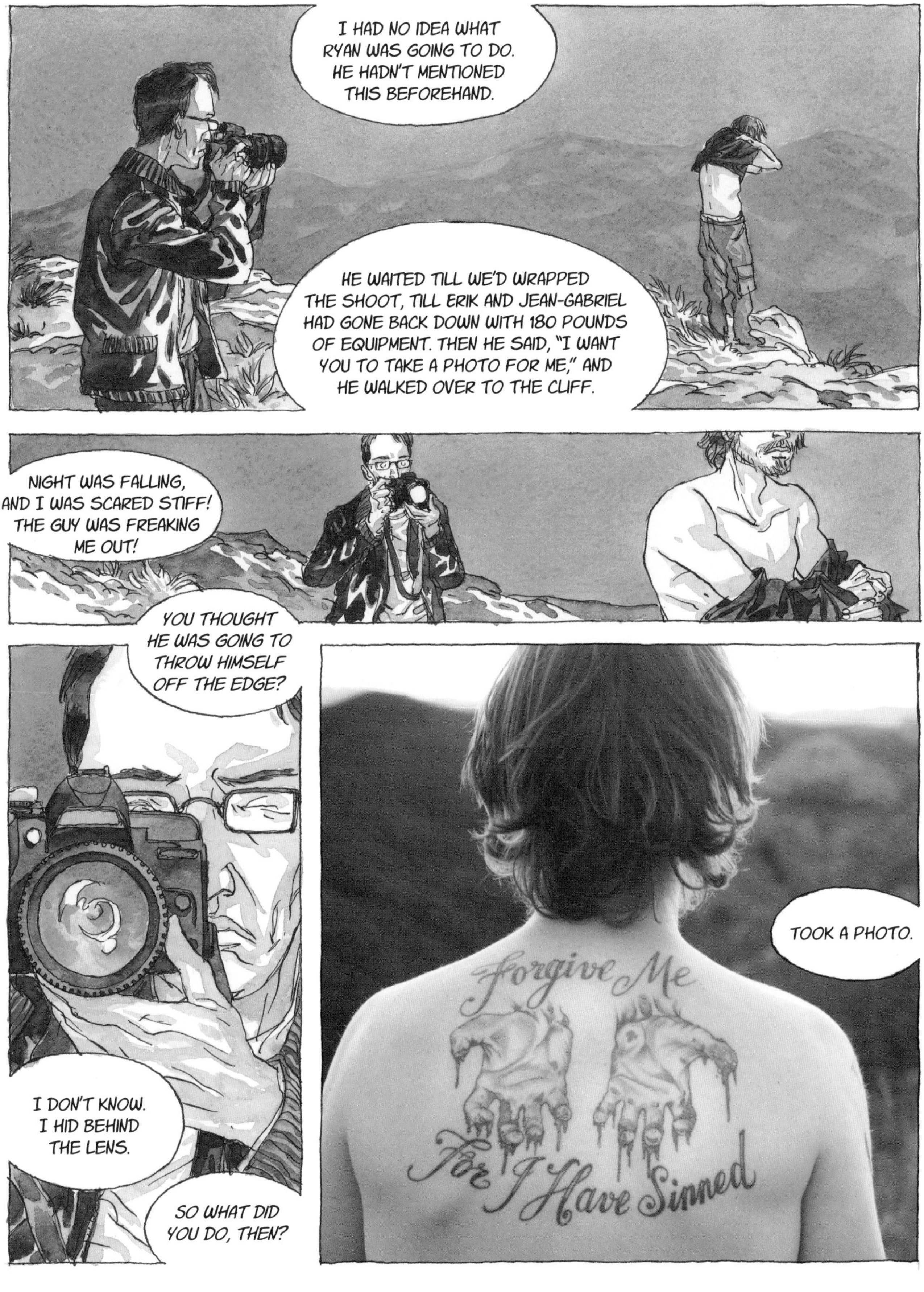
I HAD NO IDEA WHAT RYAN WAS GOING TO DO. HE HADN'T MENTIONED THIS BEFOREHAND.
HE WAITED TILL WE'D WRAPPED THE SHOOT, TILL ERIK AND JEAN-GABRIEL HAD GONE BACK DOWN WITH 180 POUNDS OF EQUIPMENT. THEN HE SAID, "I WANT YOU TO TAKE A PHOTO FOR ME," AND HE WALKED OVER TO THE CLIFF.
NIGHT WAS FALLING, AND I WAS SCARED STIFF! THE GUY WAS FREAKING ME OUT!
YOU THOUGHT HE WAS GOING TO THROW HIMSELF OFF THE EDGE?
I DON'T KNOW. I HID BEHIND THE LENS.
SO WHAT DID YOU DO, THEN?
TOOK A PHOTO.
Forgive Me
For I Have Sinned

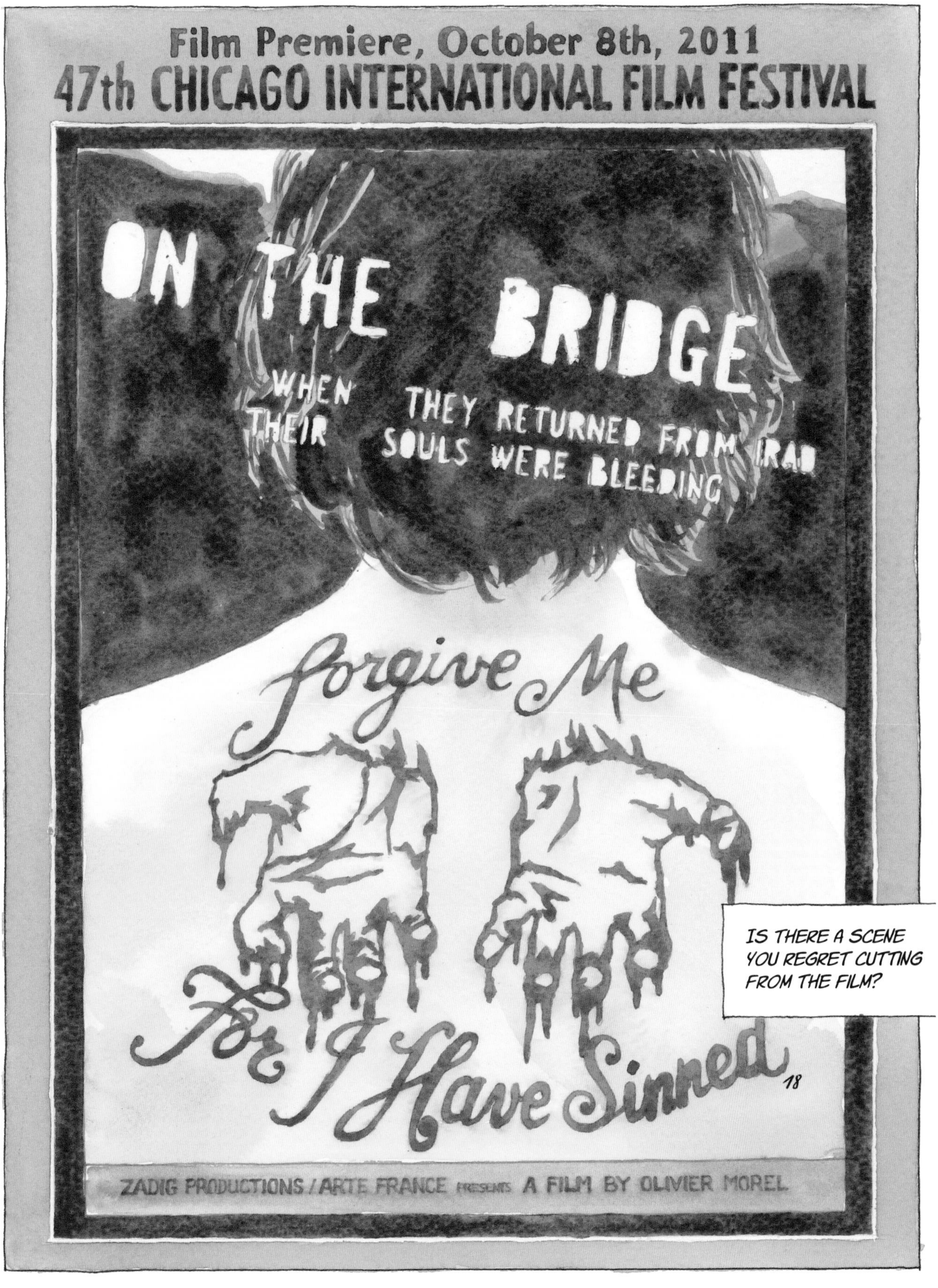
Film Premiere, October 8th, 2011
47th CHICAGO INTERNATIONAL FILM FESTIVAL
ON THE BRIDGE
WHEN THEY RETURNED FROM IRAQ
THEIR SOULS WERE BLEEDING
Forgive Me For I Have Sinned
18
ZADIG PRODUCTIONS / ARTE FRANCE PRESENTS A FILM BY OLIVIER MOREL
IS THERE A SCENE YOU REGRET CUTTING FROM THE FILM?

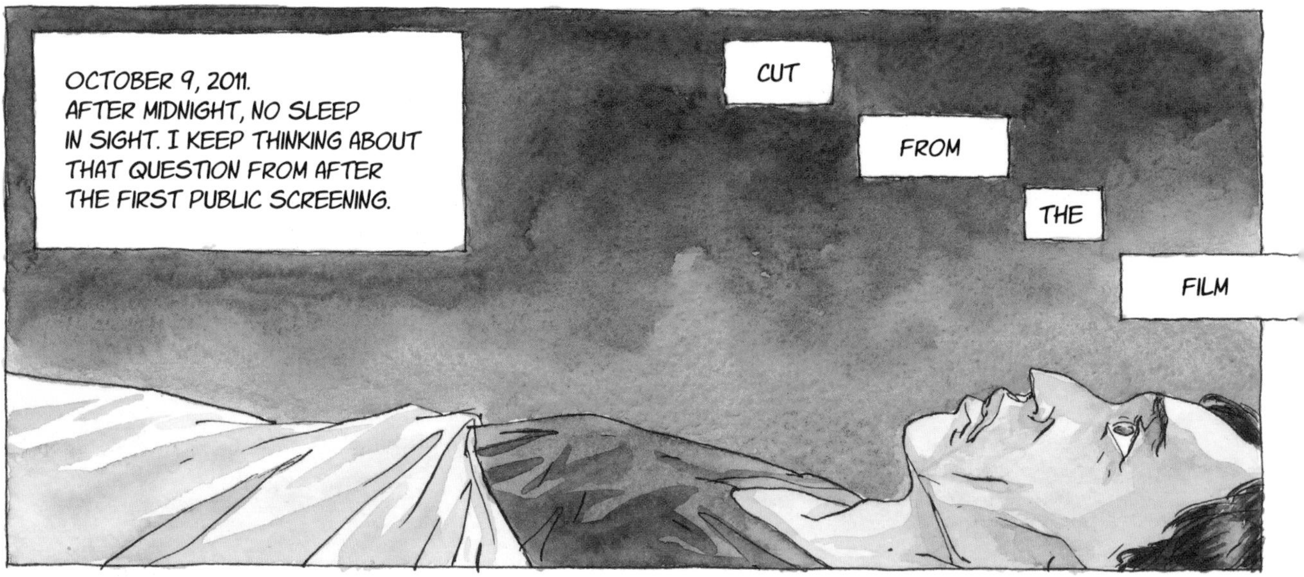
OCTOBER 9, 2011.
AFTER MIDNIGHT, NO SLEEP IN SIGHT. I KEEP THINKING ABOUT THAT QUESTION FROM AFTER THE FIRST PUBLIC SCREENING.
CUT
FROM
THE
FILM

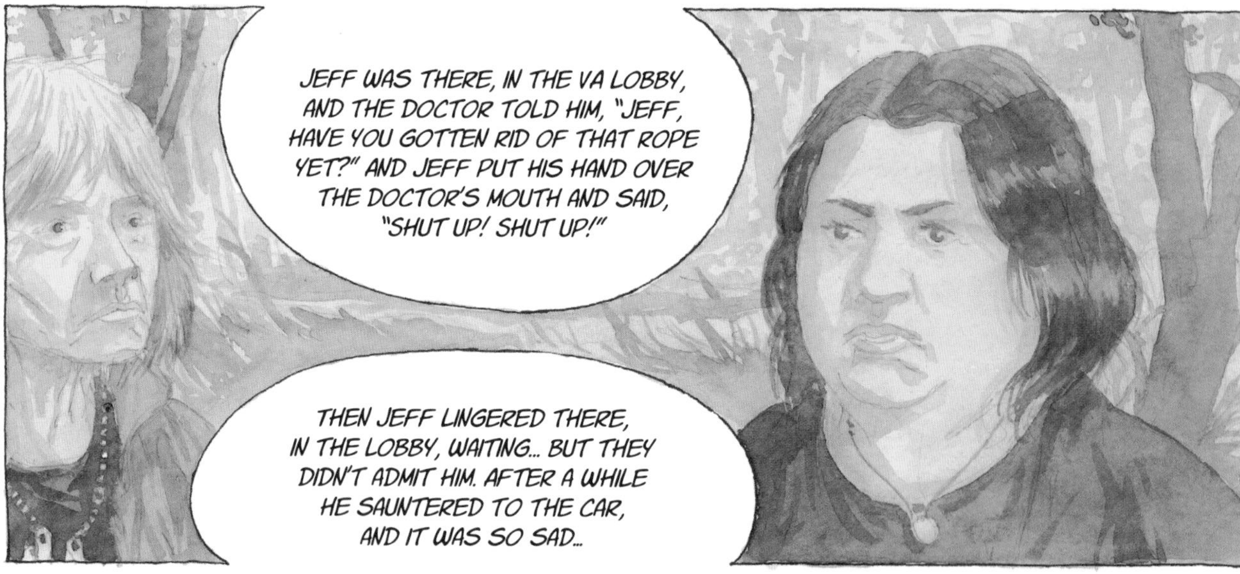
JEFF WAS THERE, IN THE VA LOBBY, AND THE DOCTOR TOLD HIM, "JEFF, HAVE YOU GOTTEN RID OF THAT ROPE YET?" AND JEFF PUT HIS HAND OVER THE DOCTOR'S MOUTH AND SAID, "SHUT UP! SHUT UP!"
THEN JEFF LINGERED THERE, IN THE LOBBY, WAITING... BUT THEY DIDN'T ADMIT HIM. AFTER A WHILE HE SAUNTERED TO THE CAR, AND IT WAS SO SAD...

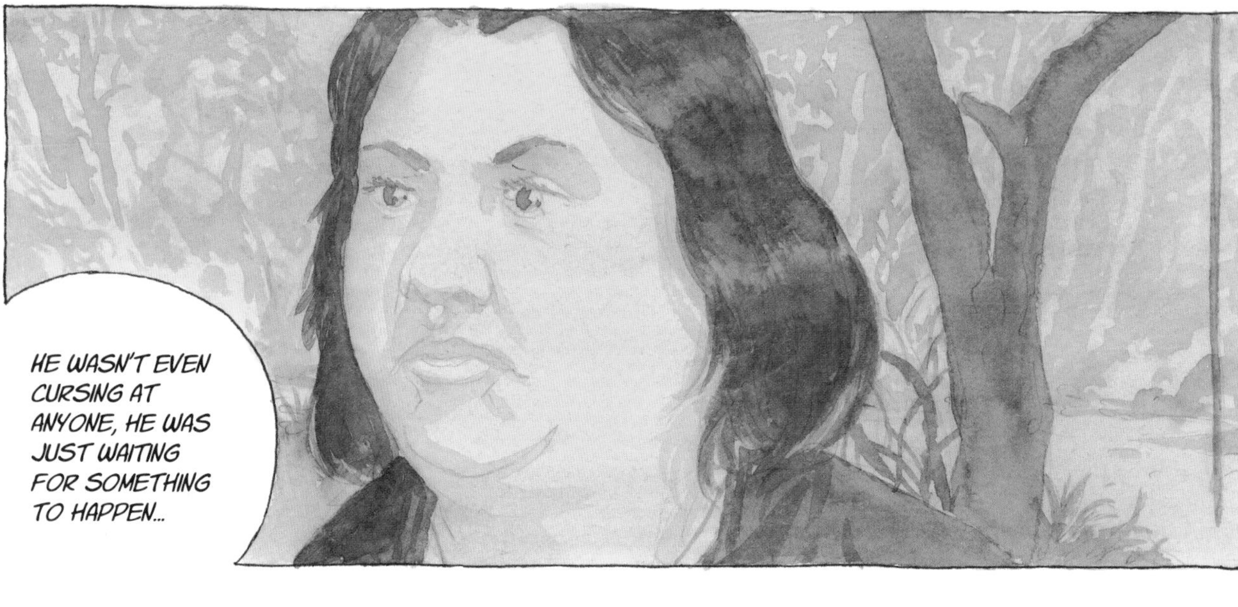
HE WASN'T EVEN CURSING AT ANYONE, HE WAS JUST WAITING FOR SOMETHING TO HAPPEN...

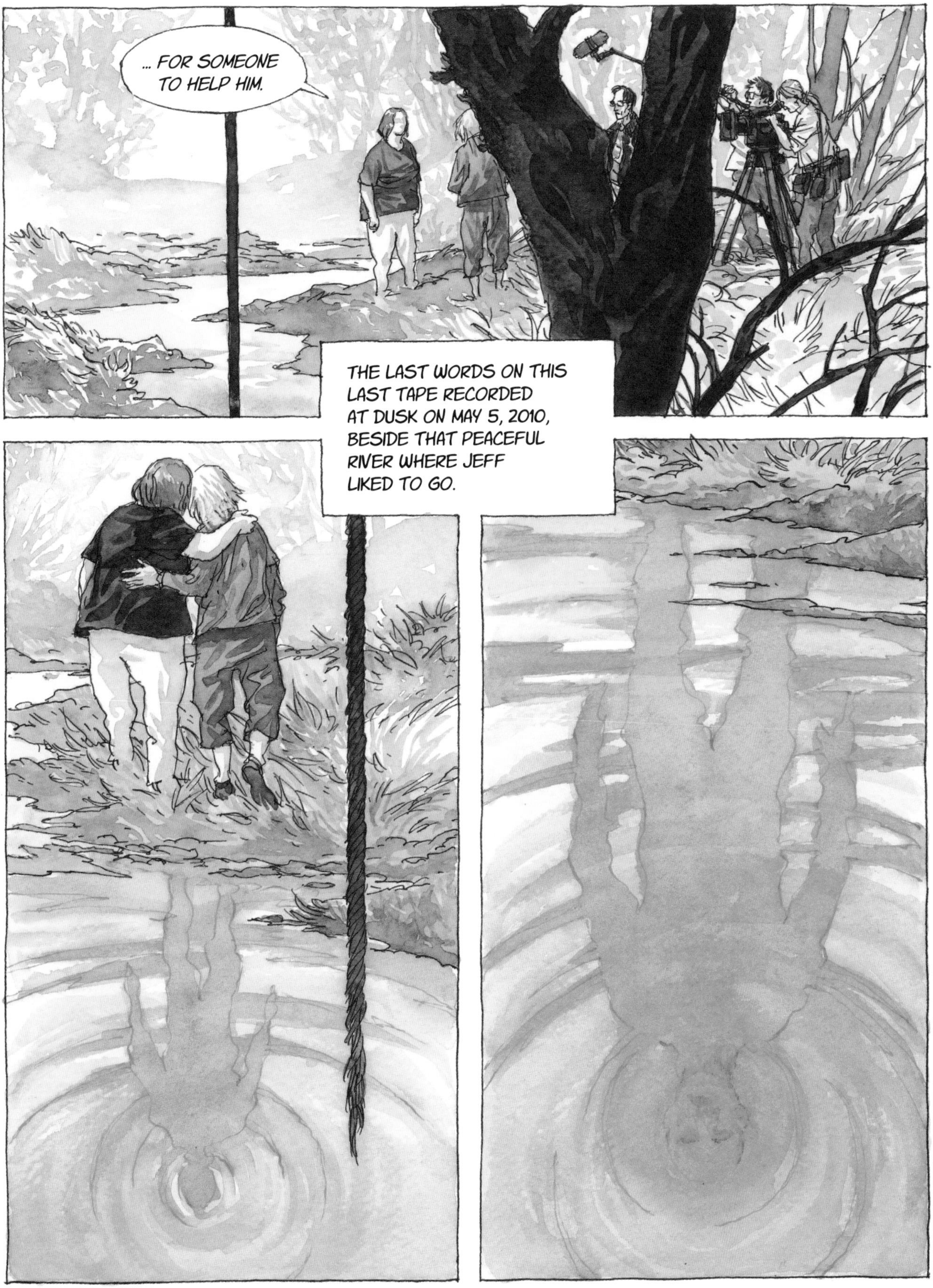
... FOR SOMEONE TO HELP HIM.
THE LAST WORDS ON THIS LAST TAPE RECORDED AT DUSK ON MAY 5, 2010, BESIDE THAT PEACEFUL RIVER WHERE JEFF LIKED TO GO.

DON'T LEAVE ME!

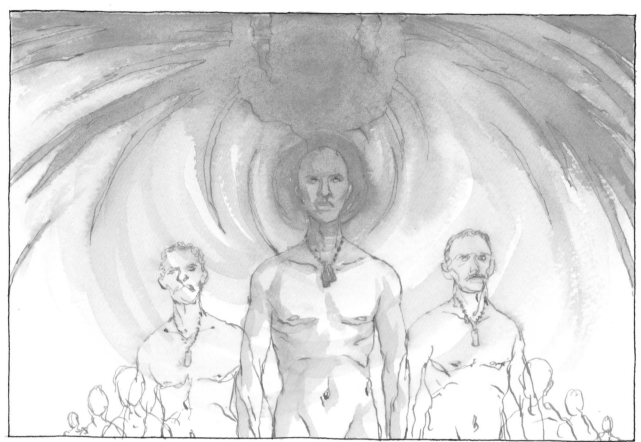

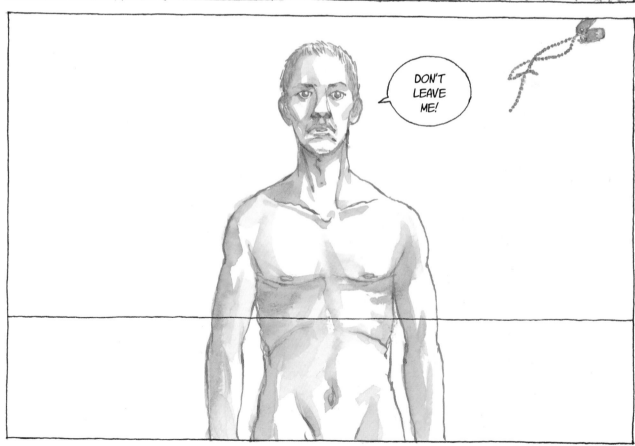

Maël - Morel - Juin 2013

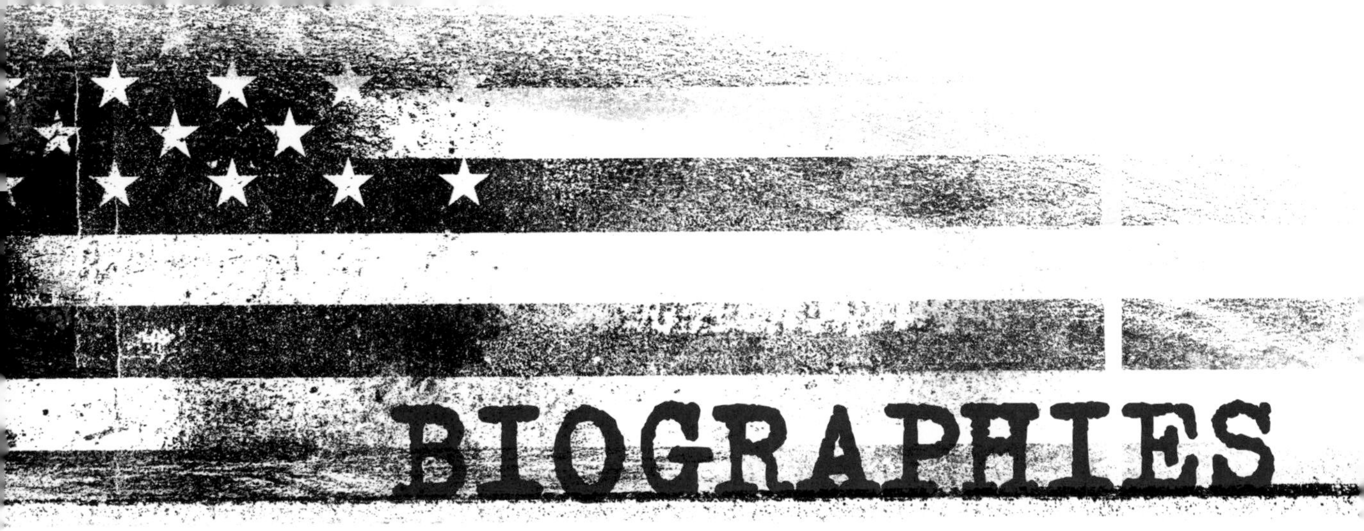

BIOGRAPHIES

Shortly after 9/11, *Wendy Barranco* joined when she was just 17. Three years later, she was deployed to Iraq as an anesthesia technician in a hospital in Tikrit. From October 2005 to July 2006, she took part in stabilizing and taking care of patients in the operating room.

Upon returning from deployment, she threw herself into defending the cause of women soldiers who struggle against harassment and sexual assault in the US Armed Forces. She is an activist with Iraq Veterans Against the War (ivaw.org), for which she served as chair of the board of directors.

She's had a string of odd jobs, and is now completing her undergraduate degree.

Marine *Vincent (Vince) Emanuele* took part in the invasion of Iraq from March to May 2003. He was redeployed from August 2004 to April 2005 in the highly dangerous Al-Qa'im region. During his time in Iraq, this son of a construction worker experienced his philosophical and political awakening, and became a compulsive reader.

He recovered from depression by becoming, over the years, a sophisticated intellectual. More than ever, Vince is involved in political activism and social activities, often with impoverished populations on the south side of Chicago, where he grew up.

When he's not devouring books on philosophy or social science, he hosts a weekly radio show, Veterans Unplugged (veteransunplugged.com), where he speaks as knowledgeably about unionism in the Midwest as he does about Heideggerian ontology...

***Ryan Endicott* was deployed as a Marine in Ar Ramadi, one of Iraq's most dangerous areas, in 2005 and 2006.** He still suffers from a serious wound to his arm inflicted by an IED explosion that killed his best friend.

Upon his return, he was close to homelessness, frequenting soup kitchens, and self medicated with alcohol. He is still waiting for the VA to re-evaluate his disability pension. After years of slumming around, relapses, and demeaning jobs, he married in 2013, and is studying history at UCLA.

Along with their two daughters and grandchildren, *Joyce* and *Kevin Lucey* have devoted their lives to honoring the memory of their only son *Jeffrey Michael Lucey* (1981-2004). They travel the US on awareness campaigns related to damage caused by PTSD, veteran suicide, and suicide in general.

A former United States Marine (USMC), Jeffrey Lucey participated in the invasion that led the US army from Kuwait to Iraq in 2003. He now rests in a small cemetery in Ludlow, Massachusetts.

Jason Moon was a member of the US National Guard in the final years of the Cold War. While the embers of the 9/11 attacks were still smoldering, he re-enlisted. Deployed with the National Guard in 2003 and 2004, he participated in the invasion of Iraq.

Unable to work in the months after his return, he nearly became homeless and a regular at soup kitchens, sinking into a depression that almost cost him his life in the summer of 2008. That was when he met Olivier.

Though he had not touched his guitar for a long time, he overcame the torments stirred up by filming to record an album of original songs (*Trying to Find My Way Home*) written in Iraq and after the film, one of which was about music coming back into his life.

This graphic novel got him going: not a week now goes by without him taking the stage somewhere in America, usually to fundraise for veterans with psychological issues (warriorsongs.org). He and his wife Sarah have a little girl, Penelope June, born in 2013.

After an earlier stint in the Marines from 1988 to 1992, Kevin Stendal reenlisted after the 9/11 attacks in New York. He was deployed in 2003 and 2004, notably in the Iraqi region of Al Anbar, near the city of Al-Qa'im. A few years after getting back, Kevin, almost 40, made good on a dream he once thought out of reach: studying at a university thanks to the Post 9/11 GI Bill, a program that allows veterans of the wars in Iraq and Afghanistan to attend school with tuition paid, along with a stipend for books, and a monthly living allowance.

After graduating from Columbia University, Kevin went back to live with his daughters in Southern California.

Juggling a day job and his family, he now works as a clerk in a law office.

Lisa Zepeda, reservist and single mother of a twelve-year old, was deployed to Iraq starting in 2003. She spent eighteen months there as a Medical Lab Technician assigned to a Forward Surgical Hospital at Abu Ghraib. When her time was up, the army unilaterally extended her service contract, as is its right in times of war.

Shortly after the making of *On the Bridge*, she began to live again and accept "her" past by founding a support group that gathered veterans from the wars in Iraq and Afghanistan, especially women. During this time, she also met the man she would share her days with—like her, a police officer on the south side of Chicago.

1. Iraq Veterans Against the War (IVAW)

An association founded in Boston on July 24, 2004 during the annual Veterans for Peace convention.

IVAW emerged from a group of Iraq War veterans headed by Kelly Dougherty, a woman in her thirties who had just spent a year in a medical unit in Kuwait and Iraq from February 2003 to February 2004. Born in 1979, Dougherty is the daughter of a Vietnam vet. A member of the National Guard from 1996 to 2004, she was opposed to the war in Iraq well before it began. IVAW's primary advocacy goals have been the "immediate and unconditional withdrawal of all occupying forces in Iraq; full benefits, adequate healthcare (including mental health), and other support for returning servicemen and women; reparations for the human and structural damages Iraq has suffered." The association is also among the first in the US to have vigorously protested the repeated deployments imposed on psychologically fragile soldiers, and to point a finger at the scandals linked to sexual trauma in the American military.

Like many other post-9/11 veterans' associations (like IAVA: Iraq and Afghanistan Veterans of America), IVAW mainly brings together very young servicemen and women from the lower ranks. Women are very well represented in the group. It should also be noted that many of its 1,500 members are active soldiers who, deployed to Iraq and Afghanistan, opposed the wars. One of the association's acts was to organize Winter Soldier: Iraq & Afghanistan, which consisted of public events where former soldiers spoke on any topic related to their tours in Iraq and Afghanistan, notably the dehumanization of the enemy, sexual violence, torture, the injustice of the Occupation, and the fate of veterans after their service.

See also:
Winter Soldier Iraq & Afghanistan, Eyewitness Accounts of the Operations, IVAW & Aaron Glantz (ed.), Chicago: Haymarket Books, 2008, p.3

2. La Chanson de Craonne

The famous "Chanson de Craonne" is a well-known World War I French anti-militarist song sung by mutinying soldiers who refused to fight further at the Chemin des Dames in 1917, protesting their commanders' recklessness and negligence. Most likely the effort of many contributors, the anonymously credited song was banned in France until 1974.

3. The Subprime Crisis and Crash of 2008

Triggered by a growing difficulty among Americans in paying back their mortgage loans, the so-called "subprime" crisis affected the high-risk mortgage loan sector in the US starting in 2007, and led to the crash of 2008.

Traditionally, the value of property guarantees banking institutions can repay mortgage loans should their clients prove insolvent, via the sale of that property. For various reasons—economic (rising oil prices) and regulatory (increased loan incentives, tax reductions encouraging real estate debt), as well as cultural (over-consumption and virtual standard of living) and systemic (deregulation of the banking sector)—in 2007 the number of clients unable to pay back their mortgage loans had reached a critical threshold in the US. Insolvent owners had to leave their homes en masse: prices plummeted, and no homes were sold. Lenders could not pay themselves back, which led, in a domino effect, to the bankruptcy of several large American financial institutions in September 2008.

Most of these were saved in extremis by the Federal Reserve, with the notable exception of Lehman Brothers, whose spectacular failure was a famous case. The global economy was deeply affected. Despite serious flaws this upheaval revealed in the financial system, the Obama administration's response was marked by a conspicuous refusal to call into question the system or its architects.

4. Bernard Stiegler

For thirty years now, Bernard Stiegler has believed that capitalism's teletechnological development has produced self-destructive consequences for psychic and collective individuation: after proletarianizing its workers, the system now proletarianizes its consumers. In particular, Stiegler shows how, at the very moment when Ford invented mass production in 1912, the first movie studios were being built in Hollywood; the "dream factory" is the corollary of Taylorism, symbolic of capitalism entering the era of what Stiegler calls "the time of cinema," a society without shame. The focus of capitalism is no longer to increase productivity, but to capture the consumer's libido (desires, urges). Among the central hypotheses of Stiegler's recent work is that libidinal energy has become a product like any other, whose industrial capture ("available brain time") gives rise to great symbolic poverty and generalized demotivation. The dominant industrial model tends to destroy the shame which the ancient Greeks called aidôs, and set forth along with justice (dikè) as the sublime principle and condition of political body. Thus the tendentious drop in libidinal energy provokes a devastating desublimation and a disaffected society.

In his work on teletechnologies and the way they alter memory, Stiegler cites Jacques Derrida announcing that "the future belongs to ghosts." According to Stiegler, this means we have before us the prospect of a libidinal economy via cinematography of the psyche.

Walking Wounded owes a great deal to his work.
Among Stiegler's notable books are: *Uncontrollable Societies of Disaffected Individuals: Disbelief and Discredit* (Cambridge: Polity, 2012), *Technics and Time, 3: Cinematic Time and the Question of Malaise* (Redwood City: Stanford University Press, 2010), *Decadence of Industrial Democracies* (Cambridge: Polity, 2011).

5. You Can't Be Neutral on a Moving Train

Howard Zinn, *You Can't Be Neutral on a Moving Train: A Personal History of Our Times* (Boston: Beacon Press, 2002).

Born to a Jewish immigrant family in Brooklyn, Howard Zinn (1922-2010) was a bombardier in World War II and took part in the bombardment of the French town Royan, which killed a thousand people, but only a few Germans, barely three weeks before the end of the war. In 1966, Zinn returned to Royan and befriended the locals. He learned from research that the missions were motivated only by the desire of a few military officials for their own career advancement.

Howard Zinn has often explained how these acts have affected the course of his life, influencing his work as a historian as well as his personal conduct.

After the war, he took advantage of the GI Bill to pursue a doctorate at Columbia University in New York. From that time on, his work has focused especially on the right to strike, the redistribution of wealth, and the role of the state. He began his career in the South, at Spelman College, at the time of segregation. He was a very active participant in civil rights movements. This was also the time he became established as a historian, defending an oral history of the people against the history of those in power. What interested him was people who had no say in matters. Inextricable from his research were his political commitments—civil rights on behalf of minorities and the voiceless (he influenced Martin Luther King, Jr.), protests against the wars in Vietnam and Iraq, and his critique of American exceptionalism—which make him a voice of conscience of the twentieth century. He has a considerable readership, especially among veterans of the Vietnam and post-9/11 wars.

A People's History of the United States is one of his most widely read books.

6. Halliburton

Halliburton is a multinational corporation based in Texas that specializes in services and equipment for the oil and natural gas industries, for which it is one of the largest suppliers worldwide. From 1995 to 2000, its CEO was former Secretary of Defense Dick Cheney, who went on to become George W. Bush's vice-president. The Iraq War gave Halliburton and its subsidiary KBR an occasion to profit from very lucrative contracts, awarded under circumstances whose suspicious nature (there was no public bidding) has been repeatedly denied.

7. Abu Ghraib

Located about twenty miles west of Baghdad, the Abu Ghraib complex is a prison that housed many political prisoners under the dictatorship of Saddam Hussein. When Iraq was invaded in 2003, the establishment passed into coalition hands.

In early 2004, US Central Command informed the media that an official investigation had been diligently carried out to shine light on the acts of abuse, humiliation, and torture perpetrated by a group of American soldiers on Iraqi prisoners at Abu Ghraib. On March 21, it was announced that six soldiers had been charged.

Less than a month later, on April 28, 2004, the "Abu Ghraib Scandal" blew wide open when 60 Minutes (CBS) aired a story in which several photographs of the abuses were shown. At the same time, The New York Times published a long article and photos on the subject, which made their way around the world. A few days later, Secretary of Defense Donald Rumsfeld stated that the highly publicized images were but a small number of the existing pictures and videotapes of the abuse at Abu Ghraib.

One of reporter and New Yorker writer Seymour Hersh's informants pointed out that certain "coercive" interrogation methods, similar to torture, had been perfected and used by the American military in

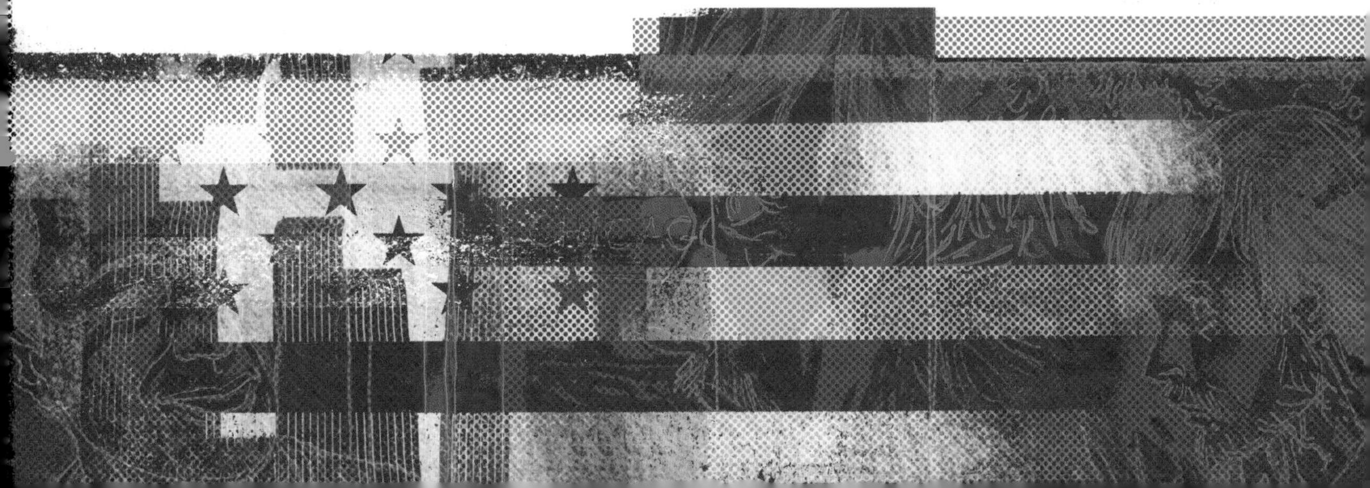

Afghanistan and Iraq. The Pentagon denied this information.

8. The Divine Comedy

La Divina Commedia is a poem in three parts (or cantos) by Dante Alighieri (1265-1321), written in Florentine Vulgar Latin from 1306 to 1321. Moving from Inferno (Hell) through Purgatorio (Purgatory) towards Paradiso (Heaven), the poet recounts a journey of initiation through the three realms of the afterlife, leading to a vision of the Trinity. Considered the first great work to be written in Italian, it was inspired by the bloody conflict between the Guelphs and the Ghibellines from 1125 to 1300, some of which Dante experienced firsthand. Immediately influential, Dante's poem was widely copied by hand before the invention of printing. This monumental work is a major account of medieval Europe.

The quotation "Abandon all hope, ye who enter here" is the final line of the third canto of the Inferno.

9. Donald Rumsfeld and Dick Cheney

Richard B. (Dick) Cheney was Secretary of Defense (1989-1993) under George H.W. Bush (Sr.), and vice-president under George W. Bush (2001-2009).
Donald Rumsfeld served as Secretary of Defense (1975-1977) under Gerald Ford and George W. Bush (2001-2006). Several human rights associations, notably in France, charged him on multiple occasions with the mistreatment and torture of prisoners under his purview.

10. "Deadly Days"

Deadly Days was written by **Vincent Emanuele** with other veterans over the course of a writing workshop. It was published in the collection *Warrior Writers, Re-Making Sense*, edited by Lovella Calica, Drew Cameron, and Aaron Hughes (Warrior Writers, Barre: 2008, p. 27-30). Vince is also the author of a text for the Winter Soldier event, which took place near Washington D.C. in March 2008: *Winter Soldier Iraq & Afghanistan, Eyewitness Accounts of the Operations*, op. cit., p.47-49.

11. Hajji

Pejorative term commonly used in the American Armed Forces to refer to people from the Near and Middle East after the 9/11 attacks.

12. Occupy Wall Street

The name of a social protest movement that began in New York on September 17, 2011, and took the form of an occupation of Zuccotti Park, in the heart of the Wall Street Financial District. Demonstrators and occupiers mainly denounced social and economic inequality, banking reforms, corporate practices, and other inappropriate ties between the worlds of politics and business. In America, the protests grew to a national scale, and have often been compared to the "Indignados" movement in Europe. One of the focal points of "Occupy Wall Street" was the distribution of wealth and income disparity in the United States, which had attained heights not seen since the Great Depression.

13. VA: Veterans Affairs

"To care for him who shall have borne the battle and for his widow and his orphan": these words of Abraham Lincoln's have become the motto of the United States Department of Veterans Affairs (VA), whose

current incarnation dates back to the 1920s and '30s. It was, notably, born from a social struggle: that of World War I veterans, tens of thousands of whom camped out on the National Mall in order to obtain the compensation they had been promised.

Answering directly to the federal government, this public service is in charge of pensions, medical and (psychological) monitoring and treatment for American veterans, largely through a network of hospitals. Since the beginning of the Iraq and Afghanistan invasions, the system has been much maligned for its lack of respect, its slowness, its bureaucracy, and the wealth of tricks it deploys to put off patients as long as possible, or simply refuse them care (disability claims, pensions) altogether.

More specifically, in January 2003—two months before the start of the war in Iraq, and less than three after war broke out in Afghanistan—the Bush administration launched a broad plan of budget cuts, slashing jobs in the VA and limiting the number of medical reimbursements for veterans. At the same time, it was revealed that higher-ups in the VA appointed by the Bush administration, received annual bonuses of up to $33,000 per year. Some of these bonuses were also correlated to employee "performance"—that is, the number of claims they rejected.

Ill-prepared for the massive influx of suffering veterans, the VA saw its ability to handle patients and cases plummet: in 2013, the average wait time for case review was 327 days for an initial claim. Putting together these claims applications is an exceedingly complex process for veterans and often requires the help of specialist peers, made available thanks to associations of former soldiers. Tens of thousands of veterans lack the physical and emotional strength to file these claims, instead swelling the ranks of the homeless.

See also Aaron Glantz's *The War Comes Home: Washington's Battle Against America's Veterans* (Los Angeles & Berkeley: University of California Press, 2008).

The first half of 2014 was marked by several scandals that lay bare before the public eye just how insufficient the care the VA system offered really was. Revelations regarding the scope of these deficiencies and dysfunctions led to the sensational resignation of Eric K. Shinseki, Secretary of Veterans Affairs, on May 30, 2014.

14. "Hold On"

In the six months after returning from Iraq, **Jason Moon** wrote music to cope with the violence of the emotions weighing on him. The result was three distinct periods: his first songs were cheerful, celebrating the joys of the here and now, of being back ("Happy to be Home"). Then came a longer-lasting phase of doubt and revolt ("The Best of Me," "Trying to Find My Way Home"), followed by a lengthy collapse. "Hold On" was the last song Jason wrote before he sank into a deep depression lasting several years. "Hold On" is the record of one man's struggle not to leave life behind.
See also www.jasonmoon.org

15. Ajax

(In Ancient Greek: Αἴας Τελαμώνιος, Aías Telamōnios) The earliest of Sophocles' plays left to us. Date of composition unknown, though it is believed to be close to that of Antigone (442 BCE). In many ways a mysterious play, it is often considered a tragedy of madness and melancholy. Ajax is depicted as a character outside the ordinary, the great hero of Homer's *Iliad*, "filled with and destroyed by a refusal of the laws that govern the civic world of which Sophocles' works are a part—the world of the 5th century BCE" (Jean Alaux, in his Introduction to Sophocles' *Ajax* (Paris: Les Belles Lettres, 2002)). An eminently political figure, Ajax plays a crucial role in the Athenian imagination, and a statue of him can be found in the Agora.

Acknowledgements
Olivier Morel expresses his gratitude:

To Martin Leclerc (Maël).
To Wendy Barranco, Lisa Zepeda, Joyce, Kevin et Debbie Lucey, Vincent Emanuele, Ryan Endicott, Jason Moon, Kevin Stendal and their loved ones, for their courage to bear witness. To David and Paulina Brooks, Jason Lemieux, Peter Sullivan, Aaron Hughes, Tomas Young (deceased) & Claudia Cuellar Young, Sergio Kochergin, Chris Arendt, Derek Giffin, Craig O'Brien, Kim Scipes, Kathleen Hernandez; to Hans (Johanna) Buwalda, Dr. John Zemler.

To Zadig Productions, producer of On the Bridge (Zadig-Arte France, France-USA 2011): Hassiba Belhadj, Céline Nusse, Paul Rozenberg, Félicie Roblin, Heidi Fleisher, Martine Michon, Florence Guinaudeau, Nadine Belkacemi, Bruno Bazanella, Benjamin Gourier, Claude Szwimer, Florian Lobstein. To Pierrette Ominetti & Christilla Huillard-Kann (Arte).

To my friends and colleagues Matthieu Augustin, Jean-Gabriel Leynaud & Erik Ménard, Jared Wright, Richard Molina, Kirsten Blazic, Marc Iantosca (film crew); Claude Gendrot, publisher; Ruth Zylberman & Bénédicte Rochas (mentors).

To my colleagues from the University of Notre Dame, Scott Appelby, Joe Buttigieg, Ted Cachey, Jim Collins, Don Crafton, Hal Culbertson, Julia Douthwaite, Anne García-Romero, Peter Holland, Anton Juan, Thomas Merluzzi, John McGreevy, Anthony Monta, Catherine Perry, Jeff Spoonhower, Alain Toumayan. To the departments of Film, Television, & Theatre, and Romance Languages & Literatures, the Institute for the Scholarship in the Liberal Arts, the Nanovic Institute for European Studies, the Kroc Institute for Peace and International Studies, the Ph.D. in Literature Program.

To Iraq Veterans Against The War, the Arlington West Memorial Santa Monica (Los Angeles), Military Families Speak Out, Iraq and Afghanistan Veterans Of America, Chicago International Film Festival, University Of Columbia in New York City, Hideout Theatre Chicago, Dryhootch Milwaukee, Gavelston Steak House Michigan City, Skydive Coastal Camarillo, 5th district of the Chicago Police.

To Marie-Françoise & Yves Morel (deceased), Rick & Gail Rice.

To Alison, Rosa & Alexa.

Watch On the Bridge on VOD:
beamafilm.com

Olivier Morel
French author and documentary director, now naturalized American and teaching film and romance languages at Notre Dame. He has worked primarily on the relationship between trauma and creativity, getting testimony from veterans of the Shoah and the Great War. This graphic novel is related to his documentary "On the Bridge" interviewing Irak War vets.

Maël
Martin Leclerc was born near Grenoble, and spent most of his childhood copying 'Lucky Luke' stories. He studied at the Political Science School of Grenoble and created the fanzine Youkaïda. He lives in Paris since 2000. Now he leads a double life. He is lead singer of a folk rock group, and also works as a comics artist under the pseudonym Maël.